JEAN GENET

A Study of His Novels and Plays

By the same Author

★

ALBERT CAMUS

JEAN-PAUL SARTRE

ALBERT CAMUS, 1913-60

JEAN GENET

A Study of His Novels and Plays

BY

PHILIP THODY

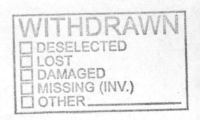

HAMISH HAMILTON
LONDON

First published in Great Britain, 1968
by Hamish Hamilton Ltd.
90 *Great Russell Street, London, W.C.*1
Copyright © 1968 *by Philip Thody*

PRINTED IN GREAT BRITAIN
BY W. HEFFER AND SONS LTD., CAMBRIDGE

Contents

PART ONE

INTRODUCTION

PART TWO

THE NOVELS

PART THREE

THE PLAYS

To Alan Milne

INTRODUCTION

CHAPTER ONE

THE MAN AND HIS WORK
(i) 1910—1942

JEAN GENET was born in Paris on December 19, 1910, the illegitimate son of Gabrielle Genet and of an unknown father. His mother abandoned him as soon as he was born, and Genet was brought up by the Public Assistance. At the age of seven, he was placed as a foster-child with a peasant family in Le Morvan, a country district north-east of the *massif central*. When he was twenty-one, Genet claimed his legal right of obtaining his birth certificate. His place of birth was given as 22, rue d'Assas. He went to the address. It was the public maternity hospital.[1]

Initially, Genet seems to have been happy with his foster-parents, and even to have enjoyed some sense of security. Thus, in his autobiographical *Journal du Voleur* (*The Thief's Journal*), he describes a dream in which he was pursued by a train. He ran from it in terror, left the tracks and cut across country. The train followed him, and stopped only when it reached a gate leading into a field near his foster-parents' home. 'It stopped', Genet told the friend to whom he was describing his dream, 'at the fence of my childhood'. Another notation in *The Thief's Journal* suggests that he may have been placed with recently deprived parents, for he mentions how his foster-mother once stole some flowers from a nearby grave in order to place them on her daughter's tomb. The more idyllic aspects of his childhood almost certainly form the basis for certain features of the description

---

[1] All notes and references are given at the back of the book, beginning on page 228. The sign * indicates that the note has some general interest.

which he gives in his first novel, *Notre-Dame-des-fleurs* (*Our Lady of the Flowers*), of Louis Culafroy's childhood, but this happiness, like that of Culafroy, did not last. By the time he was ten, Genet had begun to steal small objects and sums of money from his foster-parents' house. He was caught, punished, and labelled a thief.

In *Saint Genet, comédien et martyr* (*Saint Genet, actor and martyr*) Jean-Paul Sartre argues that Genet began to steal in order to compensate himself for being, in a traditionally-minded community, the only person with no right to own property. Alone, in this village where fields were handed down from father to son, Genet had no father and no right to any inheritance. He consequently felt, according to Sartre's analysis, that he could *be* someone only by *owning* things, and began his career as a thief for this reason. Although nothing that Genet has so far published in book form provides direct confirmation for this particular interpretation of why he stole, he did comment on his early thefts in a text presented in *Les Temps Modernes* in July 1946 as an extract from the forthcoming *Journal du Voleur*.

'When I was a child', he wrote, 'I stole from my foster-parents. Was I already conscious of the reprobation that was to be my lot because I was a foundling and a homosexual? I dare not say that I was led to steal as an act of rebellion. I already liked boys when I was very young, although I was happy in the company of girls and women. The earliest kind of love I can remember took the form of my desire to be a handsome youth with vigorous, decided gestures, whom I saw cycling past, and of my self-indulgence as I imagined what it would be like to be him. I was ten or eleven. At thirteen, I recognised the feeling of love as the sadness which came over me when I left the presence of a handsome youth of fifteen. At ten, I felt no remorse when I stole from people whom I loved and whom I knew to be poor. I was found out. I think that the word "thief" wounded me deeply. Deeply, that is to say enough to make me want, deliberately, to be what other people made me blush for being, to want to be it proudly, and in spite of them.'

Perhaps because this particular confession provided too perfect an illustration for another of Sartre's theses, or perhaps because it evoked too intense a memory, Genet did not include it when the *Journal du Voleur* was published in book form in 1949. Then, he roundly declared that he had stolen because he was hungry, and he repeated this explanation in an interview which he gave to the American magazine *Playboy* in April 1964. However, he also added in his remarks to *Playboy* that after he had stolen he felt the need to 'justify and accept' his act.

This additional comment parallels Sartre's view that Genet, as the extract in *Les Temps Modernes* indicates, deliberately chose to become a thief once he had been accused of being one. Genet was certainly sufficiently fixated in his original decision to declare, in July 1946, that 'to give up stealing would mean giving up the thief that is in me', and to defend this refusal by proclaiming that 'the thief is still the worthiest character inhabiting me, since it is by him that I am led far from the paths of banality and into the infernal regions'. Sartre's attitude towards the Genet who thus chose to defy society is, at this point in his analysis, similar to his approval for the Jew who accepts himself as a Jew or the Negro who 'picks up the word "nigger" that is thrown at him like a stone and proudly proclaims himself as black in face of the white man'. 'Genet's dignity', he writes, 'is the demand for evil', and he adds that he 'deeply admires' this child who 'grimly *willed* himself at an age when *we* were merely playing the servile buffoon'. However, as the long study in *Saint Genet, actor and martyr* of the problems which Genet encountered as a result of this 'authentic choice' indicates, it plunged him into even more contradictions than those which bedevil Negroes or Jews. To begin with, as Sartre points out, it meant that Genet was in the paradoxical position of deliberately willing something already decided. He made his decision to be a thief only after he had begun to steal for reasons which escaped him— 'I am not interested in how my taste for theft originated ("*Je ne veux pas savoir l'origine de mon goût pour le vol*")', he wrote in 1946—and his social position virtually predestined

him to join the ranks of the criminal world. He also, in
Sartre's view, carried his choice to be a thief to the point
where he wished to become the embodiment of evil. 'This
little pilferer', writes Sartre, 'aspires to the sacred moment in
which he will be penetrated, torn apart, by the great and
terrible essence of the Evildoer'. Genet thus fell victim,
thanks largely to the *'morale fruste et théologique'* ('simple
minded, theological morality') of the peasants who originally took him into their home, to all the contradictions
involved in the view that Good and Evil are absolute
entities and not simply convenient terms of social approval
or disapproval.

As will be seen, a study of Genet's work confirms
Sartre's view that the pursuit of absolute evil involved him
in a number of far-reaching personal and philosophical
contradictions. The rest of Sartre's analysis was also near
enough to Genet's own memories to have a devastating
effect on Genet himself. In the *Playboy* interview, Genet said
that after reading the manuscript of Sartre's study he felt
that he had been 'stripped naked . . . unceremoniously', and
that he was 'almost unable to continue writing'. It is
perhaps significant that, although Genet openly confesses in
a number of his books to having betrayed his friends, and
to having been a thief and a homosexual, he has always
stopped short at analysing what Sartre calls 'the original
event to which he constantly refers and which he reproduces in his secret ceremonies', and has never repeated the
statement he made in July 1946 about his first thefts. He has,
in fact, made very few direct statements about his childhood,
and begins to speak about himself in detail only when
describing his adolescence. Then, he offers two different
explanations for the next important event in his life: his
entry, as he himself says, 'at the age of fifteen years and
seventeen days', in the *colonie agricole*, or reformatory, of
Mettray.

The first explanation, in his novel *Miracle de la Rose*
(*Miracle of the Rose*), from which this unusually precise

dating is taken, is that he had gouged another boy's eye out with a knife. The second, in *The Thief's Journal*, is that he had simply drifted there 'through laziness and day-dreaming,' and this fits in with another piece of information which Sartre mentions almost in passing: that, as an adolescent, Genet went off into such deep and protracted day-dreams that he was actually placed under psychiatric observation. Genet's first explanation is not even mentioned by Sartre, though it would not be difficult to fit into Sartre's frequently expressed view that other people fix us in a certain rôle by the way they look at us. The obsessive quality of this memory, whether it refers to a real incident or not, is nevertheless indicated by the fact that eye-gouging recurs four times in Genet's work: Alberto, one of the characters in Genet's first novel, loses an eye; Village, the murderer in *Les Nègres* (*The Blacks*), and Saïd, in *Les Paravents* (*The Screens*), both put out someone else's eye; and Querelle murders a young Russian in order to 'rid himself of the horror' of having stabbed him in the eye.

Whatever the reason for which Genet was sent to Mettray, the three years which he spent there certainly did nothing to change his attitude towards society. The reformatory, to some extent an earlier version of the Borstal system whereby boys are given a chance to work in the open air, to learn a trade, and to form positive relationships with adults, had been founded in 1839 by a well-known lawyer called F. A. Demetz. The Vicomte Bretegnières de Courteilles, whom Genet in *Miracle of the Rose* refers to as a baron, had lent his patronage and assistance, and no less a personage than Alexis de Tocqueville had written an enthusiastic letter of support to Demetz. The colony's motto was '*Améliorer la terre par l'homme et l'homme par la terre*' ('Improve the land by man and man by the land') and its founders considered it capable not only of reforming delinquent boys but also of encouraging a general return to agriculture in nineteenth-century France. It occupied some sixty *hectares* of land near Tours, and was recognised, in 1853, as being *d'utilité publique*. It then received, as a gift from a Mistress Fry, of Upton, a number of pure-bred cattle of English stock. Even as late as 1940, it was described in a standard work on criminology as 'perhaps the most signal experiment in children's institutions, setting the general pattern for modern juvenile reformatory handling'.

Genet was there, if his own dates are correct, from 1926 to 1929. In autumn 1934, a journalist called Alexis Danan published a series of articles in *Paris-Soir* denouncing a number of French reformatories, and especially Mettray, as nothing more or less than *bagnes* (hard-labour camps), whose only achievement was to encourage the crime and violence they were supposed to cure. Later, as the privately printed edition of *Miracle de la Rose* indicates, Genet met Danan and discussed his own experiences at Mettray with him. This must have been an interesting encounter, for although the two writers gave basically the same account of Mettray, they each had a totally different attitude towards it. Danan wrote in conscious and deliberate protest, and the validity of his criticism was endorsed when, in 1936, a selection of letters from former inmates of Mettray was published in book form. All spoke of the brutality, the appalling food, the disgusting sanitary conditions, the homosexuality and the violence, which Danan had denounced in his articles and which Genet described in *Miracle of the Rose*. Several of these letters accused former officers of the *colonie* of causing the death of boys imprisoned there, and stated that it was quite common for boys deliberately to mutilate themselves in order to be released on medical grounds. However, when Genet describes comparable events, mentioning even the same names which occur in the letters, his attitude towards Mettray is apparently one of delight and approbation. It was, he maintains, 'a paradise', and after a description of how there was never any paper in the lavatories, he writes: 'Idiotic vandals—Danan, Helsey, Londres and others—have written that penal homes for children should be destroyed. They fail to realise that if they were, the children would set them up again. Those inhuman kids would create courts of miracles (that's the word for it!) and perform their secret, complicated rites in the very teeth of well-meaning journalists'.

Whether the original intention and final effect of such statements are not, in fact, comparable with those of Swift in his *Serious Proposal* is a question that will be discussed later in this book. It may well be, indeed, that by irony and exaggeration, both in *Miracle of the Rose* and in a shorter text entitled *L'Enfant Criminel*, Genet comes close to the common-sense, liberal attitude towards crime and the treatment of criminals which he always claims to reject. The immediate effect of his experiences at Mettray, however, was to confirm his total defiance of society and its standards. When he left Mettray, he is said to have joined the Foreign Legion in order to receive an enlistment bounty, and then to have deserted, stealing the luggage belonging to his Negro officers as he did so. He was not, however, if his friend Jean Cau is to be believed, entirely devoid of a sense of humour during his brief army career. In Syria, when the army was on manoeuvres, he told a General to whom he had to make a report that he could not possibly do so if he stood to attention; he had to make his narrative live. He began to gesticulate wildly, and the General, rightly feeling that this was a new form of dumb insolence, sent him off to prison.

It was indeed prison and crime which formed the basis for Genet's experience for the next fifteen years or more. What he actually did during this period will probably never be known with any precision. At fifteen or sixteen, according to *The Thief's Journal*, he was already a homosexual prostitute in Marseilles, 'that city dear to queers', and he made a particular choice to live by prostituting himself when he went to Hitler's Germany. 'If I steal here,' he thought to himself, 'I perform no singular deed that might fulfil me. I obey the customary order; I do not destroy it. I am not

committing evil. I am not upsetting anything. The out-
rageous is impossible. I'm stealing in the void.' In what he
felt was already 'a camp organised by bandits', the particular
form of evil-doing which he had chosen was pointless, and
he needed to 'return to a country where the laws of ordinary
morality were revered'. In Spain, he lived as a beggar, in
Yugoslavia as a petty thief, and in Holland by smuggling
drugs in collaboration with a criminal called Armand.

There seems to have been an important change in his
attitude when, sometime in his twenties, he made the
acquaintance of a professional cracksman called Guy. He
then escaped from the servility of prostitution and begging
by what he presents, in *Miracle of the Rose*, as good, honest,
virile robbery. According to Sartre, who rightly dismisses
Genet's contention that this experience made him into a
down-to-earth, practically-minded criminal, this encounter
took place when Genet was twenty-six, but in *The Thief's
Journal* Genet himself speaks of a similar change coming over
him at the age of twenty-three. However that may be, the
successful exercise of crime never seems to have inspired
Genet to make a profit from it. For all his prison
sentences, he contends that he was a skilful thief, and was
never once caught *en flagrant délit*. He also, however, states
in *Pompes Funèbres* that the police is always too powerful to
allow the existence of criminal gangs, and seems to dismiss
the possibility that crime can be a successful form of
defying society. Although this idea may be based less on
actual observation than on Genet's own paradoxical
situation of a man seeking evil in its purest form, there is an
interesting coincidence between his general portrayal of
the criminal as stupid and inefficient, and the views held by
a number of professional criminologists.* It was nevertheless the quest for absolute evil, together with the ineffectual
petty robbery and constant betrayal of confederates which
were linked with it, that seems to have taken up virtually all
his energy until, early in the nineteen-forties, he began to
write.

(ii) 1942—1948

When Genet was sixteen, Sartre tells us, he was 'taken in hand by a professional song-writer', who, according to another critic, taught him the basic rules of French versification. It was first of all through the medium of poetry that Genet began to express his view of the world, though for various reasons it is not as a poet in the strict sense of the word that he has achieved his greatest success. Initially, it seems, poetry came to him in groups of words, in units of sound, which he murmured over and over to himself as if they were incantations. Then, one day in prison, a fellow inmate declaimed a long, sentimental poem about a man who had been sentenced to death. Genet was offended by its stupidity, and volunteered to write a far better poem himself. He did so, and Sartre contends that he was wholly satisfied when his fellow convicts greeted it with howls of derisive laughter.

The poem was called *Le Condamné à Mort*, and was published at Fresnes in September 1942, on very poor paper with a large number of misprints. It is dedicated to the memory of a twenty-year-old murderer, Maurice Pilorge, who according to Genet was executed on March 17, 1939, at Saint-Brieux prison. The same dedication, with the same date, is printed at the beginning of *Our Lady of the Flowers*, but the fact that Pilorge was actually executed on February 2, 1939, indicates that not all Genet's statements can be believed, however apparently precise they may be. The poem itself is a fairly long one, in which there are interesting contrasts between form and content: invocations to crime and homosexuality are presented in language which moves from formal rhetoric to extreme obscenity, but the regularity of the alexandrines never varies with the peculiarity of the ideas. It is not, however, a very good poem. Many of its lines and much of its verbal rhythm are highly derivative, and the language is so obscure and romanticised that it is equally difficult to discover what Genet means and to sympathise with his meaning when it is found. Genet's career as an important writer begins not with his poetry but with his prose, not with the lush rhythms of *Le Condamné à Mort*, but with the alternately glamorous and ironic presentation of criminals in *Our Lady of the Flowers*.

The circumstances in which this novel was written have been recorded by Sartre and confirmed by Genet himself in his *Playboy* interview. At La Santé prison, the convicts were given sheets of brown paper from which to make paper bags. It was there, using a stub of pencil, that Genet began to write his book. Then, one day when he was appearing in Court, a warder entered his cell, found his manuscript, took it away and destroyed it. After Genet had done three days' solitary confinement for illegal use of prison property, he bought some notebooks at the prison canteen, reconstructed from memory the fifty pages he had already composed on brown paper, and completed the book.

Neither Genet nor his critics, however, have given any details about five other aspects of *Our Lady of the Flowers* which are perhaps even more intriguing than the circumstances of its composition: how Genet learned to write such brilliant and impeccable French, where he acquired the knowledge of art and literature displayed in his novel, how the manuscript was smuggled out of prison, how it found a publisher, and who was the 'amateur' at whose expense 350 privately printed copies were eventually published 'in Monte Carlo'. Jean Cocteau may well have been involved, for he states in his book *La Difficulté d'Être* that he appeared in Court on Genet's behalf as early as 1942, and was widely criticised by certain newspapers for so doing, According to Simone de Beauvoir, it was in July 1943 that Cocteau wrote to the judge of the 19ᵉ *chambre correctionnelle* in order to appeal for clemency on Genet's behalf, and this date is confirmed by an article that appeared in *Poésie* in the same year. Genet had been arrested for stealing an edition of Verlaine's poetry—'I knew its value', he told the Judge, 'but not its price'—and in spite of the fact that this was his seventh offence, his sentence was reduced to three months because Cocteau wrote a letter saying that Genet was 'the greatest poet of our time'. Simone de Beauvoir also mentions that Marc Barbezat's wife Olga used to go and visit Genet in prison, and it may be that it was through her that Genet's manuscript found a publisher. None of the copies of the first edition gives either a date of publication or the name of a publisher, though most critics do say that it appeared in 1942. It was produced with the care that characterised all Barbezat's work, and he certainly published the second, identical edition, in 1948. He also, in 1966, published the first completely unexpurgated edition to be placed on open sale.

Whatever facts may be subsequently discovered about the original publication of *Our Lady of the Flowers*, the book certainly enabled Genet, from the mid nineteen-forties onwards, to be widely accepted in French literary circles. He met Sartre in May 1944, and immediately reached a close understanding with him. This, Simone de Beauvoir writes, was based on their common feeling for liberty, and their common disgust with everything which places limitations upon it: 'nobility of soul, eternal ethical systems, universal justice, high-sounding words, great principles, institutions and idealisms'. The trial scene from *Notre-Dame-des-Fleurs* was printed next to the first edition of *Huis Clos* in the Spring 1944 edition of Barbezat's magazine, *L'Arbalète*, and in 1945 Genet's poem *La Galère*, again on the theme of the beauty of the criminal in prison, appeared in the third number of the very expensive review *La Table Ronde*, side by side with texts by Jean Paulhan, Louis Jouvet and Rudyard Kipling. In December of the same year extracts from his third novel, *Pompes Funèbres*, were published in Sartre's review *Les Temps Modernes*, and when the extracts from the *Journal du Voleur* appeared in the same review in July of the following year, there were at least two different reactions: a critic with the initials C.E.M. wrote in *Poésie* that they 'did not succeed in making us forget the admirable *Notre-Dame-des-Fleurs* published earlier in *L'Arbalète*'; and a number of surrealist writers, according to Sartre, violently attacked Genet for his praise of treason.

In March 1946, Marc Barbezat published 475 copies of a sumptuous first edition of Genet's second novel, *Miracle de la Rose*, each copy of which weighed over six pounds and could be sold only to subscribers. Like *Notre-Dame-des-Fleurs*, this novel had also been written in prison, this time at La Santé and the Prison de Tourelles, and according to Genet was completed in 1943. However, a reference to the regret which France felt as the German soldiers left her after the Occupation, indicates that Genet certainly corrected his manuscript before sending it to press and did so in a way that showed his determination not to accept any of the standards of the society which was gradually becoming more prepared to accept him.

In the spring of 1947, Genet extended his activity from poetry and novels to the theatre. He had already, on June 25, 1946, had his ballet *'Adame Miroir* danced by Roland Petit to the music of Darius Milhaud, but it was the production of *Les Bonnes*, by Louis Jouvet, at the Théâtre de l'Athénée on April 19, 1947, that was the first step in bringing his work to the attention of a wider public. Critics were sharply divided over the merits of the play, and Robert Kemp, in *Le Monde*, roundly declared that it was nonsense. Thierry Maulnier, on the other hand, then editor of *La Table Ronde*, wrote that it was 'a truly horrifying act of accusation against modern society', and gave it high praise. Inaugurating the series of *Punch*-type jokes which recur whenever this play is produced, he declared that he had actually heard a lady remark, as she left the theatre: 'It's quite untrue. My servants are very fond of me'. This first production of *Les Bonnes* ran for about thirteen weeks, and marked the beginning of Genet's gradual transformation from what *Transition* later called 'the last of the court poets', to a well-known and controversial public figure.

Genet's prose works could not, however, yet be openly published in their entirety, and 1947 also saw the private publication, '*Au dépens de quelques amateurs, à Bikini*', of *Pompes Funèbres*. Originally, it would seem, there had been a possibility that this novel might be published by Gallimard, and Simone de Beauvoir paints an amusing picture of Genet's fury when an employee at the Gallimard offices not only gave him the impression that his manuscript was lost, but also made an impolite reference to Genet's sexual tastes. However, both the extremely detailed description of homosexual activity that this novel contains, and Genet's choice of a member of Darnand's pro-German *Milice* as the hero, probably made Gallimard change his mind, and the book had to appear privately. It was Genet's first attempt to relate his preoccupations with crime and homosexuality to a wider context of historical and political events, and probably contributed largely to the rumours that he had collaborated with the Germans during the Occupation of France. Both Sartre and Simone de Beauvoir insist that Genet's proclaimed affection for the *Milice*—'If I had been young,' he writes in *Pompes Funèbres*, 'I should have been a *Milicien*'—remained purely Platonic, and it is true that, towards the end of the book, the greater vigour shown by the Resistance movement makes him find that sexually attractive too. However, the general tone of the novel showed that his frequentation of left-wing literary circles had done little to change Genet's fundamental hostility to western society. This attitude, which led him to present as heroes in *Our Lady of the Flowers* 'those whom you would call: hoodlums of the worst sort', also predominates in *Haute Surveillance* (*Deathwatch*) which was published in the important literary review *La Nef* in March and April 1947, and first performed at the Théâtre des Mathurins on February 26, 1949. It had originally been called *Préséances*, also the title of one of François Mauriac's early and more amusing novels, but it was not for this reason that Mauriac brought even more attention to Genet by publishing a violent attack on his work and admirers in *Le Figaro littéraire* on March 26, 1949.

The origin of the article was, in fact, a quarrel between Jean Marchat, the director of the Théâtre des Mathurins, and the theatre critic of *Le Figaro*, Jean-Jacques Gautier. Gautier had written, of *Haute Surveillance*, a play that deals with the prestige which murderers enjoy among their fellow convicts, that: 'The themes are filthy. The tone is odious. We witnessed, for 48 minutes that seemed like 24 hours, garbage in its pure and unadulterated state.' Marchat had replied, pointing out that Gautier had been equally unable to recognise the originality of plays as varied as Claudel's *L'Annonce faite à Marie* and Synge's *The Playboy of the Western World*, and arguing that his reaction to Genet's play represented the instinctive refusal by the French bourgeoisie of everything new and exciting in the artistic world. When Mauriac joined in the argument, it was to carry it on to a moral plane and accuse Genet of exploiting vice for literary ends. *Le Figaro littéraire* celebrated the fact that Genet was the centre of a major literary controversy by publishing a sketch of him by the actor Jean Marais on the same page as Mauriac's article, and it was apparent from what Mauriac said that *Notre-Dame-des-Fleurs*, although still officially available only in a limited edition, had been placed openly on sale in the theatre. It was, in fact, also in 1949 that a prose work by Genet was first openly published, and that one of his books became available in English. *Le Journal du Voleur* appeared simultaneously in a standard Gallimard edition as well as in a private printing of 400 copies, and in April 1949 Bernard Frechtman's translation of *Our Lady of the Flowers* was issued in a limited edition of 300 copies. It was published by Paul Morihien, who had had a long association with Jean Cocteau. In December 1947, *Querelle de Brest*, Genet's fourth novel but the first of his works to be translated into German, had appeared in a restricted edition of 850 copies, so that by the end of the nineteen-forties all Genet's major prose works had already appeared in France and two of them had been translated into other languages.

(iii) 1948—1959

It was also as a result of Genet's friendship with Jean Cocteau and Jean-Paul Sartre that he was granted, in 1948, an official free pardon for his crimes. On July 16 of that year, the newspaper *Combat* published an appeal which Sartre and Cocteau addressed on Genet's behalf to President Auriol. They recognised, they said, that Genet's work was *'en marge de la littérature et ne saurait courir les rues'* (was 'on the fringe of literature and could not be openly distributed'). Nevertheless, they argued, he deserved a pardon on two counts: the sentence which he now faced, and which would have the effect, in view of his previous record, of sending him to prison for the rest of his life, was for a crime that he himself had not committed; and his literary work, which was that of 'a very great poet', comparable to Villon or Verlaine, had had the effect of freeing him from the evil and crime which had characterised his early years. His entire life, wrote Sartre and Cocteau, was now dedicated wholly to his work.

Genet was facing a life sentence for something he had not done because he had decided to assume responsibility for a crime committed by Jean Decarnin, a friend of his killed in the Paris street-fighting at the Liberation. *Pompes Funèbres* is dedicated to Jean Decarnin, and the recurrence of this name in Sartre's letter confirms that at least one aspect of this particular novel is based upon fact. It is also interesting, in view of the argument which later took place in England as to whether Genet's work should be admitted into the country, to note that Sartre and Cocteau apparently accepted the view that it could not and should not be offered to all and every reader. It may be, of course, that this was a concession that they made in view of the need to ensure that Genet was pardoned. There is also a touch of bad faith in their claim that Genet's work had 'delivered him from evil', especially when Sartre later claimed that 'To read Genet is *to be thought by the spirit of Evil*, in complicity with it', and

Genet himself continued, in all his work, to reject every basic principle of normal morality. Nevertheless, the appeal was successful. Legally speaking, Genet was reintegrated into society.

Three years after this appeal, in 1951, the first volume of what are called Genet's *Oeuvres Complètes* was openly published by Gallimard, and a copy legally deposited at the Bibliothèque Nationale in the first quarter of the year. It contained two of his poems, *Le Condamné à Mort* and *Un Chant d'Amour*, as well as his two novels, *Notre-Dame-des-Fleurs* and *Le Miracle de la Rose*. The novels were slightly bowdlerised—the dimensions of the heroes' sexual parts, for example, had been given in centimetres in the privately printed edition, and were now omitted—but the essential of the works was conserved. Then, the following year, there came Sartre's massive study, *Saint Genet, comédien et martyr*, rather oddly classified as Volume I of Genet's complete works, and in 1953 the third volume, containing a long poem, *Le Pêcheur du Suquet*, and two novels, *Pompes Funèbres* and *Querelle de Brest*. Once again, the novels were slightly toned down, and the ending of *Querelle de Brest* was changed quite substantially. More unfortunately, some of the amusing extracts from this novel were also omitted, as well as what were obviously considered as certain over-realistic details about homosexuality. Neither the *Journal du Voleur*, nor *L'Enfant Criminel*, nor the text of either of Genet's first two plays, was included then or has been included since in what are still called the *Oeuvres Complètes*.

The immediate reception of the *Oeuvres Complètes* in France adds little to our knowledge of Genet's relationship with his public. Only one critic, the Catholic André Rousseaux, deigned to review them. His article was called *Décomposition littéraire*, and did not actually mention any of Genet's works by name. It contained, for the most part, a denunciation of Genet on moral grounds, and included only one literary judgment: Genet's poetry was that of '*un Lamartine médiocre et pourri*' ('a corrupt and mediocre

Lamartine'). Other critics who discussed Genet did so
purely in the light of Sartre's essay on him, and nobody
thought it worth while to examine his work by the normal
literary criteria of plot, character portrayal, use of language,
recurrence of images, repetition of themes, relevance to
social reality or consistency of vision. Even now, such
critical writing as there has been on Genet in France has
rarely attempted to assess his novels as anything but biographical or psychological documents. If, of course, Sartre's
claim that Genet has 'reinvented literature' is a valid one, all
normal criteria may well have ceased to be valid. It is
difficult, however, to see quite what will replace them.

Apart from a short appreciation of Giacometti, an essay
about an acrobat, and a number of prefaces to his plays,
Genet has not added to the prose works published in his
Oeuvres Complètes. This confirms his remark, in the *Playboy*
interview, that Sartre's study made him almost unable to
continue writing, and emphasises how curious the relationship between Sartre and Genet is. Had it not been for Sartre,
far fewer people would have heard of Genet, and his work
would certainly have been studied from a very different
point of view. It is also rumoured that it was only because of
Sartre's influence that Genet consented to the publication of
his *Oeuvres Complètes*, and that Gallimard agreed to under-
take it. The way Sartre uses Genet as a pretext for his own
ideas on the wickedness of bourgeois society lends weight
to Philip Toynbee's remark that their relationship is 'rather
that of the bearded lady in the tent to the voluble huckster
outside', but there is, in this respect, one significant
difference: no previous literary huckster so vaunted the
fascination of the beard that the lady became unable to grow
any further hair. This seems to be what happened to Genet,
though it could also be argued that his sources of inspiration
had virtually dried up, as far as his prose work was concerned, before Sartre ever showed him the manuscript of his
analysis. Only the *Journal du Voleur* was, in fact, published
after 1947, and Sartre is quite right to see it as a 'literary

testament, or at least a conclusion'. It breaks no new ground, and frequently seems contrived and over-intellectual when compared to *Our Lady of the Flowers* or *Miracle of the Rose*.

The nineteen-fifties were, for Genet's reputation as well as his activity as a writer, a period of consolidation and controversy rather than of creation and development. *Les Bonnes* had a second series of performances in Paris early in 1954, and was put on in English at the New Lindsey Theatre Club in June 1956. In 1957, *The Balcony* had its world *première* at the Arts Theatre Club, after it had been virtually banned in Paris by the refusal of the authorities to guarantee the safety of the actors if it was put on at the Théâtre Antoine. It was published in English in 1957, by Faber and Faber, who have since brought out both hard- and paper-back editions of all his plays. Genet's novels were, in fact, the subject of considerable controversy in 1957, when the two volumes of his *Oeuvres Complètes* ordered by the Birmingham City Librarian were impounded by the customs. The decision to prevent the works entering the country was heartily endorsed by the Chairman of Birmingham Public Libraries Committee, who was reported as saying: 'When I had the opportunity of reading translated passages from page after page of Genet's book, I felt sick to the foundations of my heart. The theme was homosexuality. I am convinced that the Customs and Excise Department has rendered a public service in impounding such a book'. It was only in 1964, when translations of Genet's novels began to appear in English, that all his works could be freely imported into this country.

(iv) 1959—1966

The most important event in Genet's career as a dramatist, and the one which was to give his work a far greater popularity than his early plays ever seemed likely to enjoy, was Roger Blin's production of his third play, *Les Nègres*, at the

Théâtre de Lutèce on October 18, 1959. The 1957 production of *The Balcony* at the Arts Theatre had not been outstandingly successful, and Genet himself had protested so violently against Peter Zadek's interpretation of his play that he had had to be restrained by main force from climbing on to the stage and denouncing the production to the audience. For *Les Nègres*, however, he had a director with whose methods and interpretation he thoroughly agreed, as well as a group of Negro actors whose presence added considerable exoticism if not always complete audibility to a long and successful series of performances. Indeed, it is said that Roger Blin and the directors of the Théâtre de Lutèce were rather surprised by the success which *Les Nègres* enjoyed. Under the misleadingly polite translation of *The Blacks*—*nègre*, in modern French, has most of the connotations of *nigger*, and Genet exploited these in his play—a production at St. Mark's Playhouse, New York, achieved an even greater triumph when it ran for over three years, from May 1961 to September 1964.

After Blin had set the pace with *Les Nègres*, Genet became a much more widely acceptable dramatist in France. In May 1960, *Le Balcon* was produced in Paris with Marie Bell in the rôle of the majestic Madame Irma, and in 1961 *Les Bonnes* was put on by the state-subsidised Théâtre de France as part of a series of performances given at the Odéon to illustrate the nature of the new French theatre. Then, in 1966, his notoriety reached its high-water mark in France by the production at the same theatre of his controversial play about the Algerian war, *Les Paravents* (*The Screens*). This play had been published as early as 1961, but widely regarded as impossible to produce. However, it was produced in West Berlin in June 1961, and in May 1966, under the direction of Jean-Louis Barrault, Roger Blin finally gave it a French production at the Odéon-Théâtre de France for a limited run of twenty performances. It played to packed houses, and was revived for a further series of performances in September of the same year. So much hostility was provoked by the first series that the Odéon-Théâtre de France had to be given special police protection against the outraged ex-servicemen who were threatening to take the theatre by storm. For an ex-convict, it was perhaps the most blatant symbol that could have been chosen to express the new attitude which society had adopted towards him. When *Les Paravents* received the *Palmarès de la Critique* for the best play of the 1966 theatrical season, the decision to perform, at the tax-payer's expense, what many critics considered as a deliberate insult to the French army seemed completely vindicated on aesthetic grounds.

In 1963, Genet had also begun to reach a wider Anglo-Saxon public. The film of *The Balcony* was shown at commercial cinemas in England, America and Canada, as well as in France itself. Also in 1963, Bernard Frechtman's translation of *Our Lady of the Flowers* was published by the Grove Press in America, and in 1964 by Anthony Blond in England. There seem to have been no serious legal obstacles in either country. In England, Anthony Blond sent the Director of Public Prosecutions a list of well-known literary figures who were prepared to appear in court to defend the publication of Genet's work, and no case was brought against him. In 1964, Bernard Frechtman's translation of *Saint Genet, actor and martyr* was published by W. H. Allen, and with the appearance of *The Thief's Journal* in the same year, *Miracle of the Rose* in 1965 and *Querelle de Brest* in 1966, all Genet's important works except *Pompes Funèbres* had appeared in English.

Paradoxically, Genet's fame as a writer has increased as his creativity has declined. Except for his later plays, he has written virtually nothing since 1949. The film *Mademoiselle*,* which was presented at the Cannes Festival in 1966 and later in London, was based on an early scenario, and contained few ideas not previously exploited in his novels and plays. Even in the works that Genet has published since 1949, there are strong reminiscences of his early work: Madame Irma, in *The Balcony*, is clearly a development of Madame

Lysiane, in *Querelle of Brest*, and the rituals of murder and impersonation which form the subject-matter of *The Blacks* already figure in *The Maids*. There were a number of new works announced as forthcoming on the flyleaf of a recent edition of *L'Atelier d'Alberto Giacometti: Le Bagne, La Fée, Elle* and *Les Fous*. However, it is rumoured that Genet recently destroyed all his manuscripts, and violently quarrelled with the person who probably did most to make his work known in English-speaking countries, his translator the late Bernard Frechtman. However suspicious one may be about any rumours connected with Genet, this particular report was partly confirmed in 1966 when *Querelle de Brest* was translated by Gregory Streatham.

It is, in fact, almost as difficult to find out anything definite about the life which Genet has led since he became a writer as it is to check up on the details of his convictions before 1947. There are occasional glimpses of him in Simone de Beauvoir's autobiography, commenting unfavourably on the sloppy appearance of the American army of liberation in 1944, or remarking to Simone de Beauvoir, of her own play, *Les Bouches Inutiles*, 'That's not what the theatre's about at all.' In 1955, the gossip column of *Carrefour* reported him as selling a non-existent manuscript to two separate publishers, while Paul Léautaud noted in his *Journal littéraire* that Cocteau had, in the same year, been ordered to remove all mention of Genet from his *discours de réception* at the *Académie Francaise*. When Genet came to England in 1957 he apparently said that he adored the English because they were such liars. Interviewed by the *Evening Standard*, he again said that he originally stole because he was hungry, declared that he disliked London intensely, and claimed to have come from France only to see the Rembrandts in the National Gallery. From the many newspaper articles published on his work in 1966, it emerged that he lived a wandering life, continually moving from hotel to hotel, owning nothing but what the magazine *Candide* called '*son éternelle veste noire, son pantalon clair et son manteau anglais à*

petits carreaux' ('his eternal black jacket, his light-coloured
trousers and his check overcoat'), still refusing to be reintegrated into the society which had rejected him as a child
and which he had rejected in turn. His homosexuality, so
flaunted in his novels, now seems to take the form of looking
after young men, in particular, according to the article in
Candide, the stepson of Lucien Sénémaud, the person to
whom his poem, *Le Pêcheur du Suquet*, was dedicated. An
artist's work, he said in the *Playboy* interview, should speak
for itself. The author must disappear completely behind it.
Asked by *Playboy* where he was directing his life, he replied:
'To oblivion.'

CHAPTER TWO

PROBLEMS AND THEMES

(i) Evil

OTHER writers before Genet have been criminals. He is not
the first to have written about homosexuality, and not the
only one to have rebelled against society or centred his
work round the problem of evil. Where he is original, and
where he differs from Baudelaire, Rimbaud or Villon as
radically as he differs from Proust, is in the point of view
from which he writes. Whereas Villon and Baudelaire write
for the most part of evil in a spirit of repentance, and even
Rimbaud finally comes to express his admiration for *'le
forçat intraitable sur qui se referme toujours le bagne'* in the past
tense, Genet claims to have nothing but praise for evil. He is
celebrating it here and now, in all his books, with no hint at
the need for repentance. He announces on the very first page
of *Our Lady of the Flowers* that the book is written to celebrate
the crimes of Weidmann, a mass murderer, of Maurice
Pilorge, a soldier who 'killed his lover Escudero, to rob him
of something under a thousand francs', and of a young
ensign who 'committed treason for treason's sake'. *Miracle
of the Rose* speaks of 'the death on the scaffold which is our
glory', of the cult which Genet himself has for murderers,
and argues that all great social movements have their origin
in evil and darkness. *The Blacks* is a hymn to hatred, *The
Balcony* insists that law, justice, religion and politics are
nothing but excuses for play-acting, and Saïd, the hero of
Les Paravents, is a traitor.

For Genet, evil is to be defended for its own sake, and not
as a necessary counterpart to good. Whatever similarities his
work has to that of Claudel, he would certainly not accept

25

the implications of the lines from *La Ville* which *La Quin-zaine littéraire* quoted as preface to an article on *Les Paravents*:

> *S'il n'est ordure ou boue dont la science ne sache tirer profit,*
> *Je pense qu'il n'est point d'être vil et si infime qu'il ne soit nécessaire à*
> *notre unanimité.*

For him, evil is evil precisely because it does not fit into a pattern. When, at the end of *The Screens*, Saïd rejects his mother, the triumphant revolution, and the reconciled world of the dead, Genet is himself pointing out the mistake of any attempt—in Cocteau's phrase—to 'Claudelise' him. The point which *The Screens* makes about evil is that it is total negation, and that as soon as it is subsumed into any overall plan it automatically becomes good. Genet's whole struggle is to prevent this happening, and his last play frequently reads like an illustration of Sartre's remarks about 'the ontological failure' of Evil, which constantly 'pursues its own nothingness'.

If, as Genet suggests in *The Screens*, evil is total negation, then it can never be defended by any form of rational argument. Once argument and justification are introduced, then what we had previously looked upon as evil becomes somebody else's good. This comes out clearly if Genet's views on crime and murder are compared with those of the Marquis de Sade. Both writers talk about crime, and both praise it. De Sade recommends robbery, arson, murder, torture and incest and pours scorn on the virtuous if they dare complain of their sufferings at the hands of evil-doers. In doing so, however, he specifically invokes another standard, which he argues is superior to the normal codes of religion and society. The criminal, he maintains in *Justine* and *La Philosophie dans le Boudoir*, is right to act as he does, because it is a fundamental principle of Nature to destroy old or existing forms of life in order that new ones may take their place. Life can exist only through death, and it is therefore legitimate that the weak, whose instincts tend towards conservation, should be sacrificed to the destructive appetites of the strong. Philosophically, this curious mixture of distorted Darwinism and hedonistic Nietzscheanism may be fundamentally unsound, in the same way as Hitler's views on race were utterly pernicious. Both Hitler and de Sade, however, differ from Genet in that they justify doing what other people consider as evil by appealing to alternative standards. In their way, they are striving after their version of the good: the freeing of Nature from artificial trammels, the purification of the race by the elimination of unhealthy elements.

Genet, in contrast, has no concept of goodness and no desire to achieve it. He is aiming at absolute evil, and the inclusion of any rational argument, of any search for pleasure, would introduce positive qualities into what must remain an entirely negative world. At times, it is true, he associates crime with the pleasures of sex: in *Miracle of the Rose*, Rocky and Bulkaen make love in the bedroom of the house that they have just burgled, and in *The Thief's Journal* Genet writes of himself, '*J'ai bandé pour le crime*' ('I was *hot* for crime'). Nevertheless, this happens rarely, never as a result of a crime of violence, and never as a consequence of a crime consciously undertaken in order to procure this kind of pleasure. When Querelle has killed his associate, Vic, Genet describes his 'self-condemnation', and writes that the criminal, after committing his crime, 'lives in a state of uncertainty, of which he can rid himself only by denying his act, that is to say, by expiation, and further, by self-condemnation.' In *Deathwatch*, Genet's characters act because they think evil has chosen them as its agents, in *Our Lady of the Flowers* or *Miracle of the Rose* because their position offers no other way out, and in *Pompes Funèbres* because they are deliberately trying to be perverse. In his books, there is no reasoned attempt, as there is in de Sade, to call into question the established values of society, to show that conventional morality is wrong because it denies the Life Force, sacrifices the vigour and originality of the rich to the timorous nature of the poor, or is based upon a mistaken concept of human

B

nature. Whereas de Sade has the romantic conception of the criminal as the man superior both by birth and qualities to his fellows—most of his main characters, like himself, are aristocrats—Genet's criminals are for the most part stupid, cowardly, treacherous and selfish. He may describe them, at times, with glowing approbation, but everything which he shows them doing underlines how little they deserve his encomiums.

Neither does Genet limit himself to showing the banality of evil by consistently refraining from ever allowing any of his characters to do anything brave, enterprising, generous or intelligent. He openly condemns both his own romantic adulation of crime, and the cult of absolute evil which he claims to be celebrating. In *Miracle of the Rose*, for example, he specifically rejects the glamorous vision of prison and prisoners that had inspired *Le Condamné à Mort*. 'Now that the prison is stripped of its sacred ornaments,' he writes, 'I see it naked, and its nakedness is cruel. The inmates are merely sorry creatures with teeth rotted by scurvy; they are bent with illness and are always spitting and sputtering and coughing... They stink. They are cowardly in the presence of the guards, who are as cowardly as they. They are now only scurrilous caricatures of the handsome criminals I saw in them when I was twenty. I only wish that I could expose sufficiently the blemishes and ugliness and what they have become so as to take revenge for the harm they did me and the boredom I felt when confronted with their unparalleled stupidity'.

In *Pompes Funèbres*, he links this disillusioned realism even more closely to the evolution of his own attitude when he writes that after all his frenzied pursuit of evil, after his obstinacy in 'sublimating a world that is the reverse of your world', he sees himself arriving 'maimed and bloody, on a bank more thickly peopled than death itself'. And, he adds, 'the people I meet there have had an easy journey, with no dangers, and have omitted nothing. They live in infamy like fish in water, and all that remains for me to do, to achieve solitude, is go back the way I came and deck myself in the virtues of your books. In the face of such misfortune, tears or anger are all that remain'.

If this is how Genet feels, then it is not surprising that his cult of evil should differ so completely from that of the Marquis de Sade. To defend evil by rational argument, and thus appeal to positive if mistaken standards, would not only be illogical and inconsistent; it would also involve going against his own experience, which has taught him that evil is both dull and unoriginal. Genet nevertheless persists in his cult of evil, and never formally goes back on his declared intention of praising it in poetic terms. Thus he writes of Harcamone, one of the convicts in *Miracle of the Rose*, that he is a synthesis of dark and light, that his crimes give off 'a fragrance of roses', that he has a 'radiant image', and that he confronted the prison governor with 'a mystery as absurd as that of a rose in full bloom'. The novel begins, in fact, with a series of images in which Genet presents Harcamone as a bearer of flowers, and the title refers to a closing passage in which Harcamone's heart becomes 'a red rose of monstrous size and beauty'. There are similar attempts in all Genet's novels to present in terms of great poetic beauty a reality which he himself also insists is tawdry and banal, and this very curious use of language simultaneously to debunk and exalt evil is one of the most intriguing aspects of his work. If he really has recognised, as he says in *The Thief's Journal*, that the disreputable areas of towns 'are without mystery', and that the most dreadful criminals are 'distressingly stupid', why does he not reject his earlier attitude, and write books about evil that are as moral and pessimistic as *Les Fleurs du Mal*?

In a way, of course, he does. If a moralising novelist had set out to demonstrate the banality and stupidity of crime, or a theologian undertaken to prove the negative, self-defeating nature of evil, they could scarcely have given a more disillusioned picture of the underworld than the one which Genet offers in *Our Lady of the Flowers*, *The Thief's Journal*, or *Miracle of the Rose*. Far from persisting in his original, 'existential' choice by showing how it enabled him to build up a consistent if heretical world view, Genet seems to be perpetually calling it into question by intelligent and perceptive reference to his own experience. Lurking behind his phrases about the glow which perfect evil possesses, and often coming out visibly into the open, there is the common-sense, agnostic view that absolute good and absolute evil are illusions, created for social convenience or inherited from a more primitive, religious age, and that the harm which it does to others is the only reasonable criterion by which an act can be judged. Even so, Genet never explicitly considers this idea, either as a basis for further defiance of society or as a standard by which to satirise his criminals. He thus provides interesting confirmation for Sartre's thesis that he originally aimed at being a thief, at being 'torn apart by the great and terrible essence of the Evil-doer', rather than at doing wrong. Had Genet wished to do wrong, or sought to present in his books characters who are evil because they do harm to others without deriving benefit from it, he would surely have tried to recreate a series of Iagos. Curiously enough, however, no one in his work attempts to be evil in this way. None of his criminals sets out, as Iago does, consciously and deliberately to harm other people. This is partly because none of them is ever intelligent enough to plan ahead—Bulkaen, Harcamone and Stilitano all give the impression of being mentally retarded—and partly because Genet pretends to see the criminal as essentially the victim of fatality. But once the evil-doer is deprived of his intelligence, his courage and his devilish cunning, he ceases to be a threat to society. Genet's criminals do very little harm to anyone except themselves, and with the exception of Querelle of Brest they are all caught by the police and spend most of their time in gaol. He shows evil as self-defeating by its nature as well as defeated by society in practice. No one could ever receive encouragement to be a criminal from reading Genet's books.

Although Sartre recognises and occasionally emphasises

the stupidity, cowardice and treachery of Genet's characters, he does not see this aspect of his work as undermining the challenge which Genet's books offer to modern society. At the very beginning of *Saint Genet, actor and martyr*, he puts forward his own, neo-Freudian view of how the concept of evil originates in human society: man is afraid of the negative aspect of freedom, of his power to say 'No' to existing institutions, and casts it out. In so doing, he creates the figure of 'the evil-doer', who is detestable because he represents the frightening part of human liberty, its capacity to criticise or destroy. When the 'good people' who received Genet into their home caught him stealing and baptised him as a thief, they were making him into a monster 'for reasons of social utility'. Good people need criminals in order to project their own evil desires on to them, and Genet was admirably suited to fulfil this role.

Sartre also acknowledges, however, that Genet did not succeed in his attempt to *be* an evil-doer, and gives two reasons why this failure was inevitable. The first is connected with his general view of the human condition put forward in *Being and Nothingness*, and consists of saying that no one ever *is* anything at all. Because man is always free to choose a new attitude, he can never have the fixity of being which characterises a stone. When he tried to *be* a criminal, Genet was chasing a metaphysical will o' the wisp. A man who steals is not 'A Thief' in the same way as a stone is a stone, and Genet's initial predicament can be rather tritely expressed in contemporary British philosophical terms by saying that he failed to observe the difference between verbs of action and verbs of being. The second reason for his failure is a sociological one: all societies have a certain percentage of criminals, and Genet's social origins destined him from the start to play his part in maintaining this for early twentieth-century France. 'He had only to go to the trouble of being born,' writes Sartre. 'The gentle, inexorable hands of the Law will conduct him from the National Foundling Society to the penal colony.' When Genet tried deliberately to assume this social predestination as if it stemmed from his free choice, he was involved in another contradiction: it is pointless to will what is preordained, and Genet was merely pushing an open door.

Sartre thus comes very close to suggesting that Genet based his original choice on a double illusion, and discovered this only when it was too late. He might therefore be expected to endorse Genet's findings as to the banality of evil, and see him as merely a victim of old-fashioned, semi-theological modes of thought. However, he does not do this, and argues instead that although Genet failed to achieve absolute evil in his life, he nevertheless succeeds through his art. 'To read Genet,' he argues, 'is *to be thought by the spirit of Evil*, in complicity with it.' Genet's poetry, he continues, is 'a deliberate damning of the reader . . . a crime without extenuating circumstances'. When 'the "average Frenchman" who adorns himself with the name of good citizen' reads Genet's works, he is tricked into recognising that there are no crimes or unnatural passions of which he is not capable. Genet wins, for Sartre, by recreating the existence of evil in other people's minds, and thus preventing them from continuing to cast out the negative part of their freedom as foreign to them.

This is an interesting theory, but not one that survives a close reading of Genet's works. As will be seen when the novels are studied in more detail, Genet never presents his heroes consistently. For example, he describes Divine, the homosexual prostitute in *Our Lady of the Flowers*, as 'a thousand shapes, charming in their grace, which emerge from my eyes, mouth, elbows, knees, from all parts of me'. Yet in other parts of the book, we are faced with reality: Divine is a toothless, bald, skinny, ageing queen. His presentation of Mignon-les-petits-pieds, Divine's favourite lover, also shifts most amusingly from the adulatory to the ironic. Mignon 'has in his supple bearing the weighty magnificence of the barbarian who tramples choice furs beneath his muddy boots'. Yet as he walks along the boulevard, wearing his Prince of Wales tweed, a gold chain on his wrist, and those 'extraordinary, very light yellow, thin, pointed shoes peculiar to pimps', he becomes a comic gangster from an Ealing Studios film or from Monicelli's *I Soliti Ignoti*. He betrays his friends to the police, and is eventually arrested for the very unglamorous crime of shoplifting. Bulkaen, Genet's great love in Fontevrault prison in *Miracle of the Rose*, is first of all presented by a quotation from Ronsard: *'La grâce dans sa feuille et l'amour se repose'* ('Grace in leaf and love at rest'). On the very same page, however, Genet admits that the end of the book will show him 'contemptible for his stupidity or vanity', and only a few lines further on he brings the reader face to face with reality when he writes that the skin of Bulkaen's neck was 'shadowy with grime'. The portrait of crime and the criminal in Genet's work is, in this respect, far more likely to reassure the ' "average Frenchman" who adorns himself with the name of good citizen' in his dismissal of criminals as misguided fools than it is to disturb his satisfaction at being on the right side of the fence.

The problem which Genet's work sets the literary critic is thus significantly different from that of other writers who use immense verbal skill to put forward a view of the world that many of their readers find unacceptable on intellectual, moral or political grounds. The case for a dissociation between aesthetic and intellectual attitudes has been most elegantly expressed by W. H. Auden, and certain stanzas of his poem on the death of Yeats seem at first sight almost to have been written with Genet in mind:

> Time that is intolerant
> Of the brave and innocent
> And indifferent in a week
> To a beautiful physique,
>
> Worships language and forgives
> Everyone by whom it lives;
> Pardons cowardice, conceit,
> Lays its honours at their feet.

> Time, that with this strange excuse
> Pardons Kipling and his views,
> And will pardon Paul Claudel,
> Pardons him for writing well.

Because Genet does write well, in the sense that he has the knack of using words effectively, a strong feeling for verbal rhythm and a gift for transmuting experience into language, it is possible to forgive him a very great deal. His case is nevertheless fundamentally different from that of Kipling or Claudel, in the same way as it is different from that of the Marquis de Sade. These three writers, whatever the immense differences between them, are putting forward ideas that are consistently formulated. Unlike Genet, they are not always cutting the ground away from under their own feet by telling us that the people they pretend to admire are really selfish, stupid and cowardly.

The fundamental difference between Genet and other writers whose world vision seems to run counter to our present moral assumptions can also perhaps be explained by reference to George Orwell's essay on Swift. After showing all the anti-human and anti-humanistic aspects of Swift's work, Orwell raises the question of whether a book can be good 'if it expresses a palpably false view of life'. His reply is that one can imagine a good book being written in 1946 by 'a Catholic, a Communist, a Fascist, a pacifist, an anarchist, perhaps by an old-style Liberal or ordinary Conservative', but not by a 'Buchmanite, or a member of the Ku-Klux-Klan'. The essential requirement, he maintains, is that the views which the writer holds 'must be compatible with sanity, in the medical sense, and with the power of continuous thought'. In the case of Swift, he adds, we have a writer who had a 'terrible intensity of vision, capable of picking out a single hidden truth and then magnifying and distorting it'.

Almost all these remarks are, to some extent, applicable to Genet. The only two political movements which he mentions favourably are Darnard's *Milice* and the Kenyan

Mau-Mau, the criminals he presents for our admiration are, he proclaims, 'hoodlums of the worst sort', and the people he most admires are traitors. This attitude might form the basis for 'a terrible intensity of vision', were it not for the fact that, in all Genet's prose works, common-sense keeps breaking in to remind the reader that this vision is not to be taken wholly seriously. It often seems, again to quote Orwell on Swift, that Genet is a good writer because he has 'a native gift for using words, as some people have a naturally "good eye" for games', and that such literary value as his work possesses has therefore nothing to do with either the consistency or the inconsistency of his world vision. The literary merit of his work can, in this interpretation, be totally separated from his lifelong dedication to evil, and Genet can be seen as 'a good writer' in spite of and not because of his peculiar moral attitudes. Anyone who had lived with criminals and convicts for as long as he had, and had a 'gift for using words', could write books that were just as good, and perhaps even better.

This is a view that Sartre totally rejects.

> 'Rubbish,' I was told by a pretentious imbecile. 'Stop looking for complicated explanations. Genet wasn't saved by his persisting in evil. If he succeeded, it's because he had talent.' Very well: and if you're a failure, it's because you haven't any. But Genet's case isn't as clear as yours. *Precisely* because he has talent. What do you think talent is? Mildew of the brain? A supernumerary bone? I have shown that his work is the imaginary aspect of his life and that his genius is one with his unswerving will to live his condition to the very end.

Genius, Sartre argues later on, 'is not a gift but a way out that one invents in desperate cases'. In his view, Genet's greatness as a writer cannot be dissociated from his total attitude and attributed to an isolated aspect of his personality which lies in the ability to use words effectively. To say that Genet emerged from the lower depths because of a peculiar technical aptitude for language would be to make no distinction between literature and cricket, and assimilate the writer of genius to the West Indian who saves himself from poverty because he has a good eye for a ball.

In the same way that Sartre denies that an author's ability to use words can be separated from his total world view, he also rejects the attempt which Joseph McMahon made in his book *The Imagination of Jean Genet* to distinguish between Genet's 'instinctive imagination' and his 'presentational imagination'. For Mr. McMahon, our intellect rejects the views of the first, while at the same time our faculty of aesthetic appreciation is enthralled by the second. This is a view which runs parallel to the attitude implied in Auden's poem, and implies that criticism can distinguish fairly clearly between form and content. For Sartre, no such distinctions can be made. 'I know people who can read the coarsest passages without turning a hair: "Those two gentlemen sleep together? And then they eat their excrement? And after that, one goes off to denounce the other? As if that mattered! It's *so* well written." They stop at Genet's vocabulary so as not to have to *realize* the content.'* With complete intellectual consistency, Sartre transposes into the field of literary criticism the holistic philosophy and psychology which led him to argue, in his *Réflexions sur la question juive*, that the intolerance and hatred which characterise the anti-semite express themselves in each and every action which the anti-semite performs. We must either accept or reject Genet completely, and Sartre does not discuss the implications of those intrusions of realism and common-sense which provide so startling a contrast with Genet's more romantic and rhetorical approach. When he mentions the cowardice and treachery of Genet's heroes, he sees it not as part of a satirical portrait of the world of crime, but as an aspect of the 'corrosive cynicism' of homosexuals which characterises all Genet's work. In his view, the dichotomy in Genet's attitude to evil and to crime fits into the general pattern of his work, which manages still to be a tribute to evil because it reduces everything to images. 'His extraordinary books,' he writes, 'are their own rebuttal:

they contain both the myth and its dissolution, the appearance and the exposure of the appearance, the language and the exposure of language. When we finish them, the reading leaves a taste of ashes since their content cancels itself out.' Genet's aim, he argues, is to 'do Evil without resorting to Being. By his action as an artist and a poet who finally realizes the unrealizable, he forces the others to support, in his stead, the false against the true, Evil against Good'. The 'honest citizen' who picks up a book by Genet in order to 'see what this chap is all about', will thus be tricked in two ways: he will realise that he himself is just as bad as Genet; and he will have spent his valuable time giving life to something that does not really exist. 'Genet gives us *nothing*', maintains Sartre. 'When we shut the book, we shall know no more than we did before about prison or ruffians or the human heart.' Like the devil who pretended to scatter gold coins, he is in fact giving us only 'dead leaves'.

This may be the case if Genet's work is read with the moral, political and philosophical presuppositions which inform *Saint Genet, actor and martyr*, and if Sartre's portrait of 'the "average Frenchman" who adorns himself with the name of good citizen' is accepted as accurate. Such a man believes in essences, both of good and evil, holds that things are exactly as they seem and cannot bear to see them altered, and totally identifies himself with the characters of any book he happens to be reading. He has never before recognised the potentially criminal and anti-social aspects of his own personality, and believes that goodness coincides exactly with what is. It is, therefore, quite probable that he will be both taken in and wholly deflated by Genet's work. If, however, Genet's books are not studied for the effect they are likely to have on this reincarnation of Monsieur Prud'homme, they take on a different appearance and set essentially the kind of problems raised in the quotations from Auden and Orwell. They also, it may be added, do tell the truth about the criminal world in a peculiarly honest and effective way. In particular, their insistence upon the way

criminals betray one another to the police shows the same
kind of realism that Malraux found in Faulkner's *Sanctuary*,
while the comments in *Querelle of Brest* on the similarity
between criminals and policemen show that the days of
Vidocq are not yet completely over.

(ii) Homosexuality

Genet's treatment of homosexuality presents both the
same originality and the same dichotomy as his approach to
the problem of evil. In both cases, there is the same initial,
apparently wholehearted, support for conduct of which
society disapproves; the same refusal to justify this conduct
by an appeal to any standards which can be rationally
formulated; the same exploration through experience of
what this conduct implies; and, finally, the same simultaneously enthusiastic and disillusioned presentation of it.

All four of Genet's novels, as well as his more openly
autobiographical *The Thief's Journal*, deal extensively with
homosexuality, and there is no description anywhere in his
work of the more usual kinds of heterosexual activity.
Indeed, according to Sartre, Genet first of all began writing
in order to give encouragement and permanence to his own
erotic homosexual fantasies, and *Our Lady of the Flowers* is
described in *Saint Genet, actor and martyr* as an 'epic of
masturbation'. Sartre illustrated his interpretation further by
saying that when Genet succeeded in giving himself an
erection by writing out descriptions of his imaginary
characters, it was 'as if Flaubert had described the poisoning
of Madame Bovary in order to fill his own mouth with ink'.
Yet here again, Genet is completely different from any other
author who has written sympathetically about homosexuals
and tried to argue that society is wrong to persecute them.
His work contains nothing like the argument from nature
which Gide put forward in *Corydon*, nothing comparable to

the implication in *Les Faux-Monnayeurs* that a homosexual relationship between an older and a younger man may help the latter to come safely through the difficult period of adolescence, nothing like the appeal for sympathy, understanding and tolerance that informs Peter Wildeblood's *Against the Law*, nothing like the presentation of homosexuality as innocent but persecuted passion which gives almost a tragic note to Fritz Peter's *Finistere*. In the same way as Genet's criminals make no attempt to justify what they are doing by the Vautrin-type argument that the general corruption of society compels all men to commit crimes out of the sheer need to keep alive, none of his homosexuals ever argues that his mode of behaviour is natural and legitimate.

It may be, of course, that this is because all Genet's characters are already outlaws because they are criminals. Society does not persecute them for being homosexuals for the very good reason that they have already incurred its displeasure by more serious misdemeanours. Consequently, they do not feel the need to reply to this persecution by pleading a case for themselves on rational grounds. Moreover, in the exclusively male world of prison and reformatory, which so much of Genet's work describes, the choice is quite simply between homosexuality and no sex at all. Even so, there is something deliberate in his refusal to present any kind of positive case for homosexuality, and it is linked with the remark that he is said to have made about Gide: that he was 'of doubtful immorality', and therefore somebody whom Genet preferred not to meet. What Genet meant was that anyone who tried to defend so-called unnatural or illegal behaviour by rational argument, as Gide had done in *Corydon*, had already gone over to the side of the good. If he was not a respectable citizen as yet, he was striving to become one; and if his form of sexual activity was not yet accepted as normal, he was trying to make it so. It is, in this respect, consistent for the person who wrote, in *Pompes Funèbres*, that he had willed himself to be 'the traitor, the thief, the plunderer, the man of hatred, destruction, scorn and cowardice' not to want the way he enjoys sex to become socially acceptable.

This refusal to justify his own sexual taste also accompanies a portrait of homosexuality that is just as unflattering as the description which Genet offers of crime. Sexual relationships, in Genet's world, are never accompanied by affection or fidelity. In *Our Lady of the Flowers*, for example, he comments that homosexuals are 'great immoralists' and writes: 'In the twinkling of an eye, after six years of union, without considering himself attached, without thinking that he was causing pain or doing wrong, Mignon decided to leave Divine. Without remorse, only a slight concern that perhaps Divine might refuse ever to see him again.' In *Miracle of the Rose*, where Genet describes the homosexuality which flourished both at the *Colonie de Mettray* and in Fontevrault prison, all the relationships are characterised by lack of affection, brutality and ruthlessness. At Mettray, Genet himself is 'sold' by his friend Villeroy to another boy called Van Rey, in exchange for a few pieces of cheese. In *Pompes Funèbres*, the German soldier Erik watches his lover Riton treated with great brutality by his comrades and makes no attempt to interfere. In *The Thief's Journal*, Armand makes Genet smuggle cocaine into Belgium, and is completely indifferent to the long prison sentence which his friend will undoubtedly receive if he is caught. Not even Proust, denying his own homosexuality and satirising it in the Baron de Charlus, gave quite so unsympathetic a portrait of what Genet himself calls, in *Querelle of Brest*, 'the monstrosity of masculine loves'.

This is not, it is true, always the case in every page of Genet's works. A number of passages in his novels do seem pornographic in the sense of being written to excite sexual desire, and some of the characters in his work have, when first presented to the reader, that curiously unreal air of the male models sketched or photographed in magazines with titles like *Male Physique* or *Model He-Men*. It is doubtless this fact which led Ronald Bryden, in an article published in the

Observer in September 1966, to claim that 'no other writer seized more strongly on the imagination of the 1950's, creating a literary cult of the tough, the "butch" and bisexual, the English and American equivalents of Genet's world of the hustlers, ponces and drag queens of Montmartre'. The themes of Genet's work, Bryden argued, had been 'diluted and absorbed into the broader fashions of sexual permissiveness, butch clothing (leather jackets, tight trousers and the rest) and general anti-establishment bolshiness'. These remarks do draw attention to one of the several ways in which Genet's novels enlarge the reader's imaginative experience by enabling him to see how the world can appear to the homosexual: inhabited by eminently desirable males, whose trousers, belts, thighs and shoulders glow with the same kind of sexual qualities which most men find in the latest fashions of female attractiveness.

However, just as Genet begins by singing the praises of evil and then shows how banal it is, the splendidly attractive males whom he presents in his poems and in certain pages of his novels are soon revealed in a very different light. Maurice Pilorge, for example, is addressed in *Le Condamné à Mort* as a beautiful Greek shepherd, with eyes like roses and hair powdered with clear stars of steel. Yet on the very first page of *Our Lady of the Flowers*, we learn that he killed his lover, Escudero, to rob him of less than a thousand francs. Stilitano, whom Genet follows around Spain and Holland with dog-like devotion, is a coward, Divers, the handsomest boy at Mettray is syphilitic and betrays his accomplice Harcamone to the police, and even Querelle, the most virile and enterprising of Genet's criminals, feels the need to expiate his crimes by a masochistic relationship with a brothel-keeper and a policeman. Genet's insistence on ramming the stupidity and cowardice of his heroes down the reader's throat is the most effective anti-aphrodisiac that a moralising writer could find, for there is a wide difference between showing that love can still persist in spite of weaknesses and perversity, and the decision to deprive one's characters of any redeeming features whatsoever apart from a somewhat ambiguous sexual charm. Indeed, Genet goes so far as to suggest in *Our Lady of the Flowers* that all homosexual desires are, in the final analysis, doomed to frustration: the attractive male is desirable because of his virile masculinity, but he immediately loses this attraction when he responds to the homosexual's advances. After all, the clearest sign of virility is an intense and exclusive liking for real women. Mignon-les-petits-pieds may well proclaim that 'A male who fucks another male is a double male', but as Genet suggests, and as Sartre makes explicit, this is not at all the case. He is merely 'a female without realising it', and the longer Mignon associates with Divine the more feminine he becomes.

Sartre acknowledges that Genet gives a very hostile portrait of homosexuality, but he does not interpret this as a reassurance to the ordinary reader that his sexual tastes are, after all, preferable to those of Genet. Instead, he presents those passages in which Genet speaks lyrically of the boys he finds sexually exciting as yet another way in which he revenges himself, through literature, on the society that originally used words to brand the term 'thief' upon him. 'Homosexual because of the power of words', he writes, 'we taste for a moment, in the realm of the imaginary, the forbidden pleasure of taking a man and being taken, and we cannot taste it without horrifying ourselves.' This may be true for some readers, but a number of criticisms can be made of this new variation on the theme that 'When reading Genet, the Just Man becomes Jean Genet . . .', and is thus '. . . *thought by* the spirit of Evil'. The first is that Sartre's picture of the Just Man is a figment of his imagination, a caricature based on a selection of ideas from highly conservative, reactionary, late nineteenth-century authors such as Maurice Barrès and Paul Bourget. Sartre himself seems to recognise the weakness of his approach when he writes that 'the ideal Just Man does not read anything', and it is only someone who had never opened a book or listened to the radio, who could still imagine, in this post-Freudian age, that he possessed total sexual normality. 'All right,' the modern Just Man might say, 'so I can see what it is like to be a homosexual when I read Genet. I could see what it was like to have a passion for under-age girls when I read *Lolita*, and this probably means that a part of me is that way inclined as well. It also means that Genet and Nabokov are good writers. But if I am to believe what psychologists tell me, everyone is a bit odd. An eminent anthropologist once said to me of Pauline Réage's *Histoire d'O*, "*Je défie quiconque de le lire sans bander.*" It struck me at the time that he was an honest man.'*

The second criticism is a more purely literary one, and concerns the theory of reading assumed as correct in *Saint Genet, actor and martyr*. When we read, argued Sartre, in *What is Literature?*, we bring the characters in a novel to life by lending them our ability to feel passion, impatience, anger or excitement. Unless we willingly allow ourselves to be alienated in this way, the novel will remain merely a series of inanimate signs. This is a valid point, but Sartre then goes on, in *Saint Genet*, to write as if the reader of a novel were totally alienated and completely deprived of any power of critical reflection. For the theory of reading that Sartre assumes in *Saint Genet* to be true, everyone would have to be like the lady who leaped from her seat during a performance of *Othello* and screamed: 'You great big black fool, don't you *see*!', or the Arabian tribesmen who shoot at the villain when they see a Western. The 'willing suspension of disbelief' applies just as much to the novel as it does to the theatre. If it did not, then the reader of *Great Expectations* would not be able simultaneously to feel Pip's embarrassment when Jo comes to visit him in London, and condemn this embarrassment as snobbish and unjustified.

In the case of the homosexuality in Genet's novels, the reader's ability to retain a certain critical detachment is strengthened by the knowledge that the young man described with such evocative appreciation will, as has been said, turn out to be cowardly, stupid, dishonest and unfaithful. Bulkaen, for example, in *Miracle of the Rose*, is a character whose initial description by Genet leads Sartre to write: 'If I have the slightest inclination for men, even if it is repressed to my very depths, I am caught, constrained, in the shame of avowing my tastes to myself.' The subsequent development of the plot, however, can only reassure the Just Man that he was quite right to have repressed whatever homosexual leanings he possessed. Otherwise, he would have had to confront Bulkaen's grimy neck, bear with his lies, stupidity and cowardice, and never be sure which other person he was really shacking up with. Sartre remarks that Genet's worst enemies are to be found among homosexuals, and the statement is not difficult to believe. The final impression left by Genet's novels is, in this respect, analogous with the impact of Laclos's *Les Liaisons dangereuses*: both authors begin by describing a certain form of sexual behaviour—seduction of the innocent and heterosexual promiscuity for Laclos, homosexuality for Genet—in terms that imply approbation and excite both connivance and approval; the further one reads, however, the less attractive the activity becomes, until in the end it is not difficult to believe Laclos's claim that his novel was meant to be moral, or to present Genet as a critic of the sexual tastes that he himself flaunts. The comparison should not be taken too far, since Laclos is writing from a consistent moral viewpoint whereas Genet is not. Nevertheless, it does highlight the wide difference between Genet and those authors who, like Gide or D. H. Lawrence, put forward an unorthodox view of sex which they are prepared to support on moral and social grounds. To have denied entry into England of Genet's works on the ground that they might deprave and corrupt shows that they can have been read only rather superficially, in the same way that the prosecution of Flaubert for having written an immoral book in *Madame Bovary* was undertaken on rather inadequate evidence.

(iii) Poetry, realism and the theatre

In the interview which he gave to *Playboy*, Genet did in fact criticise some of his own works by saying that on those occasions when he wrote in order to excite sexual emotion, he was using literature and art incorrectly because he was not being true to 'poetry'. Although few critics have argued that Genet's poems were poetic in any sense other than the purely formal one of being written in conventional metres, writers as different as Jean Cocteau and Philip Toynbee have recognised a poetic quality in his work as a whole. In so doing, they have undoubtedly responded to Genet's intention, for he wrote of *The Thief's Journal* that: 'The aim of this account is to embellish my earlier adventures, in other words, to extract beauty from them, to find in them the element which today will elicit song, the only proof of this beauty.' Earlier in the same book he completely subordinates ethical to aesthetic considerations when he contends that 'the beauty of a moral act depends upon the beauty of its expression. To say that it is beautiful is to decide that it will be so. It remains to be proven so. This is the task of images, that is, of the correspondences with the splendours of the physical world'. At least in theory, his books transcend the ugliness of his life, which thus becomes sacred by the art which it inspires. 'My victory is verbal,' he writes in *The Thief's Journal*, in a phrase which Sartre takes as the title for his chapter on Genet's aesthetic achievement, 'and I owe it to the richness of the terms, but may the poverty that counsels such choices be blessed.'

These are far-reaching ambitions, and a study of Genet's work tends to reveal the same gap between declared intention and actual achievement which characterised his treatment of evil and homosexuality. In the same way as satirical writers of the past have emphasised the banality of lower middle-class life by describing it in mock-heroic terms, the high-flown, poetic language which Genet uses to describe his own miserable adventures serves only to underline how very tawdry and depressing the reality was. He comes near to recognising this in a passage in *Miracle of the Rose* when he writes: 'It is not to be wondered at that the most wretched of human lives is related in words that are too beautiful. The magnificence of my tale springs naturally (as a result of my modesty too, and my shame at having been so unhappy) from the pitiable moments of my entire life,' and there are moments when his books become either deliberately or accidentally funny because of the extreme contrast between his glamorous style and his drab subject matter.

There are two other reasons for questioning Genet's claim that he writes only to realise his own ideal of poetry. The first of these is that the claim applies only to one aspect of his work and apparently discounts those features of his novels which English critics, in particular, have found especially valuable. They have nearly all echoed Simon Raven's judgment that while 'Genet the preacher is an inflated bore', there must be praise for 'Genet the chronicler of low life', and there is no doubt that, especially in *Miracle of the Rose*, Genet gives a superb picture of prison life, its physical horror, emotional atmosphere and social complexity. In *Our Lady of the Flowers* and *Querelle of Brest* he also offers a fascinating account of homosexual problems and behaviour, one all the more intriguing because it is based on no conventional ethical standards. Moreover, anyone who reads Genet's novels primarily for the transfiguration of his experience into poetic terms is almost bound to be disappointed. Relatively few of his pages even try to achieve this, and they are surrounded by much more immediately interesting realistic passages. There is also a second problem in the definition which Genet himself gives of poetry, for this rarely seems to apply to any of the phrases in his books which do contain language used in its highest, most sensitive and most perceptive form.

Thus he writes, in *Our Lady of the Flowers*, that poetry 'always pulls the ground from under your feet and sucks you into the bosom of a wonderful night'. A poetic work, he maintains, annuls conflicts, and poetry itself is *'la rupture (ou plutôt la rencontre au point du rupture) du visible et de l'invisible'* ('the break [or rather the meeting at the breaking point] between the visible and the invisible'). This may or may not be the case, and the accuracy of these definitions is quite obviously not a question which can be decided by rational discussion or analysis. Anyone who maintains he has had a poetic experience of this kind is rather in the position of a mystic who claims to have had an intuition of God: what he says is in no way empirically verifiable. What is empirically verifiable, however, is that Genet's work contains many phrases which are poetic in a more traditional sense of the word. Thus when he speaks in *Miracle of the Rose* of *'un peuple invisible à force d'être nombreux'* (a people invisible by virtue of their number'), or describes, in *Our Lady of the Flowers*, a street as being *'morne comme un matin d'insomnie'* ('dismal, like a morning of insomnia'), or describes Divine as writhing about *'comme un copeau né sous la varlope'* ('like a shaving from a turning lathe'), he is using images of a fairly traditional kind and doing so very successfully. Similarly, his remark that each object *'apporte dans la chambre sa fascination du larcin bref comme un appel des yeux'* ('brings into the room the fascination of petty theft that comes as swiftly as a glance'), does convey something of his own attitude to theft. Nor are all his images totally devoid of humour. In *The Screens*, a character is insulted by being told that his skin is as depressed as *'un vieux cache-col en soie autour du cou d'un instituteur laique'* ('an old silk scarf round the neck of a lay schoolteacher'), and the imaginative accuracy of the social observation in this phrase never failed to raise a laugh when the play was performed. There are, it is true, many phrases in Genet's work where the poetry and images defy analysis. His description of the popular novels as being written on *'un papier spongieux—comme l'est, dit-on, la conscience des vilains messieurs qui débauchent les enfants'* ('as spongy as the consciences of nasty gentlemen who debauch children') is one example, and the remark that someone has *'des genoux païens si beaux qu'ils refléteraient l'intelligence désespérée du visage des mystiques'* ('pagan knees so lovely that they reflected the desperate intelligence on the faces of mystics') is another. Nevertheless, it is not impossible to imagine a satisfactory explanation for the curiously effective impression which such phrases do leave on the mind, and one which would not involve the annulment of all intellectual faculties which Genet's own definition seems to involve. In short, there is often the same dichotomy in Genet's literary work between formal statement and actual achievement as there is in his attitude towards society and towards sex. In practice, he is constantly moving away from the position which he claims to be taking up, criticising the cult of evil and the practice of homosexuality when he claims to be endorsing them, communicating with his reader in more or less traditional literary terms while at the same time denying that any such communication is his aim. His theatre, in this respect, is no freer from this dichotomy than his novels.

Theoretically, and in the views of most of his critics, all his plays exemplify the aesthetic credo which he put forward in his preface to *Les Bonnes* in 1954 and in his *Lettres à Roger Blin* in 1966. In both these texts, he argues that the theatre should not reflect social reality, should not create character, and should not entertain the spectator. It should, in the image chosen by Martin Esslin for his chapter on Genet in *The Theatre of the Absurd*, create a 'Hall of Mirrors' in which man is 'inexorably trapped by an endless progression of images that are merely his own distorted reflection'. Another analysis of Genet's theatre that he himself would probably be prepared to underwrite is the one put forward by Robert Brustein, in his *Theatre of Revolt*. There, the argument is that Genet's plays represent the application of Antonin Artaud's theory on the theatre of cruelty, and are thus a liberation of man's violent, irrational, subconscious drives. This is certainly how Genet seems to see the function of the theatre, for in his 1954 preface to *Les Bonnes* he speaks with approval of what the theatre would be like with the Mau Mau—an explosion, presumably, of the kind of primitive violence evoked at times in *The Blacks*. Genet's plays undoubtedly do possess the qualities which Martin Esslin and Robert Brustein describe, and he is consequently well within the mainstream of mid-twentieth-century avant-garde writing. Like Ionesco and Beckett, he does show a world in which man is alienated from himself by language and self-consciousness, and like Antonin Artaud or the Peter Weiss of the *Marat-Sade*, he does try to create a kind of inspired rapture in the theatre by concentrating on themes of extreme violence. Nevertheless, in the same way that his novels both sing the praises of evil and homosexuality and show them in an ironic, critical light, so, in his plays, reality keeps breaking through and offers a more conventional type of theatrical experience in addition to the avant-garde challenge.

Thus *Haute Surveillance* (*Deathwatch*) makes a statement about a particular type of criminal and a particular feature of prison life, *The Maids* is a study in the psychology of resentment and *The Balcony* is about the relationship between real and imaginary power in modern society. Both *The Blacks* and *The Screens* deal with the problem of violence in a colonialist or neo-colonialist context, as well as with the wider issues of dignity and self-awareness among recently oppressed people. The treatment of these social and psychological themes is, of course, never realistic in the conventional way. As Genet himself said in *Our Lady of the Flowers*, we must lie in order to tell the truth. His plays are presented with every insistence upon fiction and theatricality, but they nevertheless, by a strange and effective paradox, give insight into a reality which is both recognisable as our own and revelatory of what lies behind everyday appearances.

(iv) Sainthood and language

There is one further theme in Genet's work that should be mentioned before each of his books is discussed separately.

It is that of sainthood. Genet says that, for him, *la sainteté* is the most beautiful word in human language, and he claims that both he and a number of the characters in his novels and plays are inspired by the desire to become saints. Solange, in *The Maids*, speaks of 'the eternal couple of the criminal and the saint', and Genet says of Divine, the homosexual prostitute of *Our Lady of the Flowers*, that he will 'gradually deliver her from evil, and, holding her by the hand, lead her to saintliness'. His own ambition, he claims in *The Thief's Journal*, is to have people say of him 'he is a saint—or, preferably, he was a saint'. Few aspects of Genet's work are more difficult to understand and appreciate than this insistence upon sainthood, especially as the concept is never integrated into the plot of his novels and plays in the way that his treatment of evil and homosexuality is. It thus remains on the surface of his work, apparently a purely verbal manifestation of that desire to shock the bourgeois reader which has characterised so much French literature since romanticism.

This, indeed, is the explanation which Sartre tentatively puts forward at one point in his study in order to explain the frequency with which Genet mentions sainthood in the most unlikely contexts. Genet, he writes, takes pleasure in 'constructing aberrant notions, the aim of which is to shake the tranquil assurance of honest folk'. Later in his analysis, it is true, Sartre rejects his particular explanation, and states that Genet's sainthood should be seen as part of his misguided attempt to live on a mode of pure existence rather than of effective action, but it is nevertheless difficult to dismiss the first possibility absolutely. Indeed, it is sometimes tempting to go even further than this, and to interpret some of Genet's remarks about sainthood as deliberately satirising the more extreme implications of the remark by Péguy which Graham Greene placed at the beginning of *The Heart of the Matter*: '*Nul n'est aussi compétent que le pécheur en matière de chrétienté. Nul, si ce n'est le saint.*' Thus when Genet writes in *Miracle of the Rose* that sainthood 'is also recognised by the following: that it leads to Heaven by way of sin', he is carrying Mauriac's attitude towards Thérèse Desqueyroux and Graham Greene's view of Pinkie to their logical conclusion: if these characters are saved because of their sin, then Harcamone, the child-murderer, and Divers, the traitor, have an even greater hope of salvation. Once the sinner is equated with the saint, and the theological virtues of faith, hope and charity discounted in favour of the clearer perception of reality afforded by actually sinning, there is no limit to the claims that can be made.

It is extremely doubtful, however, if Genet ever consciously satirises anyone's views. Although a number of passages in *Pompes Funèbres* or *The Thief's Journal* often produce complete revulsion from the ideas or institutions which he enthusiastically praises, this is almost certainly unintentional. There seems no reason to doubt that he intends his remarks about sainthood to be taken seriously, in spite of the fact that he completely distorts the normal meaning of the word. What he does is take only two aspects of sainthood—the quest for absolute humility and the renunciation of all human pleasures—and present them as if they were the whole thing. He totally ignores the fact that sainthood has all the other connotations of holiness, patience, moral perfection and genuine devotion to the well-being of others. The characters whom he describes as saints in his books act for the most part in complete defiance of these moral and spiritual values, whose existence Genet does not even mention.

This Humpty Dumpty-like attitude towards language raises yet another literary and philosophical question: can a writer expect his readers to follow him when he takes a word and strips it of so many of its normal connotations that he virtually gives it a new meaning? As long as Genet is writing down his stories on sheets of brown paper, and intending them for no eyes other than his own, then there can be no possible objection to his use of any private language he likes. He was exactly in this position when he first wrote *Our Lady of the Flowers*, and there is no reason to doubt that he did, at the time, think he had fulfilled some of the conditions of sainthood by seeking out the modes of humiliation which he describes retrospectively in *The Thief's Journal*. Yet he seems to forget, when he moves to the second stage of his career as a writer and allows his books to be printed so that other people can read them, that words have a public as well as a private meaning. If he is not deriding the very concept of sainthood by showing how completely its other aspects can be forgotten in the quest for personal humiliation, then his continued use of the word shows that, here at least, he has totally abandoned the use of language for communication.

If Genet were always unintelligible when he writes about religion, the critical problem raised by his use of the words 'saint' and 'sainthood' would be less acute. He could be classified as an author with a blind spot, a man whose King Charles's Head intrudes every time a particular subject arises. This, however, is far from the case. The very brilliant pages about religion in *Our Lady of the Flowers* show that Genet can be just as original, perceptive and ironic on this subject as he is on crime or homosexuality. Indeed, he presents the same problem in each case, alternating between a complete defiance of normal linguistic and moral standards and an implicit acceptance of them, an acceptance which he then uses as a basis for communicating a new vision to the reader. Thus, not long before his reference to how Divine, whom he qualifies as a saint, deliberately causes the death of a two-year-old girl, Genet writes the following passage about the Virgin Mary:

> To be the human mother of a divinity is a more disturbing state than that of divinity. The Mother of Jesus must have had incomparable emotions while carrying her son, and later, while living and sleeping side by side with a son who was God—that is, everything and herself as well—who could make the world not be, His Mother, Himself not be, a God for whom she had to prepare, as Josephine did for Marie, the yellow corn mush.

There is a parallel alternation, this time between defiance and acceptance of normal moral values and reactions, in Genet's description of a murder trial in *Our Lady of the Flowers*. Thus, at one point, he writes that 'the crowd was ashamed of not being the murderer', and declares a little further on that the murderer's body was as 'prodigiously glorious as the body of Christ rising aloft, to dwell there alone and fixed, in the sunny noonday sky'. Yet he also writes, in the same description, that the general public comes to murder trials 'only insofar as a word may result in a beheading and that it may return, like Saint Denis, carrying its severed head in its hands'. This is a perceptive comment on the popularity of murder trials, and one which could well be fitted into an argument criticising capital punishment because of the openings which it provides for vicarious cruelty. It is also, in French, a very clever pun on the ambiguity of the possessive pronoun. The crowd will return *'tel Saint Denis, portant sa tête entre ses mains'*. The *'sa'* can refer both to the decapitated saint and to the crowd which has gone to get 'its' head as a huntsman goes to get 'his' fox or a murderer 'his' victim.

In this particular scene the rapid switching from one set of values to another is aesthetically successful, for it reinforces the point which Genet is making about the incompatibility between certain kinds of crime and the 'due processes of law' used to condemn them. In the passage in *The Thief's Journal* where he talks about 'the difficult, painful ascension that leads to humiliation', and yet suddenly protests against the fact that he is required by the French police to produce 'the humiliating "anthropometric card"' to prove his identity, he is on more dangerous ground. It is surely fair comment to point out that he cannot have it both ways: either he is seeking all forms of humiliation, and he should welcome the insistence of the French police that beggars should prove their identity by having a card showing their finger-prints; or he is arguing that it is wrong to treat people as if they were merely immatriculated animals, and is therefore accepting the rational and humane standards that he pretends to reject. As will be seen when *Miracle of the Rose* is examined in more detail, the facts that Genet adduces about prison and reformatory life are wholly consistent with an enlightened policy which would not treat criminals as the total outcasts and make them even more vicious by wanton acts of cruelty. Yet he persists in stating, with an insistence that becomes almost hysterical, that this is not what he wants, and that Mettray, where he suffered most, was 'a paradise'. Whatever he discusses, whether it be crime, homosexuality, sainthood or prison reform, Genet always presents the reader with the same dichotomy between what he claims to think and the totally opposite conclusion which the reader cannot fail to draw from the facts which Genet also presents to him.

Were Genet not also a brilliant prose writer, and did his effects not sometimes come off, he could perhaps be dismissed as a kind of practical joker who deliberately sets out to put forward contradictory ideas for the pleasure of baffling his readers. Yet he possesses, in spite of his total inability to cast his ideas into a consistent world view, an extraordinary capacity to create atmosphere and character and to exploit all the poetic and intellectual potentialities of the French language. His technical skill is indeed so great that it often seems as though only his refusal to hide the disillusionment which he feels about crime prevents him from presenting a consistent and persuasive philosophy of evil. His lack of consistency clearly stems from deliberate choice, and accounts for the basic contradiction in his work, whereby he is both a self-indulgent romantic, pretending to refuse all communication with his fellows on any but his own terms, and, as he himself says, a 'disenchanted visionary', whispering to the bourgeois reader whom he claims to insult all the most reassuring secrets about the banality of evil and the disappointments of homosexuality.

PART TWO

THE NOVELS

CHAPTER THREE

OUR LADY OF THE FLOWERS

ALTHOUGH Genet himself never uses the word to describe any of his books, *Our Lady of the Flowers* has three qualities which justify discussing it as a novel: it tells a story, albeit in a disjointed and untraditional way; it creates characters which give the illusion of being real people; and it describes life in a particular social milieu. It is also an autobiographical work, in which Genet's own experiences are used as a basis for creating the main character in the novel, as well as an analysis of homosexuality, and a series of experiments with words and concepts. At times, as when Genet describes the smell and atmosphere of prison, it is realistic. At others, as when he makes Divine, his own dream creation, imagine another character called Marchetti, who then re-enters Genet's own dream and plays a part in the events he is describing, it is like a hall of mirrors in which nothing is real. In this respect, it looks forward to the world of his plays, and there are a number of phrases in *Our Lady of the Flowers* which take on their full meaning only when seen in the context of Genet's work as a whole.

The book tells the story of a young country boy, Louis Culafroy, who comes to Paris and lives as a homosexual prostitute styling himself—or, rather, herself—as Divine. The confusion of genders is Genet's own, and from time to time he uses both masculine and feminine on the same page in order to indicate that some of the remarks refer to the character's life as Culafroy, and some to her experiences as

Divine. Much of the book is taken up with describing
Divine's affaires with those of her lovers whom she takes for
her pleasure: Mignon-les-petits-pieds, a thief and pimp
whose real name is Paul Garcia; Gabriel, a soldier, whom
Divine christens the Archangel; a teen-age murderer,
Notre-Dame-des-Fleurs, more prosaically known as Adrien
Baillon; and a negro called Seck Gorgui. Mignon lives for
six years with Divine, before deserting her for another
homosexual called Mimosa II, and ending up in prison for
shop-lifting. Divine then lives with Gorgui and Notre-
Dame, until the latter is arrested and guillotined for having
murdered a middle-aged homosexual called Ragon. Divine
herself dies of tuberculosis.

The story is not told in straight chronological sequence,
and Genet insists from the very beginning that the characters are figments of his imagination, vaguely modelled upon
criminals he has known, and never to be considered as real
people. The book begins with a description of Divine's
funeral, and the narration is frequently interrupted while
Genet meditates on his character and own situation, as a
prisoner in La Santé gaol awaiting his trial. Divine's
memories of her childhood as Culafroy, of the homosexual
relationship which, as Culafroy, she had with an older boy
called Alberto, are mingled with Genet's own memories of
the different cells in which he has been imprisoned, and
events such as Notre-Dame's eventual confession to the
police are mentioned in passing long before they are actually
described. This deliberate disruption of the time sequence
recurs in each of the books by Genet that can be broadly
considered as novels—*Our Lady, Miracle of the Rose, Pompes
Funèbres* and *Querelle of Brest*—and marks him out as an
avant-garde novelist just as much as his exploitation of
violence and mirror images in his plays puts him in the
tradition of the mid-twentieth-century drama. It would be
interesting to know whether he had read Faulkner, for his
treatment of time, and presentation of the main events in his
novels as having already occurred, are very reminiscent of

The Sound and the Fury. It is not at the moment possible, however, to find out how Genet acquired the extensive culture which he scatters a little self-consciously through the pages of *Our Lady*, and whether he was influenced by any writer apart from the popular novelists whom Sartre claims he is imitating. He may have read Faulkner, or he may simply have hit upon a similar technique of narration because he too wishes to present a world in which man has lost control over his future.

It is impossible, in analysing *Our Lady of the Flowers*, to separate a study of Divine as a fictional character either from Genet's study of homosexuality or from the use which he makes of his own experiences. In her homosexuality, Divine both is and is not Genet. Yet in both cases the inspiration for the creation of her as a character seems to stem just as much from what Genet was as from what, in one way, he would have liked to be. Divine lives as a homosexual prostitute, and also develops strong attachments for other men who do not pay to sleep with her. In *The Thief's Journal*, Genet makes no bones about the fact that he found homosexual prostitution 'better suited to his indolence' than the more active career as thief, and his relationship with Stilitano, which he describes in the same book, is often similar to Divine's relationship with Mignon-les-petits-pieds. Both Divine and Genet are attracted by the flamboyant masculinity of their male partners, both see through them completely in that they recognise their fundamental cowardice and treachery, and both are treated with the same ruthlessness and lack of affection. Another similarity between Divine and the Genet who describes his own homosexuality in his other books lies in the fact that both live through torments of jealousy whenever their lovers are unfaithful. Perhaps the most powerful scene in the whole of *Our Lady* describes a 'drag ball' which Divine attends with Notre-Dame and the Negro, Seck Gorgui, and in the course of which the young murderer and the Negro become so violently attracted to each other that they quite neglect Divine. As a study in jealousy, it is much better than the passages in *Miracle of the Rose* because it is condensed, highly dramatic, and full of movement. It also has a particular interest for the relationship between the real Genet and the fictional Divine in that it shows Divine managing to carry off a situation in a way that Genet clearly dreamed of doing but never, it would seem, actually achieved.

As the three characters leave the ball, they decide to take a taxi 'in order to escape the vexation of a commonplace return'. Divine, excluded by the two others, flirts outrageously with the taxi-driver, and thus escapes, for the time being, from the humiliation of being the odd one out. This ability to transcend a humiliating situation by plunging so deep into it that she comes out triumphantly the other side also occurs in another scene in the novel when Divine, sitting one evening in a queer bar, utters so violent a shriek of laughter that the little coronet of false pearls that she is wearing falls off and scatters all over the sawdust-covered floor. This is Divine's opportunity. 'She lets out a burst of strident laughter. Everyone pricks up his ears: it's her signal. She tears out her false teeth from her open mouth, puts them on her skull and, with her heart in her throat but victorious, she cries out in a changed voice, her lips drawn back in her throat:

"Dammit all, Ladies, I'll be queen anyhow." '

The difference between Divine and the Genet who describes his own misadventures in *The Thief's Journal* can be seen by his description of what actually happened in Barcelona when Stilitano forced him to put on women's clothes. When a woman in a bar asked him if he liked men and 'When did it start', as when a young man caught his foot in his dress, all Genet could do was mumble a feeble protest or stammer a reply. Yet, in the midst of his embarrassment, he felt 'a beautiful actress smouldering within him' ready to scream out: 'I won't have people limping in my dress.' This, or probably something even more devastating for the poor young man, is undoubtedly what 'Divine la Cascadeuse' would have shrieked, turning the situation wholly to her advantage by a kind of farcical behaviour which can be highly comic or deeply tragic according to the point of view adopted to judge it. This, indeed, is part of the originality and honesty of Genet's treatment of homosexuality in *Our Lady of the Flowers*: in the same way that Divine is both a screaming old queen and a rather timid, simple and superstitious country boy with the ridiculous name of Culafroy (cold arse), so homosexuality is shown as both glamorous defiance of the dullness and conventionality of the bourgeois world, and a sterile and basically sordid way of behaviour. Divine herself attains at times the stature and fascination of a proletarian Charlus, and with none of his advantages of rank or wealth she protects herself in a much harder and more brutal world. At the same time, she also embodies the deep despair of the ageing homosexual who is reduced to paying her lovers and is intensely sensitive to the insults which are heaped upon her.

For Sartre, Divine was born of the 'only human feeling' which Genet still retained after his systematic pursuit of evil: 'the fear of growing old.' 'Perhaps one day,' he writes, 'the adolescent will awaken: he will go to a mirror and see the image of an old, faded fairy.' This may well be true, for the life which Genet led between the ages of sixteen and thirty, joining the foreign Legion and then deserting, wandering round Spain as a penniless beggar, in and out of prison in every country he visited, must have been a very wearing process. But this fear of ageing, though undoubtedly present in the insistence on Divine's bald and toothless state, is not the only element of his personality which Genet put into his creation of Divine. Her insolence and bravura are a kind of wish-fulfilment of Genet's ambitions, but her sensitivity to insults and obsession with humiliation also provide a directer expression of Genet's more general situation and unhappiness. Thus he writes of Divine that 'calling herself an old, whorish whore, she simply forestalled mockery and insults' and underlines how she reflected his own experiences when he says of himself, in virtually the same words, 'if I declare I am an old whore, nobody can do better than that, I discourage insult'. In his own case, however, such insults were not aimed solely at his homosexuality, and it is interesting to see how he introduces his general situation and uses it to make Divine an extreme incarnation of the homosexual's dilemma in modern society: deny what you are by pretending to be normal, or flaunt what you are and forestall ridicule.

Thus when he was sent to Mettray, Genet was mocked and bullied by the other boys who were, as he says 'stronger and more malicious (*plus méchants*) than I'. He describes his reaction as being 'to keep no place in my heart where the feeling of my innocence might take shelter. I owned to being the coward, traitor, thief and fairy they saw in me'. This deliberate search for humiliation plays an important part in Genet's conception of sainthood, and thus provides a link between his own experiences and his insistence, in certain parts of the novel, that Divine is on the way to being a saint. Its immediate relevance to his treatment of homosexuality, however, lies in the expression which it enables him to give to the situation of those homosexuals who, as Genet was at Mettray, are basically ashamed of being what they are, whose homosexuality invades their whole personality, and who exaggerate their difference from other people by blatantly flaunting it.

No other novel by Genet is quite so dominated by its central character as *Our Lady of the Flowers* is by Divine, and in no other character does Genet provide so fascinating an account of his own dilemma and situation. It is, indeed, partly because Divine assumes such a stature and is seen in so many different roles that Sartre's remark about *Our Lady of the Flowers* being 'an epic of masturbation' is so peculiarly inept. The most outstanding feature of what Mirabeau once called 'books to be read with one hand' is their extreme monotony and the one-dimensional nature of all the characters who appear in them. This is true even of the novels of the Marquis de Sade, in which characterisation is always sacrificed either to erotic reveries or philosophical disquisitions. In *Our Lady of the Flowers*, on the other hand, the reader never sees Divine, or indeed any other of the characters, as merely the expression of Genet's own sexual longings. Genet may very well have begun writing his novel in order to provide himself with sexual excitement, and he does refer, in *The Thief's Journal*, to his 'decision to write pornographic books'. Nevertheless, the very act of literary creation clearly took hold of him and carried him beyond this original intention, transforming what may have been, originally, a very limited aim, into the ability to use literature as a means of attaining some kind of awareness of his situation and problems. This is noticeable not only in this portrayal, through Divine, of certain aspects of the homosexual's dilemma, but also in the long passages which describe Divine's boyhood as Louis Culafroy. In these, Genet moves on from his homosexuality in order to write about three other aspects of his life: his childhood in Le Morvan, his imaginary relationship with the mother whom he never knew, and the beginnings of his career as a thief. His treatment of these subjects also reveals another side of his skill as a writer: his ability to show the way in which the human mind, and especially the memory, do in fact work.

During the description of how Divine, Seck Gorgui and Notre-Dame climb into the taxi to come home after the drag ball, Genet falls into a meditation on the implications of Divine's habit of talking about herself as 'she', and of what this means for her attitude towards real women. By association of ideas, this leads to what is apparently a long digression on Culafroy's boyhood relationship with a girl called Solange. This girl, writes Genet, was 'all of woman' for Divine-Culafroy, and 'on broiling days' the two would 'sit together curled up on a white stone bench, in a delicate little patch of shade, narrow as a hem, with their feet tucked under their smocks so as not to wet them in the sun', and tell each other stories based on local superstitions. Solange forecast that, in a year's time, a man would come and throw himself from a rock near where they were sitting, and Culafroy believed her. When, after thirteen months, nothing had happened, he 'saw another supernatural function fade away', and turned for ever away from women and towards the more fascinating world of the snake-catcher Alberto. In itself, the incident is of trifling importance, and from a rational point of view is a very inadequate account of why Culafroy should have become a homosexual. What it does do, however, is show how a whole incident in the past can be summoned up by thinking about a problem that is apparently unrelated to it (masculine and feminine pronouns, and what 'women' were for Divine), and thus how irrational the processes of the mind can sometimes be. It also, and this is perhaps more important, evokes the burning days of childhood innocence, of the magic world that existed before Culafroy ran away from home and began the career that had led him to the cold Paris dawn and the torments of homosexual jealousy.

Whatever fascination Genet's work may offer as a psychological case history, an exploration of the problem of evil, or a study of the world of the homosexual, its most substantial claim to be considered as literature rests upon the texture and quality of his prose. It is naturally impossible to experience this quality except by reading his work in French, for however well it may be translated there are always more associations in Genet's words than can ever be evoked by another language. In the passage quoted above, for example, he speaks about *'les jours calcinés'*, and the bare, rocky scenery which he evokes in the rest of his description fits admirably into the idea of the day turning itself into chalk and dust by its own heat. It is not, however, possible to convey this in another language, any more than it is possible to translate the pun at the very beginning of *Notre-Dame-des-Fleurs* when Genet talks about a conversation going on *'sous le manteau'*. The people described are, indeed, talking in the rain, but they are also characters in a book which Genet realises will be read clandestinely, that is to say, '*sous le manteau*'.

Another passage in Genet's evocation of his own childhood which is also peculiarly effective in French, but which loses a great deal in translation, occurs towards the beginning of the book when the smell rising from the blocked latrines near his cell revives his childhood memories 'which rise up like black soil mined by moles' ('*font les souvenirs d'enfance se soulever comme une terre noire minée par les taupes*'). Here, Genet is writing as the anti-Proust, showing that unpleasant as well as pleasant memories can surge up in response to physical sensation. In his childhood, like the Rimbaud of *Les Poètes de sept ans*, he sought refuge '*dans la fraîcheur des latrines*' where he could perceive life as something 'singularly sweet, caressing, light, or rather lightened, delivered from heaviness' ('*singulièrement douce, câline, légère, ou plutôt allégée, échappée à la pesanteur*') and these two implied references to other authors are an excellent example of his skill and sensitivity as a writer. The pages in *Our Lady of the Flowers* in which Genet describes both his own childhood and that of Culafroy—the experiences merge into each other, in the same way that Divine is, in Genet's own words, 'what for want of a trifle I failed to be' ('*ce que faute d'un rien je manquai d'être*')—are genuinely poetic in their recreation of the freshness and physical immediacy of the child's world. At the same time, they make *Our Lady of the Flowers* into a psychological novel by showing how Genet's childhood was divided between the bliss of what Sartre calls 'a sweet confusion with the world' ('*une douce confusion avec le monde*'), and the uncertainty about his own nature and situation.

Genet's preoccupation with the mother who, as he says in *Pompes Funèbres*, abandoned him in his cradle, recurs so frequently in his work that Sartre, ignoring the fascinating Madame Lysiane in *Querelle of Brest*, writes that women figure in his books only in the role of mother. As might be expected, there are no fathers in Genet, and Ernestine, in

Our Lady of the Flowers, is a widow. She lives in the country, in the unnamed village where Culafroy passed his childhood, and enjoys a curious reputation there because she protected her hands and face from the sun while hay-making. When, 'like all provincials', she comes to Paris in order to have an operation, she is not shocked when she discovers how Culafroy earns his living now that he has become Divine. Indeed, she even thinks to herself that he has a bank between his buttocks (*'un Crédit Lyonnais entre les fesses'*). On one occasion, however, when Culafroy lay ill in their home in the village, she had tried to shoot him with a revolver. In the psychological framework of *Our Lady of the Flowers*, this attempted murder parallels the real murder of Ragon by Adrien Baillon, for both of them are depicted by Genet as suggested and inspired by a physical object: Baillon strangles his victim because the latter's neck-tie is invitingly tight, and Ernestine's gestures as she tries to kill her son are virtually dictated by the large army revolver which she takes out of its drawer. Within a different psychological context, however, her action is almost disquietingly easy to explain in semi-Freudian terms: as far as Genet's real mother is concerned, he is as good as dead; like him, Culafroy is alive only through an accident, since Ernestine missed, and the bullet 'shattered the glass of a frame containing an honorary diploma of her late husband'. The symbolic murder which Genet's mother committed when she abandoned her son also remained, through no fault of her own, on a symbolic level.

The transition between Culafroy's childhood and his life as Divine took place when Culafroy, for some reason which is not mentioned in the novel, ran away from home. The description of the nights which he spent wandering about the streets, waiting until the Angelus announced that the churches were open to 'old maids, real sinners and tramps' (*'aux vieilles filles, aux vrais pécheurs, aux clochards'*), is introduced by another one of those semi-interior monologues that show Genet's awareness of the way in which the mind can skip from one idea to another by purely verbal associations. Divine, lying in the little bedroom overlooking Montmartre cemetery—she will later be buried by a gravedigger whom she watches from her window but never meets—hears a church clock strike five in the morning. It is through the two meanings of the word *cloche* (bell, and, in slang, extreme poverty), that Divine is taken back to the days when 'having run away from the slate house, she landed in a small town, where, on golden, pink or dreary mornings, tramps with souls—which, to look at them, one would call naive—of dolls, accost each other with gestures one would also call fraternal. They have just got up from park benches where they have been sleeping, from benches in the main square, or have just been born from a lawn in the public park.' ('. . . *enfuie de la maison d'ardoises elle échoua dans une petite ville où, les matins dorés, roses ou blafards, des clochards à l'âme—qu'à les voir on croirait naïve—de poupée, s'abordent avec des gestes qu'on dirait aussi fraternels. Ils viennent de se lever d'un banc des Allées où ils dormaient, d'un banc de la place d'Armes, ou de naître d'une pelouse du jardin public.*')

This lyrical and yet realistic description of the world of tramps and outcasts will be taken up again by Genet, not quite so successfully, in *The Thief's Journal*, and is one of the best passages in *Our Lady*. Its introduction by an association of ideas evoked by the two meanings of the word '*cloche*' is also a fairly typical example of Genet's technique of narration in his first novel, for a number of other passages describing Culafroy's childhood are introduced in the same way. One of the most interesting of these, especially in view of his obsession with sainthood, is Culafroy's discovery of 'the emptiness of God', which springs to Genet's mind through his memories of the work which a fellow prisoner was given to do in his cell. Clément Village is painting toy soldiers, and one of them breaks. This reminds Genet of a plaster bust of Marie Antoinette which belonged to his foster-parents, and which one day broke to reveal a similar emptiness. This, in turn, leads to a passage where Culafroy, creeping into church and opening the tabernacle to see whether there was any truth in the legends about profanated Hosts, knocked over the ciborium 'which made a hollow sound' as it fell on the wool of the altar carpet. The technique whereby these three different kinds of emptiness— the toy soldier, the plaster cast, the sound of the ciborium falling—are linked together is a fairly familiar one, reminiscent both of Proust's involuntary memory and of the Joycean stream of consciousness. Nevertheless, Genet uses it very well, and the building up of Divine's character from these various, apparently disparate elements, is wholly consistent with the overall atmosphere of the book. Genet constantly reminds us that he is writing it in a prison cell, allowing his memories to take control in a very loosely connected daydream, which he hopes will take his mind off the worry about his forthcoming trial and the horror of being judged. The advantage of this technique is that it enables Genet to present Divine in a number of different ways: as the boy Culafroy who, like Genet himself, 'stole because the others thought I was a thief'; as the Divine who accustoms herself to a life of luxury by climbing into first-class railway compartments and then deciding not to travel, or reserving rooms in luxury hotels and then not occupying them; as the screaming old queen of Montmartre and yet the basically tender-hearted, devoted friend; and as the would-be saint, who deliberately loves what she abhors. If this final aspect of her character does not come over very convincingly, it is because Genet has limited himself to talking about her sainthood instead of showing it in action. When he wants to show Divine trying to be tough and masculine in order to attract the delicate and flower-like Notre-Dame-des-Fleurs, he writes an excellent and amusing passage describing her imitating the boxers she admires and constantly being knocked down for her pains. When he talks about her as a saint, the only incident which he mentions is her deliberately causing the death of a two-year-old child who was in the habit of wandering into her room. If Genet's books were capable of corrupting their readers, it is far more probable that they would do so by passages such as this than by the descriptions which he gives of homosexuality.

Immediately next to Divine in the general structure of *Our Lady of the Flowers* come her lovers: the Negro, Seck Gorgui, Notre-Dame and Mignon-les-petits-pieds. Apart from the additional atmosphere which he gives the novel, Seck Gorgui is interesting for two main reasons: he provides a link between *Our Lady of the Flowers* and *The Blacks*, in that he is said to be based on the same actual criminal, Clément Village, who gives his name to the main character of Genet's play; and the description which Genet gives of the crime for which Village is in prison offers one of the most graphic and haunting passages in the novel. He had killed his mistress, in a brawl over the insufficient amount of money she had earned for him, and then walled her up in their room. This he had done in a virtually somnambulistic state, concentrating the whole of his mind on the practical problem of building a wall without letting anyone see what he was doing, knowing that if he relaxed for just one moment he would run to the police station and confess his crime. The intense strain under which he had performed this act comes out again in his mingled rage and terror as the toy soldiers which he is given to paint in his cell gradually increase in number until he is virtually submerged in them and they raise 'a swell which makes the room pitch'. Like Querelle of Brest, Village is no joyful murderer. He is haunted, obsessed by his crime, totally unlike the kind of heartless, brutal murderer whom one would expect to find in a book which opens, as does *Our Lady of the Flowers*, with the remark that it is written in honour of a number of recent killings.

Seck Gorgui lives for some time with Divine and Notre-Dame, and is magnificently attired in full male evening dress when he accompanies his two friends to the drag ball at *Le Tavernacle*. He is also the subject of another description

of how the mind works, in a passage which recalls David
Hume's remark about always finding, when he looked inside
himself, only a 'bundle of sensations'. *Il s'éveillait par de
lentes imprégnations des objets et des êtres, d'abord de lui-même.
Il se sentait être. Il émettait quelques idées timides: chaleur, un
garçon inconnu, je bande, thé, taches sur les ongles (le visage de
l'Américaine qui ne voulait pas serrer la main à un de ses amis),
huit heures dix.*' ('He was being gradually impregnated with
objects and things, and first of all with himself. He felt
himself being. He emitted a few timid ideas: heat, an
unfamiliar fellow, I got a hard-on, tea, spots on his nails
[the face of the American girl who did not want to shake
hands with one of his friends], ten after eight.' What is most
curious is that Genet himself claims, immediately after the
long and extremely moving description of Village's crime,
that all he can remember of him is his sexual performance.
This may be true for one side of Genet's own character and
literary intentions, and the scenes of homosexual love-
making in which Gorgui figures are described in fulsome
and evocative detail. Yet it is patently false for the other
Genet, the one who recreated the horror which Village felt
for his crime and described how he felt when he woke up.
If this other Genet did not exist, *Our Lady of the Flowers*
would never have contained some of its finest passages.

Divine's two other lovers, Mignon and Notre-Dame, are
twice stated in the novel to be father and son. Neither of
them knows this, and they therefore commit incest without
knowing what they are doing. This aspect of their relationship is described in considerably more detail in the original
edition of *Notre-Dame-des-Fleurs*, where Genet declares that
he finds incest between father and son 'an exquisite form of
love', but is omitted both from the official Gallimard text
and from the 1964 English translation. The two men meet
by accident just after Notre-Dame has killed Ragon, and
live luxuriously off the money stolen from him. Then, after
Mignon has deserted Divine, Notre-Dame takes his place
and lives with her until he is arrested, condemned to death

and executed after he has spent the regulation forty days in the condemned cell. Like Seck Gorgui, Notre-Dame is also said to be inspired by a criminal whom Genet knew, the young Maurice Pilorge to whom *Our Lady of the Flowers* is dedicated. Like all the men described in the novel, he is a character whom Genet finds sexually exciting, but once again this is only one aspect of his personality, and the two most effective scenes in which he figures have nothing at all to do with sex.

The first of these describes Notre-Dame's arrest by the police, and his subsequent confession of how he had killed Ragon. In the course of a routine search for cocaine, the police come to a studio apartment where Notre-Dame is living under the pseudonym of Pierrot-le-Corse, the name he used when engaged in drug smuggling. For Genet, the moment when Notre-Dame is arrested is one of timeless horror, and his description of it in these terms may be a confirmation of Sartre's view that Genet is constantly reliving, in all his books, the moment when he himself was caught and labelled a thief when still a child. The interesting feature of the scene to note from a literary point of view, however, is the use which Genet makes of a quotation from Pascal. The policemen come forward '*dans un silence effrayant comme le silence éternel des espaces infinis*', and cast both Notre-Dame, who is undergoing arrest, and Genet, who is describing it, into equal dread. Genet makes extensive use, in *Our Lady of the Flowers*, of literary and artistic references, but they very rarely fit so precisely into the atmosphere of the scene he is describing.

The strangeness and nightmare quality of Notre-Dame's arrest do not, however, end here. In the apartment which the police come to search, there is a tailor's dummy, and this gives the policemen the momentary illusion that they have stumbled upon a different crime and discovered a murdered man. The irony, for Notre-Dame, lies in the fact that this false corpse does eventually lead the police to the discovery of a real crime, for its presence so infuriates them that they take

Notre-Dame to the station for further questioning. There, the confession of his murder comes 'from his liver right up to his teeth'. He cannot hold it back, blurts out that he has killed a man, tries to retract, is subjected to further questioning which, by enumerating all the unsolved murders, gives him *'l'inutile révélation de l'extraordinaire ignorance de la police'* ('the needless revelation of the extraordinary ignorance of the police'). Eventually, his confession is complete and he is brought to trial.

Genet attributes this *'histoire ahurissante où un faux meurtre en faisait découvrir un vrai'* ('astounding story in which a false murder led to the discovery of a real one') to the influence on Notre-Dame of Divine. Her strange, feminine ways, he maintains, affect everyone with whom she comes into contact, and it was her influence which had led Notre-Dame to steal the tailor's dummy and keep it in his apartment. It is certainly true that Divine is depicted as gradually making all her lovers become more feminine. She does it to Mignon, in particular, and thus brings out the paradox of the passive, female-type homosexual who is attracted to virile males, but has to bring out their hidden feminity if she is to enjoy them sexually. But a more literary influence in this particular episode of *Our Lady of the Flowers* is that of surrealism, whose cult of the absurd is here exploited for semi-realistic ends. The crazy logic of the scene, which looks forward to the theatre of the absurd and back to the early films of Salvador Dali, affects the plot in a manner which remains basically credible. Inexplicable and absurd though the incident of the tailor's dummy may appear on rational grounds, it becomes psychologically acceptable because it provides the occasion for the guilt which haunts the criminal to manifest itself.

The description of the trial which follows this arrest is in many ways the climax of the novel: it shows Genet using language in his most skilful way, both defying society from his own point of view and criticising it intelligently from a more orthodox standard; it adds yet another dimension to his treatment of homosexuality, since it enables him to present Divine and her friends in a different social context; and it marks the virtual end of the plot. Before Notre-Dame is arrested, Mignon has already been put in prison, and Seck Gorgui has disappeared. After the trial, Divine will die, and Genet himself returns from his imaginary world. Unlike Fontevrault, the setting for *Miracle of the Rose*, La Santé is not a prison for long-term sentences, and the description of Notre-Dame's trial is mirrored, within the book itself, by the trial which Genet himself will soon undergo, and which may, he says, involve a ten-year sentence.

During Notre-Dame's trial, an official psychiatrist reads out a report which describes the murderer as 'psychically unbalanced, non-affective, amoral', but nevertheless concludes that, since there was in his act 'an element of volition which is not due to the complicity of things . . . Baillon is partly responsible for the murder'. No detail that Genet gives about his hero gives any reason for doubting the validity of the diagnosis, and his refusal to lend criminals glamour by disguising their genuine stupidity fits into the realistic and disillusioned account which he gives of the criminal world. He nevertheless describes Notre-Dame's smile as beautiful enough to 'damn his judges, a smile so azure that the guards themselves had an intuition of the existence of God and of the great principles of geometry', and however curious this switching from one set of values to another may be in intellectual terms, it is aesthetically justifiable. Its effect is to make the account of Notre-Dame's trial a peculiarly apt description both of the rightness and the wrongness of the law, of its necessity in society and its curious inapplicability to any one, existing individual.

Genet accepts the need for courts of law, but does so only ironically. He points to the rather suspect circumstances of Ragon's death when he writes that society 'has to protect rentiers, who sometimes live all the way upstairs, beneath the roof, and put to death children who murder them', and he also has a number of phrases which underline the complex cruelty involved in any murder trial and which parallel the passage already quoted in Chapter II. For example, when Notre-Dame's lawyer makes a poor speech in his defence, the Court 'curses him for not even according it the satisfaction of overcoming the pity it should normally have felt'. The poetic phrases which Genet uses to describe Notre-Dame—he is 'cut out of a block of clear water', and 'invested with a sacred character, like the kind that expiatory victims . . . had in olden times, and which kings and Jews still have today'—do enable him to make by aesthetic means a certain intellectual point: there are some crimes which, precisely because they defy all logic and reason, transcend our normal, rational categories. Notre-Dame's is one of these, and although society cannot choose but punish, it is wholly wrong to think that it understands what has happened or that it is, itself, acting morally in any meaningful sense of the word. Society is represented by the crowd, which 'twists its faces' in unison with the judge who 'twists his beautiful hands', and by the only member of the jury who looks as if he is following the trial, and whose eyes are 'as hollow as those of a statue'. If the description of Notre-Dame's trial is one of the passages in Genet's work where his challenge to society is most effective, this is less because he succeeds in glorifying the criminal than because he shows crime as something which society is neither willing nor able to understand. Crime, he is saying, may be petty, and criminals may be stupid. But the real motives governing their acts are as inaccessible to the rational mind as the phenomenon of natural beauty which is also incarnated in Notre-Dame.

When Divine and her friends attend the drag ball at *Le Tavernacle*, Genet evokes a most amusing picture of proletarian homosexuality when he speaks of how 'good-looking butcher-boys are sometimes metamorphosed into princesses with flowing gowns', and he enlivens his account of Notre-Dame's trial by a similar vision of the duplicity of social roles which homosexuality can involve. All the homosexuals in *Our Lady of the Flowers* have their *nom de guerre*, and the milkroundsman for whom Mignon deserts Divine rejoices in the appellation of Mimosa the Second. When Divine and her friends appear to give evidence at Notre-Dame's trial, they are obliged to reveal their real names and suddenly appear as prosaic, ordinary people. Première Communion is called Antoine Bertollet, Pomme d'Api is Eugène Marceau and Mimosa the Second, René Hirsch. The contrast between their assumed and their real names reflects the contradiction in their personality and social roles which Genet sums up in the phrase *'misère bariolée'* ('misery in motley'). There is also a useful reminder here, paralleled by some of the points which Peter Wilde-blood makes in his *A Way of Life*, that sexual peculiarities are by no means the exclusive feature of middle-class intellectuals, but extend to all points of the social scale. When Divine herself, announced as 'Le Sieur Culafroy Louis', enters 'supported by Ernestine . . . the only real woman in the trial', the screaming queens of Montmartre are reduced to their final banality.

Genet's presentation of the man who stays longer with Divine than any of her other lovers, Mignon-les-petits-pieds, is an interesting example of the kind of problem which he sets both his translators and those readers who approach his work in search of information about the behaviour and psychology of professional criminals. Genet was once described as 'the Racine of Existentialism', and as long as some sense of proportion is observed, the remark is not wholly ludicrous. As *Miracle of the Rose* and *Deathwatch* show, he is obsessed with the idea of predestination, and has, in many ways, a fundamentally Jansenistic vision of the world. He also, like Racine, works so close to the central genius of the language that his most subtle effects are almost bound to be lost in translation. Thus the name, Mignon-les-petits-pieds, has, in French, a wealth of associations which the English translation of Darling Daintyfoot inevitably lacks. In its full form, the name ironically evokes the Berthe aux grands pieds of Villon's poem, and thereby recalls another criminal who was a poet. At the Court of Henri III, as in the entourage of Louis XIV's brother, the *mignons* were handsome young men who, like Genet's Mignon, had ambivalent sexual habits but undeniable physical grace. Mignon's very name, both by its similarity to that of a legendary female beauty and by its historical associations, thus prepares the reader for the later revelation of his sexual duplicity. At the same time, it also evokes a grace and delicacy which the English Darling has not retained to anything like the same extent.

When he introduces Mignon, Genet states that he was '*ondoyé*', that is to say, privately baptised before his birth. This leads to the statement that he was 'beatified too, practically canonised, in the belly of his mother', and thus fits Mignon into the rather curious theological atmosphere of the novel which is also conveyed by the name of Notre-Dame-des-Fleurs. The verb '*ondoyer*', however, also has another meaning, which is to wave gracefully in the wind, and a person can be described as having '*une démarche ondoyante*'. Genet never actually applies the word to Mignon in this sense, but it is so implied by all his insistence upon his grace of movement that the two verbs, normally quite distinct from each other, become closely associated in a new and original manner.

A third aspect of Mignon's personality which is virtually impossible to translate effectively is his profession—or, as he himself insists when he is arrested, his lack of profession, for he proudly tells the police that he does not work. Genet states that he is *un mac*, which has to be translated into English as ponce or pimp. At no point in the novel, however, is Mignon described as living off the immoral earnings of any women, and within the strangely autonomous world that Genet creates in his novels the word *mac* acquires a number of rather different associations. By a rather curious process, it has been transformed in modern slang to *mec*, which simply means a man or a bloke. This enables Genet to use the word, in all his books and plays, not only in the sense of pimp, but also in the general one of man as opposed to woman and active as opposed to passive homosexual. Since the immediate connotation in English of the word *pimp* is with *pimple*, the associations of aggressive but ambiguously virile masculinity with which Genet manages to endow the word in French are inevitably lost.

The fact that Mignon is a pimp who does not run any women, but lives instead off the earnings of Divine, another man, is also linked to the problem of whether Genet's work can be considered as giving any kind of realistic account of the Paris underworld. It is certainly realistic about prisons, both in the extended descriptions of *Miracle of the Rose* and in the more occasional notations of *Our Lady of the Flowers*. In prison, Genet writes in this book, 'they close more doors than they open', and he evokes the typical prison smell rising insistently from the blocked latrines, the anonymous eye perpetually watching through a spy-hole in the cell door, and the days which 'make your life longer than broad' (*'font la vie plus longue que large'*). One of his descriptions in *Our Lady of the Flowers* evokes not horror or pity but laughter. He notes that on the main entrance of one prison the following inscription is carved in marble: 'Inauguration of the Prison: March 17, 1900', and this brings to his mind the image of 'a procession of official gentlemen solemnly bringing the first prisoner to be incarcerated'. In the details which he gives about the life that his criminals lead when they are not occupied in crime or serving a prison sentence, he insists upon their sexual habits, their extreme laziness, and their delight in luxury. Mignon and Divine lie in bed all day, smoking cigarettes and listening to a stolen radio, and when Notre-Dame and Mignon spend the money stolen from Ragon they do it in luxurious hotels which can give them the illusion of permanent wealth and comfort.

Genet's main concern in *Our Lady of the Flowers* is not, however, to describe the criminal world realistically, and Sartre, as has been seen, goes so far as to deny that his novels have any relevance to social reality whatsoever. He is projecting his own desires and concerns on to a number of fictional characters, and thereby achieving both an escape from his immediate anxieties and an increased understanding of his situation. These characters, and especially Divine, come convincingly to life partly because of the way in which Genet makes them talk, and here again he works so close to the central core of the language that it is not easy to translate his effects into another idiom. Thus, when he reproduces Divine's conversation, he makes very effective use of the fact that adjectives and pronouns have, in French, different masculine and feminine forms, which can be used in the place of nouns. In French, it is both easy and quite natural for Divine and her friends to talk about themselves in the feminine, and when they say *'Je suis la Toute-Toute'*, gradually eliding it to *'La T'T'*', or *'Je suis la Toute-Persécutée'*, there is no difficulty in imagining them forming the actual words. In English, however, it is linguistically unnatural for anyone to say: 'I'm the Quite-Quite', or 'the Quite-Persecuted', with the result that whole passages of dialogue from Genet have an air of improbability in English which they never have in French.

The impossibility of rendering Genet's conversational effects into English parallels the difficulties already discussed in translating both his puns, his implied historical references, and his poetic use of language. A problem of translation also arises when his novels are considered as attempts to recreate the atmosphere of a particular social milieu, and this problem is once again linked to a basic difference in the structure of French and English. This difference can be summed up in the remark that French four-letter words do not have four letters in them, and have never been systematically excluded from ordinary speech and from literature. Thus when a Duchess, in a play by Anouilh, wishes to teach a flower-girl to adopt U speech habits, she tells her to say *merde* and not *crotte* as an expression of displeasure. In translation, Genet's characters seem to speak much more harshly and crudely than they do in the original French, where their language, though uninhibited, retains much closer associations with ordinary speech. This feature of popular language also helps to maintain the unity of *Our Lady of the Flowers* in that it lessens the difference in verbal tone between those passages where Genet is dwelling on the sordid nature of his own surroundings and those where he describes the wind as kneeling at the foot of the prison wall (*'aux pieds des murailles de la prison, le vent s'agenouille'*) or speaks of Divine's certainty that she is now old unfurling within her 'like the hangings formed by the wings of bats' (*'cette certitude se déployait en elle comme des tentures formées d'ailes de chauve-souris'*). In English, this difference of tone is very much greater, and is reinforced by the fact that the published translation of Genet's novels uses exclusively American slang and American turns of speech. This means that Genet's characters, for the English reader, are situated in a doubly alien environment: they are French, but they also speak a very particularised dialect which situates them in Skid Row and not in Montmartre or Piccadilly. This difficulty is less insuperable than some of the other problems raised by a translation of Genet's work, but it does underline the fact that his best effects are lost in translation.

There are a number of reasons for considering *Our Lady of the Flowers* as Genet's best novel, and the work in which his vision of reality is given its most effective expression. It has a unity which stems from its concentration upon a single character, and Genet's projection of his own problems on to Divine creates a detachment and irony that are not repeated in any other of his works. Because it is consistently presented as a dream creation, the ideas which *Our Lady of the Flowers* expresses are less vulnerable to rational criticism than they are in *Miracle of the Rose* or *Querelle of Brest*, which both contain a supposedly realistic account of experience and a conscious statement of a particular point of view. In *Our Lady of the Flowers*, everything remains fictionalised, and yet precisely because of this seems to attain a kind of higher reality: we know that Notre-Dame is a petty criminal and that Mignon-les-petits-pieds is stupid, but because Genet does not ask us to see them as real, the poetic statements which he makes about their attractiveness remain acceptable within the framework of the novel. This is how a man thinks when he is lying in a prison cell, with sufficient verbal skill and sufficient imaginative persistence to cast his dreams into a permanent mould. He knows that what he is putting forward to his readers can be accepted only within certain conventions, and he respects these by constantly reminding his audience that nothing is real in the ordinary sense of the word. This does not, of course, prevent the reader from seeing certain aspects of the novel as realistic, and Genet's analysis of a particular type of homosexuality in *Divine* is a brilliant achievement. Yet in spite of the interest which the overall pattern of *Our Lady of the Flowers* provides, it remains a book whose most important qualities are, in several senses of the word, untranslatable. It is when the book is read in French that sentences such as the following description of popular, sentimental songs, take on their full poetic quality. '*Mais que dire d'un des plus étranges phénomènes poétiques: que le monde entier—et le plus terriblement morne de lui-même, le plus noir, calciné, sec jusqu'au jansénisme, le monde sévère et nu des ouvriers d'usine—soit entortillé de merveilles, qui sont les chansons populaires perdues dans le vent, par des voix riches, dorées, diamentées, pailletées ou soyeuses.*' ('But what is to be said of one of the strangest of poetic phenomena: that the whole world—and the most terribly dismal part of it, the blackest, most charred, dry to the point of Jansenism, the severe, naked world of factory workers—is entwined with marvels, the popular songs lost in the wind, by profoundly rich voices, gilded and set with diamonds, spangled or silky.') As will be seen from *Miracle of the Rose*, Genet is extremely conscious of how voices differ in quality and texture, and he here combines this awareness with a peculiarly apt reference to Jansenism to bring together several different elements of his vision: the intermingling of beauty with everyday reality, the necessity for certain social classes to find this beauty only in cheapened artistic forms, and the curiously paradoxical charm which emerges from something that is essentially fake. Not all Genet's works possess the overall architecture of *Our Lady of the Flowers*, but they do all offer passages of similar poetic interest. He is adept at suddenly showing a picture or a philosophical idea in a new light, as when he writes of Raphael that he *'n'est peut-être si chaste que par ce qu'implique son nom de pureté, car il éclaircit le regard du petit Tobie'* ('is so chaste only because of the purity that his name implies, for he lit up the gaze of little Tobias'), or states that he realises *'que le pauvre Démiurge est contraint de faire sa créature à son image et qu'il n'inventa pas Lucifer'* ('the poor Demiurge is forced to make his creature in his own image and that he did not invent Lucifer'). Even when his over-all picture of society is totally unacceptable, his verbal skill remains intact. This is as true of passages where he looks forward to his creation of *The Maids* by writing that the prisoners' New Year greetings are 'furtive and whispered, as, among others, those of proud servants and lepers must be', and of those in which he speaks ironically of the moon rising in the sky *'avec une solennité calculée pour impressionner les humains sans sommeil'* ('with a solemnity calculated to impress sleepless humans'). To read the actual words that Genet uses is less an experience of the 'spirit of evil' than of the richness and variety of human language.

CHAPTER FOUR

MIRACLE OF THE ROSE

In 1949, Genet published a talk entitled *L'Enfant Criminel*, originally intended to be broadcast on the French radio as part of a series known as *Carte Blanche*. His original aim, Genet wrote in the preface to the printed version, had been to have his talk preceded by an interview in which he put certain questions to a magistrate, the director of a reform-tory, and an official psychiatrist. All, however, refused to appear in the programme, and when the radio authorities read Genet's text they refused to allow it to be broadcast. Edwin Morgan, commenting on this refusal in *Sidewalk* in 1960, wrote that there was, in Genet's brief sentence 'All refused to take part', 'a comment on our society which is as damning as any judgment the non-participators thought they were passing on Genet'. If the text is examined in more detail, however, this refusal is not too difficult to under-stand.

Genet's argument, in *L'Enfant Criminel*, is that the harsh treatment which juvenile delinquents were forced to undergo in France corresponded to their deepest wish, and that the reforms recently introduced were consequently a mistake. The penitentiaries in which children used to be housed, he wrote, were indeed 'the projection, on the physi-cal plane, of the desire for severity which lay deep in the hearts of the young criminals', and the cruelty to which the children were subjected in them was 'born and developed necessarily from the ardour of these children for evil'. It was, he argued, because children had committed crimes that they were locked up in such places, and it was consequently dishonest to make them lead a life indistinguishable from that of young apprentices. Anyone who treated delinquent children gently was guilty of lessening their power to revolt and thereby attain salvation. It was, he said, to criminal children that he was speaking, and he asked them 'never to blush for what they have done, and to keep untouched within them the revolt that makes them so beautiful'. Society, he maintained, had been right to treat the children at Mettray with the severity that it had shown when he was there, locking them in cells whose walls were painted wholly in black, allowing them to be tormented by brutal punishments and by the violence of their fellow inmates, and making no attempt to reform them. This was how the best traditions of crime were continued.

It would, indeed, have been difficult for an official psychiatrist or the director of a modern reformatory to reply to this talk. Had they agreed with Genet's declared meaning, they would have shown themselves totally unsuited, by any civilised standards, for the job they were doing; had they disagreed with him, Genet would have accused them of being hypocritical, and only pretending to treat young criminals humanely. Had they simply replied to Genet that he was being ironic, he would certainly have refused to have his ideas brought down to such a prosaic level. Nevertheless, this would have been the only possible reply for them to have made. Like Genet's second novel, *Miracle of the Rose*, *L'Enfant Criminel* reads exactly like an ironical work written to criticise the treatment which society metes out to its criminals. Treat young offenders with cruelty and lack of understanding, he seems to be saying, and they will become brutal and defiant, welcoming the punishment you inflict on them as proof that they were right to reject society by committing crimes. The penal reformers who have criticised the use of corporal punishment on the ground that it justifies the violent criminal by answering him in only violent terms are saying no more. Genet's pretended praise for the brutality which he underwent seems, in this context, an easily recognisable rhetorical device, comparable to Swift's recommendation that the best way to solve Ireland's over-population was by selling the children of the poor as suitable food for the rich man's table.

Although Genet would undoubtedly have rejected this interpretation, there are two points which he makes at the end of *L'Enfant Criminel* which suggest that the talk may be a piece of conscious social criticism. The first is that no scientist would ever take '*la morale des manuels scolaires*' ('the ethic of school manuals') at all seriously, and that society does not really believe in the official values to which it tries to convert delinquent children. The second is that society shows a fundamental dishonesty when it derives so much of its entertainment from stories about crime and yet persecutes the criminal himself. '*Your* literature, *your* paintings, *your* after-dinner amusements all celebrate crime. The talent of your poets has glorified the criminal whom you hate in real life. Allow us, in turn, to despise your poets and your artists.' Both of these are intellectually valid points, and the second suggests that Genet's work may perhaps be aimed at replacing the romantic view of crime by a more accurate and realistic portrayal. Edgar Wallace, apparently, several times declared that the ordinary criminal was 'too lacking in ideas and too spiritless in performance for his offences to be able to be used as a model for the crime novel', and Genet's criminals are almost parodies, by their stupidity and ugliness, of the cunning villains normally presented in fiction. It is, however, a fundamental characteristic of Genet's work that he never presents a consistent and integrated intellectual attitude, and does not, in this particular instance, link the deliberate social criticism at the end of *L'Enfant Criminel* with the possible irony of the first part. It again resembles *Miracle of the Rose*, where he jumps from a glorification to a debunking of crime and calls Mettray a heaven and a hell on virtually the same page. The result is that, in both books, the reader never knows what Genet's real opinion is or whether his most telling social criticism is deliberate or accidental.

It is perhaps in *L'Enfant Criminel* and *Miracle of the Rose* that this particular dichotomy between Genet's declared intentions and actual achievements as a writer is most blatant. However easy it may be, and however justified by the kind of information he gives, to see both books as reasoned and reasonable social criticism expressed through the use of irony, nothing that Genet has ever said about himself indicates that he would endorse such an interpretation. It is, nevertheless, especially tempting to see both the plot and atmosphere of *Miracle of the Rose* as an indictment of the French prison and reformatory service, and a protest against the cruelty and suffering which it creates. The novel tells how Harcamone, a former inmate of Mettray, is betrayed to the police by another former inmate called Divers. Harcamone then deliberately kills a prison warder in order to escape from the living hell of a life sentence, and is executed after spending forty-five days chained up in the condemned cell. Genet comments on how deliberate Harcamone's action was, and pretends to reply to the objection that a mere petty thief could not build up his life 'minute by minute, witnessing its construction, which is also a progressive destruction'. We must remember, he says, that Harcamone was 'a former colonist of Mettray who had built his life there minute by minute, one might almost say stone by stone, as had all the others, in order to bring to completion the fortress most insensitive to men's blows'. The tone is that of the rebel who, as Genet says in *L'Enfant Criminel*, is speaking to the ordinary reader 'as a poet and an enemy', trying to defend the nobility of crime. The facts as set down, however, show both the failure of society and the complete lack of honour among thieves: all Mettray did was to toughen and brutalise Harcamone, giving him the strength of desperation which enabled him to commit a pointless crime; what placed him in the position where he had to kill an innocent man or spend the rest of his life in gaol, was the treachery of his companion in betraying him to the police.

In the criminal world as Genet describes it, such acts of betrayal are extremely frequent. Genet hints at the reasons for this when he writes in *Our Lady of the Flowers* that

Mignon served the police 'so as to return to his place among human beings through having served order, and at the same time to depart from the human through deliberate baseness', and in one of the extracts from the *Journal du Voleur* published in *Les Temps Modernes* in July 1946, he said much the same of himself when he declared that by informing against his companions he re-established his links with society. This is, in fact, precisely the paradox of the man who is seeking to be evil rather than to do wrong. The person interested in qualities admires people for what they are rather than for what they do, and Genet is less interested in the harm which his criminals do to society than in the bad qualities such as cowardice or treachery which their actions bring into being. Although Sartre himself does not specifically repeat in *Saint Genet* the distinction which he made in his essay on Baudelaire, Genet is far more a rebel than a revolutionary. He seeks, that is, to defy an existing social and moral order, not to destroy it and put something else in its place. The form which his defiance takes is that of being wicked rather than trying to attack society, and Genet's insistence upon betrayal fits quite logically into this ambition: the treacherous criminal strengthens society by selling his confederates to the police, but he uses only evil in his reinforcement of the standards which he rejects.

Sociologically, the frequency with which Genet returns to the theme of betrayal, pointing out that it was universal at Mettray and making the plot of *Miracle of the Rose* revolve around Divers' betrayal of Harcamone, is an essential part of the extremely unflattering picture which he gives of the criminal world. In a way, it strangely contradicts his own personal behaviour, for Sartre and Cocteau tell how Genet deliberately ran the risk of a life-sentence by assuming responsibility for a crime which he had not committed, but which stained the memory of his friend Jean Decarnin. He may talk, in *The Thief's Journal*, about the joy of betrayal, and describe in *Pompes Funèbres* how he sold one of his friends to the police and insisted on being paid in his presence, but in real life he practically did a Sidney Carton. In practice, he thus confirmed what Frank Norman says in *Bang to Rights* about there being 'a certain code even among convicts', which leads criminals to go to prison for quite long sentences and for crimes which they have not committed rather than 'grass on their mates'. What Genet did, however, is perhaps less typical than what he describes in his books, for a remark by Christopher Hibbert in *The Roots of Evil* suggests that whatever Genet's conduct might have been, his insistence upon betrayal does reflect an important aspect of criminal life. The criminal, writes Christopher Hibbert, 'instinctively distrusts the people around him and so sets great store by his own loyalty to the gang and the gang's loyalty to him. The informer is the lowest form of life—the stool-pigeon, the rat'. Even if Genet is not describing what actually happens, he is giving a very perceptive account of the criminal's subconscious obsessions. Social groups, like individuals, condemn most fiercely the sins by which they feel themselves most tempted.

The prison in which Harcamone kills the warder in order to escape the life sentence brought about by Divers' treachery is called Fontevrault. It is, as Genet points out, the burial place of the Plantagenet kings, and the warder who registers Genet's arrival makes a little joke about the similarity of names. More important than this fact, however, is the situation of this ex-Cistercian Abbey, which became a prison in 1808: it is situated near Tours, some twenty-five miles from Mettray. The *Colonie agricole*, in Genet's words, thus 'blossomed curiously in its heavy shadow', and the theme of the relationship between the prison and the reformatory recurs both in the language which Genet uses and in the actual plot of *Miracle of the Rose*. The boys at Mettray, he writes, 'lived beneath the stern gaze of the Prison, like a village at the foot of a feudal castle inhabited by steel-clad knights', and looked upon the convicts as their heroes. Every act they performed was modelled on those of the prisoners, and they longed for the time when they would graduate, as it were, from this Eton to that King's. Most of them, in fact, succeeded in this ambition, for both Harcamone and Divers are old boys of Mettray, and Genet is first attracted to Bulkaen, a much younger prisoner, by the fact that he too had been at Mettray. Genet's own attitude towards prison, however, has evolved since he left Mettray, and the account which he gives of this change reinforces the impression that *Miracle of the Rose* can be read as a novel directed against the way in which society transforms juvenile offenders into hardened criminals. It also, in a number of respects, aims at destroying a romantic conception of crime which Genet now regards as dangerous and misleading.

Near the beginning of the novel, Genet describes the different kinds of punishment that exist in prison: 'the simplest is loss of canteen privileges, then dry bread, solitary confinement, and, in the state prisons (*centrales*), the disciplinary cell.' In this cell (*salle de discipline*), the prisoners march all day in an endless circle, and when Genet is punished on his arrival at Fontevrault he feels that he has grown up 'without stopping in my round'. 'What I mean', he adds in an apparently unconscious repetition of 'Shades of the prison house begin to close/Upon the growing boy', is that 'Mettray, though now destroyed, carries on, continues in time, and it seems to me too that the roots of Fontevrault are to be found in the vegetable world of our children's hell'. *Miracle of the Rose* emphasises the extent to which Genet's choice to be a criminal was in fact a mere endorsement of his predestined role as outcast and scapegoat. What he did when he insisted that he was evil—and thus, in Sartre's view, affirmed his dignity—was to lend his own unnecessary approval to the inevitable process whereby a neglected and abandoned child moves from institution to foster-home, from foster-home to reformatory and from reformatory to prison. When he calls Mettray 'a hell', he is going completely against the views he expresses both elsewhere in the novel, where he says it was 'a paradise', and in *L'Enfant Criminel*. He is also giving support to the idea that both these works can legitimately be seen as ironic and critical, and this impression is reinforced by his description of how different the real Fontevrault is from the prison of his childish dreams.

When he was at Mettray, he had dreamed of splendid criminals, handsome and courageous, and enough of his dream seems to have remained with him for him to write about them in glamorised terms in *Le Condamné à Mort*. He had not then realised what he says in *Miracle of the Rose*— 'that prison days were poor days, that the jailed pimps had a sickly pallor, that they were bloated and unhealthy and that the youngest and least husky of the guards considered it fun to beat them till they cried for mercy with the humility of a famished dog'. Similar passages denouncing the horror and boredom of prison life recur quite frequently in this novel, and echo the tone of disillusionment introduced early in the book when Genet recognises that criminals in prison are only 'the scurrilous caricature of the handsome criminals I saw in them when I was twenty'. Nevertheless, Genet does not use this realisation to provide either the main framework or the ostensible purpose of the book, which is to glorify Harcamone and show how his death gave rise to the miracle announced in the title. On the contrary, *Miracle of the Rose* opens with a passage celebrating Harcamone for having attained the 'death on the scaffold which is our glory', and thus fulfilled Genet's own 'aspiration to heavenly glory' and to 'a saintliness of muted brilliance'. Its closing pages, which describe Harcamone as enjoying a veritable apotheosis, present a complete contrast with Genet's earlier tone of disillusioned realism.

Harcamone has already been sentenced to death for killing the warder when Genet sees him at Fontevrault, the first time they have met since they were at Mettray together fifteen years earlier. Harcamone's wrists have been chained together, and in Genet's imagination this chain is transformed 'before our astonished eyes into a bracelet of flowers'. Genet happens to have been cutting his toe-nails with a pair of scissors when Harcamone appears, and he uses these scissors to cut off 'the loveliest rose, which was hanging by a supple stem near his left wrist'. This flower imagery is continued when Harcamone, brought before the prison governor after he has killed the warder, is described as presenting him with 'a mystery as absurd as that of a rose in full bloom', and reaches its climax in the closing passage of the novel. There, the prison governor, the executioner, the chaplain and a judge come to fetch Harcamone to the guillotine. When, however, he stands up in his cell to greet them, he becomes so huge that the 'four black men shrink until they are no bigger than four bedbugs'. The chaplain and executioner climb up his thigh, pass through a forest, a deserted fair-ground, and meet up with the judge and the governor, who have entered an immense maze through the doorway of Harcamone's ear. Together, they go down a corridor, and on entering Harcamone's heart of hearts find before them 'a red rose of monstrous size and beauty'. They rush in, 'pushing back the petals and crumpling them with their drunken hands, as a lecher who has been deprived of sex pushes back a whore's skirt', until they reach the heart of the rose. There, they are seized with a kind of giddiness, and topple into the 'deep gaze' of the well lying at the heart of the rose.

Like the account of Notre-Dame's trial, this highly poetical account of how a murderer is taken off to be executed enables Genet to end his portrayal of the criminal world on a note of lyrical exaltation. Perhaps more than any other passage in his work, it does come near to satisfying the definition of poetry suggested in *Our Lady of the Flowers*: a poem 'always pulls the ground away from under your feet and sucks you into the bosom of a wondrous night'. Again like the account of Notre-Dame's trial, this passage can be interpreted as making a point central to existentialist philosophy: that the living individual can never be comprehended by the systematised concepts represented here by the judge or the chaplain. The idea of an alliance between beauty and evil, which is fundamental to Genet's formal aesthetic, is perhaps more convincingly realised here than in any other part of his work. Whether this passage is intellectually as well as aesthetically convincing is, however, quite another matter.

Although Genet told Sartre that he detested flowers, he constantly uses images associated with them in the descriptive passages of his books. The opening of *The Thief's Journal*, for example, moves from the statement that 'The convict's outfit is pink-and-white striped' to the assertion that '*there is a close relationship between flowers and convicts*. The fragility and delicacy of the former are of the same nature as the brutal insensitivity of the latter'. The sustained flower-image at the end of *Miracle of the Rose* is based on the same Pascalian idea that '*les extrêmes se touchent*': Harcamone is guilty not only of murdering the man 'who had bullied him least during his two years at Fontevrault', but also of having killed a nine-year-old girl, the crime for which he had originally been sent to Mettray. He is thus, from a rational point of view, at the furthest possible remove from an innocent flower. In the closing pages of *Miracle of the Rose*, Genet does far more than dissociate the ethical from the aesthetic. He maintains that the greatest beauty is linked to the greatest perversity and stupidity, and that the conventional link between goodness and beauty is therefore completely unjustified. He thus sets himself the greatest possible difficulty if he is interested in communicating his vision, for it is one thing to say that some types of crime are as inexplicable as naturally beautiful objects, and quite another to argue that they evoke or deserve the same admiration. The ending of *Miracle of the Rose* is certainly a brilliant piece of imaginative writing, with the haunting and enveloping effect of a nightmare in which ugliness is changed into beauty while still remaining just as full of horror. But in the same way that a person waking up from a nightmare recognises that he has been afraid only of shadows, so the reader who puts down *Miracle of the Rose* rapidly ceases to believe in the inversion of all values which Genet's description implies.

Lyrical passages such as the description of Harcamone's last moments do not, however, constitute more than a relatively small part of *Miracle of the Rose*. Perhaps even more than *The Thief's Journal*, it is a direct essay in autobiography, and couched for the most part in realistic terms. Genet's account of Mettray is horrifying but unoriginal, for it is only his attitude of apparent approval that distinguishes his account from the comparable horror stories which figure in almost every history of the way in which society has treated juvenile offenders in the past. In a passage omitted from the 1951 edition, Genet tells how the *colons* at Mettray were forced to crawl across the floor and howl like dogs in order to obtain a half ration of soup, how one of the teachers told a boy who rejected some rotten meat because it was 'not fit for pigs' that 'You are worse than a pig', and comments upon the way in which the cruelty of the authorities at Mettray merely reflected the general attitude of society. A reward was offered to anyone bringing back a boy who tried to escape, and Genet claims to have seen a peasant bring back one boy he had caught and request a further fifty francs reward for one he claimed to have shot. For all his insistence in *L'Enfant Criminel* that young criminals long for harsh treatment, and in spite of his proclaimed scorn for the journalists who sought to reform it, Genet does quite specifically condemn the way he was treated at Mettray: he speaks of the 'vile measures' with which the new arrivals were greeted, writes ironically of the 'few formalities still accorded to humans' before their life as *colons* began, points out that none of the children at Mettray ever played, that he never saw a newspaper and had to wait three years to learn that Lindbergh had flown the Atlantic, and describes how the children's bare feet were practically stripped of their flesh by the clogs they had to wear.

What makes the description which Genet gives of his sufferings at Mettray so moving is his statement that when he grew 'weary of his orphaned solitude and his soul yearned for a mother', he found that Mettray possessed 'everything that one associates with women: tenderness, slightly nauseating whiffs from the open mouth, deep, heaving bosom, unexpected punishment, in short, everything that makes a mother a mother'. This longing for a mother inspired the curious figure of Ernestine in *Our Lady of the Flowers* and recurs in the triumphant creation of The Mother in *The Screens*. In *Miracle of the Rose*, it is ironically underlined by the fact that the strongest and most brutal of the *colons* were appointed as prefects, called 'elder brothers', and given every licence to bully the younger and weaker boys. Genet claims that the homosexuality which was rampant at Mettray enabled him thus to satisfy the taste for incest which he also flaunts in *Our Lady of the Flowers*, but the remark that 'I was sixteen years old. I was alone in the world. The Colony was my universe. No, it was the Universe. Family B was my family' leaves a very different impression. In the same way as Genet's description of the visit he made to Mettray after it had been closed down recalls the traditional visit which the romantic hero pays to the deserted ancestral home, so the account which he gives of his childhood in *Miracle of the Rose* also has similarities with the romantic theme of the lonely and misunderstood child. The difference lies in the fact that Genet has genuine cause for grief, and the curious tone of defiance in which he writes of Mettray only underlines the intensity of his suffering. At times, *Miracle of the Rose* thus has almost a Dickensian note, as if *Oliver Twist* had been written by one of Fagin's successful but sentimental pupils.

Again near the beginning of the novel, Genet speaks of an earlier period in his life when he did attain 'the clear simplicity of manliness' by becoming a professional cracksman and acquiring the technical skill needed to burgle houses efficiently. He freed himself, he writes, from 'a state of painful torpor, from a low, shameful life taken up with prostitution and begging . . . by and for a prouder attitude', and the passage in which he describes this change is unique in his work for a number of reasons. As Sartre points out, it is almost certainly not a fundamentally correct account of his personality, and is thus different both from the imaginary transposition of his homosexuality into Divine and from the direct description which he gives of his childhood in the rest of *Miracle of the Rose*. These passages not only ring true aesthetically, but also fit in with the rest of the self-portrait which Genet offers in his work. Even in *Miracle of the Rose*, for example, he admits that the Divine side of his character is still there when he writes that his 'wild nature will always be visible through a thousand and one cracks' and describes how his main concern, when stealing, had originally been to imitate the elegant gestures of the thieves he found sexually attractive. His account of how he became a good, honest robber is, moreover, completely contradicted by the rest of his career. Good, honest robbers feel no more need to explain or explore their experience through literature than do competent electricians or chartered accountants: they commit their robberies, do their bird, and die in enviable anonymity. Only the Genets of this world need to save themselves through literature.

The second reason for which this passage is unique lies in the kind of challenge which it offers to the morally self-confident reader, the Sartrian 'Just Man'. This challenge is presented in a rather curious and negative way by Genet when he confesses that he was always accompanied, on his robberies, 'by one agonising thought: the fear that honest people may be thieves who have chosen a cleverer and safer way of stealing'. It is a fairly banal remark, but one that has curious affinities with the principal contention that J. B. Mays puts forward in his *Crime and the Social Structure*: 'The main argument of this book,' he writes in his conclusion, 'has been to show that society itself is in some respects criminogenic and to a considerable extent precipitates its own delinquency. My plea is therefore that we should concentrate more on the concept of crime as essentially normal and not abnormal behaviour.' What is unusual in the passage from *Miracle of the Rose* is that Genet should be questioning the official values of society within the same basically rational framework that society normally uses to justify them. As has already been argued, the irony which he seems to use in order to criticise society's treatment of its criminals is almost certainly unintentional. In his prose works, it is only here that his defence of wrong-doing is couched in terms reminiscent of Diderot's *Le Neveu de Rameau* or of the case which Adeimantes and Glaucon make for injustice in Book II of *The Republic*.

The rarity of such passages in Genet's work is explained partly by Sartre's remark that 'had he been called a thief at the age of seventeen, Genet would have laughed. That is the age at which one liquidates paternal values'. Had he not been accused at an impressionable age, when he still totally accepted 'the simple-minded, theological morality of property owners', he would have been able to 'challenge the principles of public morality in the name of a Nietzschean or anarchistic ethic'. As it was, however, Genet never really freed himself of the official values which condemned him. He may have come to realise intellectually that there was no such thing as an absolute standard of morality, but he never succeeded in integrating this realisation into his personality. In this respect, of course, he remained faithful to his initial concern with being rather than doing. By using the positive qualities needed by the professional criminal—skill, intelligence, perseverance, initiative—he would have ceased to be evil by the very fact that he was successful in doing wrong.

There is another passage in *Miracle of the Rose* which stands out in Genet's work not only by the fact that it challenges society in basically rational terms, but also because it is obviously intended to be funny. It is the description of the visit which the Bishop of Tours makes to the *Colonie agricole*. At Mettray, the *colons* offered prayer eight times a day, so that the Bishop's visit was clearly a great occasion. Even the toughest of the 'big shots', whose indifference was 'normally so like an absence that I can say they did not even go to church', wanted to be in the front row, and hear the sermon in which they were addressed as 'stray lambs'. As might be expected, the Bishop has no inkling of what is really going on in the minds of his 'young friends'. He speaks of Fontevrault as 'that house of detention whose proximity should be a continual, a daily reminder of what is right and wrong', but as soon as he mentions the prison the boys listen to his remarks in quite a different frame of mind, 'hoping that a personage so well-dressed, so escorted, so learnèd, so close to God, would reveal something startling about Jo with the Golden Voice', one of the criminals whose career they wish to emulate. The speech, written in perfect ecclesiastical French, is in its way as amusing as the address which Colonel Craven gives to Brendan Behan and his friends in *Borstal Boy*, with its complete confusion between the colonel's own reminiscences of public school life and the reality of life in Borstal. As criticism of society, however, both the Bishop's and the Colonel's speech are detached from reality because of the crudeness of Genet's and Behan's caricature. Like the quotations from Maurice Barrès and Paul Bourget which Sartre puts at the end of *Saint Genet* to illustrate how the 'Just Man' conceives society and morality, the Bishop's remarks represent a social attitude which can no longer be meaningfully satirised for the simple reason that it no longer exists. Both *The Blacks* and *The Screens* show that Genet's vision of Western society is curiously fixated at about 1890, and his account of the Bishop's visit looks forward to his theatrical achievements in two ways: it shows him temporarily abandoning his lyrical and introspective style in order to cast his ideas into an externalised, dramatic mode; and it emphasises how little his vision of society changed when he ceased to write in prison and began to be accepted in the outside world.

Mettray not only prepared boys for Fontevrault by hardening their opposition to society and making them incapable of following any but a criminal career. It also initiated them into the kind of absolute social distinctions which seem to characterise all prison and criminal society, and which give it at times as mysterious and hierarchical an air as the social world described by Proust. At Mettray, there were two basic distinctions: the jerks (*cloches*), whose inferiority was manifest in the apparently permanent newness of their clothes; and the big shots (*marles*), who managed immediately after their arrival to give their uniform the worn and battered look which emphasised their experience and authority. There were also other distinctions based upon the kind of work the boys did (*cloches* tended to work in the fields, *marles* in the workshops), the nature of the sexual relationships they enjoyed, and the tattoo marks which a clandestine committee allowed them to have. The divisions seem to have a rigidity comparable to that of the Indian caste system, and neither at Mettray nor at Fontevrault could the inmates change from one category into another. This curiously Jansenistic concept of a humanity divided by an inexplicable predestination in.ɔ Elect and Reprobate forms the subject for Genet's first play, *Deathwatch*, and is, like his insistence upon betrayal, an example of how his own preoccupations reflect an aspect of social reality while at the same time offering his own particular version of it. Frank Tannenbaum writes in his *Crime and the Community* that 'There is no more caste in the heart of India than in an American penitentiary', and Genet's description of Fontevrault suggests that this was also true in France. Where Genet differs from other writers about crime, however, is in the prestige which he maintains that other prisoners have for the *mac*, the ponce or pimp, who is normally depicted as the lowest of the low. His explanation of this prestige casts an interesting light both upon his own attitude to the *mac* in his novels and plays, and on a fairly widespread attitude in the normal world.

One of the most important divisions in Fontevrault is, in fact, between *macs* and *casseurs* (pimps and cracksmen) and it is significant in a number of ways that Genet should classify himself with the second. The *mac* despises the *casseur*, and enjoys a considerable reputation with the other prisoners because he is 'the man who has not been taken in by love. The knight stronger than love'—a curious reversal of the traditional view which sees the pimp as the 'eternal cuckold'. What is interesting is that the definition which Genet gives should reflect a not uncommon scale of masculine values in which a man enjoys prestige if he can show his independence of women. In many golf clubs, for example, the man who hurries home in order to keep an appointment with his wife loses face immediately. What Genet does is take one aspect of this scale, separate it from its normal concomitant of exclusive possession, and then treat it as embodying the whole of the scale in its purest form. He sometimes does the same with the word 'sainthood', but is then less successful in presenting society with a critical mirror image of its own values than he is when he analyses the appeal of the *mac*. In his prose, he offers such an image relatively rarely, and seems for much of the time to accept the prison hierarchy as something to be treated with respect rather than irony. Almost always, in *Miracle of the Rose*, the facts which Genet presents would support a critical or amused attitude to the society he describes, but the tone in which he speaks is one of connivance if not of direct approval.

Genet's own uncertainty about what attitude he really does adopt towards his material in *Miracle of the Rose* is perhaps the greatest flaw in the novel. He makes wholly inconsistent statements about his own character, presenting himself at one point as a hardened cracksman, and at another as a feeble, passive dreamer lost in admiration before 'the poetry of the great birds of prey'. He regrets the fact that he will never become a great criminal and thus embody this poetry, but states when writing as a 'disillusioned visionary' that this poetry is, in any case, a complete illusion. The struggle between his intelligence and his existential choice comes out more clearly in *Miracle of the Rose* than in any other text, and it is interesting that he himself provides a comment in this novel on the different attitudes which it contains.

'At the beginning of this book,' he writes, 'I spoke of a kind of disenchantment with prisons. It came about gradually as I began to examine delinquents and criminals purely from the standpoint of practical reason. From this point of view, all criminal acts may seem foolish, for the gain is trivial compared to the penalty incurred if you fail, to the risk you run, and prison seemed to me—which it also is—a pack of poor devils. But if I go further, if my lights illuminate the interior of the big shots, I understand them better, I feel exactly as I used to about them and their work. My understanding was complete when Bulkaen once said to me: "When I do a job, when I break into a house, I get a hard on, I lubricate." The reader will therefore not object to my presenting Bulkaen as a liberator.'

In other words, Genet tells us, he has ceased to believe that there is anything admirable about crime, and remains faithful to his earlier vision solely because a young man he is attracted to finds robbery sexually exciting. This may be good enough reason for him, but the disturbance which his work is supposed to produce in the 'Just Man's' conscience will probably be small indeed after such a confession. This is particularly the case when Genet paints so depressing a picture of homosexuality and abstains from justifying his own sexual tastes by anything but a subjective preference for unpleasant characters. The 'Just Man's' reaction to *Miracle of the Rose* is much more likely to be sorrow and pity for criminals, mingled once again with the comfortable feeling of reassurance that he himself is on the right side of the fence.

The fact that Genet never seriously follows up the challenge implicit in his remark that 'honest people may be thieves who have chosen a clever and safer way of stealing' only partly explains his failure to make *Miracle of the Rose* into a book which, he claims, will be 'as treacherous as the mirror systems that reflect the image of you which you did not compose'. Genet's own anticipation of Sartre's contention that he makes us share his guilt is also unjustified because *Miracle of the Rose* never attains the intellectual or aesthetic unity necessary to a work of this kind. Not only is the reader positively invited to escape from this mirror system by Genet's contradictory statements about crime and his apparent inability to maintain the same attitude for more than a few pages; he is also enabled to slip out through the many gaps left by the loose construction of the novel and by Genet's refusal to tell a coherent or compulsive story. Far from being a finely spun spider's web exquisitely constructed to catch and destroy the reader's mind, *Miracle of the Rose* is a series of episodes connected by only the most general of plans. There is nothing like the steel chain which Goethe found running through the apparent discontinuity of Diderot's *Le Neveu de Rameau*, and which effectively prevents the reader who shares the conventional moral views of Diderot's official self from refuting the cynical hedonism of his *alter ego*. It is, in fact, only too easy to read *Miracle of the Rose* in isolated passages, skipping Genet's attempt to discover what Bulkaen is really doing in order to pursue a more interesting ancedote about life at Mettray, or dodging one of the more unpleasant descriptions of what it is like to defecate in public in order to follow up what happens when the bandit Botchako tries to escape.

Genet states at one point that he is writing his *Miracle of the Rose* 'without pleasure', and that he seems to have lost the capacity to plunge headlong into his dreams. This remark underlines a fundamental difference in atmosphere between *Our Lady of the Flowers* and *Miracle of the Rose*, for in spite of the fact that Genet's first novel is no more rigorously constructed than his second, it did possess a greater unity of tone which stemmed from its dreamlike quality and from Genet's closer identification of himself with the events and characters he was describing. In *Miracle of the Rose*, he is no longer the self-hypnotised visionary who believes so strongly in his own world that everything which he writes conveys the force of his dreams to the reader. The book consequently lacks both the significant form of a classical work and the inner conviction which gives organic unity to the best romantic creations. Although it does have considerable literary qualities, these often seem to stem less from Genet's cult of evil than from a more general ability to note down both his own behaviour and the events around him with originality and accuracy.

As in *Our Lady of the Flowers*, this ability shows itself in a number of different contexts. There is, first of all, his alternately realistic and poetic description of prison: it is full of 'lying mouths' and mysterious questions of precedence, of prisoners who make calendars covering twenty years so that they can embrace their whole sentence at one glance, and a place where a ceaseless watch is kept over Harcamone from the day he is sentenced to death, and fattened up as for a sacrifice, to the moment of his execution. A man in prison, says Genet, is so cut off from reality that he seems to be walking through a kind of cotton wool, and the time he has spent in gaol is so like a dream that the memories which surge back when he is released are those of the moments immediately preceding his arrest. Prisoners, according to Genet, often live in close proximity for years without meeting. All they know of one another are their voices, and it is Genet's description of the way in which they talk and sing that is one of the most original features of his characterisation in *Miracle of the Rose*.

Divers, for example, has a 'guttural, big shot's voice', which is 'firm and solid, so that a long speech could be hacked out of it . . . composed of the same hard matter as his body and the pattern of his gestures'. It is, in fact, the complete projection of his personality, and Genet can never hear it without feeling profoundly troubled. When Botchako, the man with the toughest reputation in the whole of Fontevrault, sings one of the sentimental ballads favoured by prisoners, the 'irritating hoarseness' of his voice is 'transformed into a very sweet, velvety strain' in which its cracks and scratches 'become the clearest notes'. Genet moves on from this description to the general notation that 'beauty is the projection of ugliness, and that by "developing" certain monstrosities we obtain the purest ornaments', and in this particular instance he does come close to putting his formal aesthetic into practice. Perhaps more significantly, he offers not only an example of how ugliness is transformed into beauty but also an analysis of why this should sometimes happen: it is another elaboration of the Pascalian idea that *'les extrêmes se touchent'*, this time with Genet's favourite dialectical notion of a quality reaching such a degree of intensity that it becomes its opposite. Like his comment at another point in the novel that 'the beauty of a living thing can be grasped only fleetingly', it reveals him as a writer with a highly original aesthetic vision and an aptitude for analysis.

There are two other kinds of passage in *Miracle of the Rose* in which Genet's skill as a writer seems to owe relatively little to his existential choice as such, however closely it may be related to his temperament and to the experiences which stemmed from this choice. They are the continuation of the study which he began in *Our Lady of the Flowers* of his own homosexuality, and his analysis of the violence and ceremonies connected with the criminal world. According to Genet himself, his acquisition of the technical skill and self-confidence which characterise the professional cracksman affected his sexual attitude by making him feel less attracted by the butch hoodlums whom he evoked so ambiguously in his first novel. He now felt that he was one of their equals, and even began to talk slang, which in the world of *Our Lady of the Flowers* was 'like the language of men among the Caribees . . . a secondary sexual attribute', denied to the passive homosexuals. What Genet himself calls this 'living of his youth at thirty' is accompanied by a desire for sexual encounters with younger men, represented in *Miracle of the Rose* by Bulkaen. However, this is shown to be as frustrating in its way as Divine's longing for tough, virile males. Because she brought out all the subconsciously feminine side of her lovers, they eventually deserted her, attracted in their turn by more virile males. This was why Seck Gorgui and

Notre-Dame became attracted to each other after they had lived with her for a time. Precisely because Genet is a homosexual, and retains his essential femininity in spite of his new affectation of toughness, Bulkaen is not really interested in him. He is constantly moving away from Genet, attracted by more genuinely tough characters like Botchako. Where the Gidean concept of pederasty evoked in the relationship between Edouard and Oliver in *Les Faux-Monnayeurs* would have led to a mutually satisfying *affaire* between Genet and Bulkaen, Genet's more realistic vision shows the fallacy of such concepts. Bulkaen is killed while attempting to escape from Fontevrault, significantly enough in Botchako's company. Genet never sleeps with him, and the failure of his attempt to relive at thirty the boyhood delights of Mettray underlines the fallacy of the homosexual dream in which the young man is supposed to offer youth in exchange for wisdom. The Mignon-Divine *ménage* collapses through what Genet presents as the inevitable infidelity of homosexuals, as well as through the effect which Divine has on her lovers. The Genet-Bulkaen idyll comes to nothing because Bulkaen instinctively sees through Genet's supposed toughness and glimpses the femininity which this hides. If one of the stories which Genet tells about himself in *The Thief's Journal* is true, there is just as little possibility of two young men finding satisfaction in each other. When Genet suggests to his friend Robert that they might have sex together, the latter repulses him with the remark that because they are of the same age 'there'd be no fun' ('*ça ne serait pas marrant*').

Genet's recognition that he is not really a tough, that the 'poor quality of his nervous system' will always oblige him to act a part, is nevertheless one of the more fruitful inconsistencies in *Miracle of the Rose*, for it gives rise to some very interesting accounts of how he overcame this poor quality in order to survive in the criminal world. At Mettray, for example, he learned how to transform the way he trembled from fear into a 'trembling from anger', and eventually to obtain the objective results if not the inner certainty associated with the aggressive role he adopted. But precisely because he was not naturally and instinctively tough, he had the self-consciousness to see the play-acting involved in the criminal world, and this enables him to present his own behaviour with the detailed break down of actions and emotions of a slow motion film. Thus, on one occasion, Botchako paid Genet the great compliment of offering him a drag from his cigarette. Genet was reluctant to acknowledge the implications of this honour, but felt that he must accept out of politeness. He was on the point of taking the butt-end when he suddenly noticed another prisoner whom he had known at Fresnes. He greeted him noisily, drawing back the hand he had stretched out to accept Botchako's offer, and moved downstairs to accompany his new friend. 'Then,' he writes,

> thinking that my gesture might look like too-premeditated insolence, and thus lose the element of contempt I wanted it to have, I suddenly stopped on the third stair and acted like a person who has just forgotten something. I turned around and started to go up again. The pimps (*macs*) were watching me. Seeing Botchako only in profile, I sensed that his face was clouded with shame. I felt that the brute's decency was being tortured and was muddled in a confused episode in which I appeared and disappeared as disdainfully as an actress. He was also hurt because I was a crasher, a guy who was hostile to pimps. I ought to have been up there with him, and here I was, going downstairs and laughing with the young hustler. I scowled and flipped my hand the way one does when deciding not to bother about some trivial matter, and I went downstairs. In that way, my gesture did not seem calculated, and my contempt for his advances, which were sought by others, sometimes in a cheap way, disturbed Botchako deeply. I could hear him say, in a gentle, trembling tone, to the fellow next to him:
>
> 'Drag, Milou.'
>
> It was a triumphal moment for me, and I went downstairs, carried away by a sudden friendship for the pimp (*mac*) who had been feared at Fresnes and whom farsighted destiny had called forth to give my exit grace and brilliance.

This passage shows the same acuity of observation as the analysis of Divine's behaviour in *Our Lady of the Flowers*, but differs from it in a way that is particularly significant for the relationship between the literary value of Genet's work and his choice to be evil. Only a person who had chosen himself as one of the insulted and humiliated could have written the scene in which Divine plants her false teeth on her head and pretends they are a crown. Genet's description of his tactics in dealing with Botchako could have been written by any novelist with an experience of prison life and an interest in psychological analysis. The same thing is true of many other passages in *Miracle of the Rose*, and these also have another important quality: they lack the ambiguity frequently created elsewhere in the book by the dichotomy between Genet's lyrical presentation of his criminals and his recognition of their drabness and stupidity. When Genet is talking about convicts' voices, studying his own reactions to violence, or reporting on the behaviour of homosexuals, the reader can at least see what he is doing. When he is saying that Harcamone possesses the beauty of a flower because his brutality is at the furthest possible remove from the fragility and delicacy of a rose, it is more difficult to see quite how the reader is expected to react.

There is no doubt that Genet needed his vision of crime as poetry and sainthood, of Mettray as a paradise, of the murderer and traitor as heroes, to provide him with a driving force to write his books. In rather a different context, Zola needed the naive determinism of Claude Bernard as an intellectual framework for the Rougon-Macquart series. It is also a truism that Genet's books would have been very different if he had not spent some fifteen years of his life in and out of gaol. But in the same way as Zola's scientific theories add little to the literary value of his work, so Genet's formal views and experience in the pursuit of evil often seem unrelated to the effects he produces. His most remarkable poetic effects, like the description of Harcamone's final apotheosis, are indeed inseparable from his vision, but he himself invites the reader not to participate whole-heartedly in them by the reminders which he scatters through his work of how deliberate an illusion this is. The tone in which he speaks of Mettray is certainly highly individual, but the facts which he describes could be presented very differently and still produce the same horror.

CHAPTER FIVE

POMPES FUNÈBRES

Pompes Funèbres was the first of Genet's works not to be written in prison, and is at the moment of writing the only one not translated into English. A possible reason for this may be that it gives even more elaborate details about homosexual activity than any other of Genet's novels, or it may be that Genet's inversion of customary standards becomes totally unacceptable when it is linked with the politics of the 1939–1945 war. The hero of *Pompes Funèbres* is a member of Darnand's pro-German *Milice*, and his lover a German soldier called Erik. At one point in the story, Hitler appears and has sexual relations with another French boy called Paulo, who is said to be half-brother to Genet's friend Jean Decarnin. The Berlin public executioner is also presented as a symbol of desirable sexual vigour, and makes an important contribution to the general atmosphere of the book.

In *Our Lady of the Flowers* and *Miracle of the Rose*, Genet referred only in passing to the historical events which were taking place while he was writing his books. In the first, he thinks as he lies in his prison cell of the five million young men who are going to die 'by the cannon that erects and discharges', and writes that Mignon's virility 'has the penetrating force of the blond warriors who, on June 14, 1940, buggered us so soberly and seriously, though their eyes were elsewhere as they marched in the sun and dust'. In *Miracle of the Rose*, which Genet wrote on the sheets of white paper from which he was supposed to make paper bags in the La Santé and Tourelles prisons, the war made itself felt in three ways: the prisoners were constantly hungry because their already meagre rations had been cut by half; at Fontevrault, the work they had to do was 'make the camouflage nets that will be the enormous tulle which veils the phalli of the Nazi cannons when they spit'; and innocent people are sent to prison, thus making the criminals who have earned the right to be there feel that the prisons lose their hardness and glitter. In neither book, however, does Genet make a sustained effort to relate his private concerns to the political world of his potential readers. His references to the German army reveal far more of what Cyril Connolly called 'the obsession with the male organ which is really the obsession of a female nymphomaniac' than any serious attempt to associate his cult of evil with the political ambitions of the Nazi movement. His half-mocking, half-serious references to the mistakes which Destiny makes in putting honest people in gaol also belong more to the peculiar world depicted in *Deathwatch* than to the political ideas suggested by *The Balcony* and *The Screens*.

Pompes Funèbres was written in September 1944 and dedicated to Jean Decarnin. It was, in fact, inspired by Decarnin's death, which Genet says took place on August 19, 1944, when he was shot during the street fighting which accompanied the liberation of Paris. Genet also states in the text that he had known Decarnin since 1940, and had been his lover for the three months immediately preceding his death. In giving the book the title of *Pompes Funèbres*, Genet was not introducing a new element into his work: *Our Lady of the Flowers* had opened with a description of Divine's funeral, and *Miracle of the Rose* contained the account of the funeral of two boys, Rigaux and Rey, who died while at Mettray. Indeed, Genet himself comments at the beginning of *Pompes Funèbres* on this fondness for funerals, and one of his most recent French critics, Claude Bonnefoy, sees death as the main and most important theme in his work. Only *Pompes Funèbres*, however, deals with this theme in the context of Genet's other preoccupations with crime and homosexuality. Indeed, when Genet writes at one point in *Pompes Funèbres* that we act 'in order to obtain a glorious burial with full funeral honours', he is subordinating life to death in a thoroughly romantic manner.

The story of *Pompes Funèbres* is presented by Genet as being purely a figment of his own imagination, and in this respect the book is close in technique to *Our Lady of the Flowers*. *Querelle of Brest*, on the other hand, written immediately after *Pompes Funèbres*, resembles *Miracle of the Rose* in that it presents events as having actually happened, and this alternation between an openly imaginative and a supposedly realistic aesthetic gives an interesting balance to Genet's first four prose works. What sets Genet's imagination going in *Pompes Funèbres* is a visit which he makes to a cinema during the period immediately after Decarnin's death. He is overwhelmed with grief for his friend, and has several times been to see Jean's mother, who is hiding one of her lovers, a German soldier called Erik, in her apartment. In the cinema, he sees a newsreel depicting the end of the street-fighting in Paris and the capture of the few remaining members of the *Milice* who had been shooting at the Resistance fighters from the roofs. When the screen shows a close-up of one of the *Miliciens*, Genet sees that he is a pale, terrified boy. The cinema audience boos and jeers, and for a moment Genet shares its hatred for the boy, whom he names quite spontaneously Riton. His hatred, however, is so intense that it corresponds, for him, 'to the firmest love'. He decides that it is Riton (whose name, by its similarity to 'raton', inevitably evokes the idea of 'rat') who has killed Jean, and he is suffering so intensely from his lover's death that he wishes to use any means available to free himself from this memory. The best trick, he feels, that he can pay 'that fearsome brood that we call destiny', and which delegates a child to do its work, is to endow this very child with the love which he had borne his victim. Thus, in the same way that he had earlier decided to embrace the social destiny which made him an outlaw and a criminal, to will what he was condemned to become, Genet decides to identify himself with the very person whom he imagines as responsible for the death of his friend. The rest of the book becomes a description of the twelve days which Riton spends on the roofs of Paris, accompanying Erik and a group of German soldiers, until he is finally captured and photographed in the newsreel which Genet sees.

Genet is helped in the attitude which he adopts towards Riton by the fact that the insults hurled at the boy by the cinema audience seem, to him, yet another ovation to the young *Milicien*'s glory. Because the whole of France now detests the *Miliciens*, it becomes natural for Genet to identify himself with them, and this in spite of the fact that by the time he was writing *Pompes Funèbres* he had already met Sartre and a number of other left-wing writers. The plot of *Pompes Funèbres* develops in a dream-like manner consistent with this account that Genet gives of how and why he invented the story. In addition to the description of how Riton meets Erik, has sexual relations with him, is brutally treated by Erik's companions while his lover looks calmly on, and finally kills him as they stand together on the roof, the novel also depicts a number of other events. However, the two episodes which take place in Germany—the affair between Erik and the Berlin public executioner, and the sexual encounter between Hitler and Paulo—are only loosely connected with what Genet presents as the main theme of the book. The socially observant Genet makes a brief appearance when Erik's relationship with *le bourreau de Berlin* enables him to adopt 'some of the comfortable habits of which his working-class childhood had dreamed', and there is a nice touch of Genet's deflationary humour when Hitler 'the fabulous emblem of a nation fulfilling Satan's orders' comes down to live 'in that humble dwelling constituted by the puny body of an old queen, a screaming queer'. Perhaps naturally, in view of its subject-matter, *Pompes Funèbres* contains fewer ironical notations than either of Genet's two previous novels. It thus enables the reader to make a more consistent imaginative effort to enter into Genet's world, and Sartre reports a worthy professor of economics as being overwhelmed by the book and declaring that no one speaks of love like Genet. Intellectually, however, *Pompes Funèbres* does not possess a similar consistency of tone and content. Once again, Genet destroys with one hand the cult of evil which he is apparently trying to establish with the other, so that in his attitude to politics, as in his glorification of crime, common sense will keep breaking through.

The defiance of conventional values implied by Genet's decision to make his hero a member of the *Milice* is echoed at several points by statements which he makes about his own political attitude. He would, he says, have joined the *Milice* if he had been younger, and he declares that he was 'happy to see France terrorised by armed children'. It was natural, he says, that 'the extravagant banditry of the Hitlerian adventure' should provoke the hatred of honest folk while at the same time inspiring him with deep admiration and sympathy. In another passage, omitted from the standard Gallimard edition, he illustrates this mixture of moral and aesthetic enthusiasm by writing of Hitler that:

> As a poet, he knew how to use evil. We should be crazy to believe that he did not see that the morality dictated by our emotional principles, by religion and customs, is not on the side of a more or less egalitarian communism. He destroyed to destroy, he killed to kill. Nazism, as an institution, sought only to stand proudly upright in evil, to erect evil into a system and raise a whole people, as well as itself at the head of this people, to the most austere solitude. From the most abominable human condition, from the infamous submission of tyranny, Hitler obtained the finest effect by the artifice of pride which is called art.

In *The Thief's Journal*, Genet links his admiration for the *Milice* to his other main preoccupations by writing that he was attracted to it because it contained his 'three theological virtues' of treason, theft and homosexuality, and in *Pompes Funèbres* he declares that the *Milice* was 'born to betray'. There are, however, a number of reasons why these statements are difficult to take at their face value, and constitute an inadequate guide to Genet's final attitude. The first is that they are so exaggerated as to appear, like the praise for Mettray in *Miracle of the Rose*, highly ironic; the second is that Genet once again specifically criticises his own cult of evil in a manner now familiar to the reader of his first two novels; and the third is that he acknowledges the secret longing which he had for goodness, and even gives the appearance, at times, of holding the 'correct' political attitude.

Again in *The Thief's Journal*, Genet quotes a satirical poem which he says was written by a Communist to attack the Spanish Fascist movement, and whose first stanza runs as follows:

> We're all Good Catholics,
> We're all good killers too,
> To hell with the republic,
> Let's have some good floggings,
> Let's talk to castor oil.

Genet maintains that though this poem was written against 'the warriors of the Blue Legion, the fascists, the Nazis', it actually 'hymns them'. This may be true for him, but the majority of readers would surely find no difficulty in taking this poem at its surface meaning, as a crude but totally unambiguous condemnation of Fascism. In *Pompes Funèbres*, there is often the same dichotomy between what Genet says and how the average reader reacts to his words. Indeed, when he states that the pro-Fascist police force found most of its recruits 'among the former ponces of Marseilles or of Lyons', and insists upon the brutality, treachery and dis-honesty of its members, he is merely confirming what the most politically narrow-minded liberals have always main-tained: that anyone attracted by Fascism must be a criminal. By the time Genet wrote *Pompes Funèbres*, no view was more frequently and publicly expressed in France than the brand-ing of all supporters of the Vichy régime as traitors. For Genet to claim that he found this treachery attractive was an unusual point of view, but one that merely repeated the standard opinion in an inverted but identical form.

The passage from *Pompes Funèbres* in which Genet describes how mistaken he was in thinking that he would be alone if he chose to follow evil has already been quoted in the second chapter of this study. In the original edition, Genet compares himself in this respect to a naturalist who had 'dreamed of giving his Museum the finest collection of butterflies in the world'. 'He spent thirty years in the jungle,' Genet continues, 'risking innumerable and varied forms of death, and when he brought his Museum his multicoloured insects, he saw a collection which was even rarer than the one which had cost him so much trouble. In the face of so much misfortune, our only refuge is tears or fury'. Like his denunciation in *Miracle of the Rose* of the dullness, ugliness and stupidity of criminals, such a passage is not surprising for its content, however effective the central image may be. What is surprising is that Genet should, in both *Pompes Funèbres* and *Miracle of the Rose*, pursue such contradictory aims: praise a traitor because treachery cuts a man off from society, and yet admit that nothing is more frequent than treachery; proclaim his devotion to crime, and yet recognise its pointlessness. He says in *Pompes Funèbres* that it was when General Koenig put up posters asking people to change sides and inform the police about their friends that he came to see how commonplace and official treason had become. If that was so, it is hard to see why he still thought he was going against the usual standards of society by presenting a traitor as his hero. It is already difficult to believe that Genet maintained until the age of thirty-four his belief in the monolithic integrity of bourgeois society, and discovered the cracks in it only when he witnessed the rapid changes of allegiance which character-ised the ending of the Second World War. This is what he implies when he writes in *Pompes Funèbres* that he had tried, by being a traitor and thief, to attain 'a moral solitude where no one in the world would join me', but now realises that he is 'on a bank more densely peopled than death itself'. What is even more difficult to understand is why he included a palinode of this kind in a book which he knew that he was writing for publication.

One possible explanation is that he intended to turn *Pompes Funèbres* into what *Miracle of the Rose* sometimes promises to become: the denunciation of a society which, though dishonest itself, sends men to prison for being dishonest. Perhaps Genet is suggesting that since everyone now betrays everyone else, we should honour the *Milice* for carrying our practice to its logical conclusion, but such an explanation is tempting rather than convincing. There is no irony in the tone of the passage where Genet acknowledges once again how ordinary evil is, and any criticism which *Pompes Funèbres* contains seems directed against the *Milice* rather than at society as a whole. Moreover, in addition to undermining the effect of his plot by recognising that Riton's treachery is not a particularly original attitude, Genet also reassures his readers about their own ideals by admitting that he himself is most deeply attracted by virtue.

'If I show such passion for leaving goodness behind me,' he writes, 'this is because I am passionately attached to it', and he makes it clear what this means in political terms when he says that he admires the beauty which men show when they free themselves from tyranny. The approval which he also expresses for the Resistance movement because of the new sexual vigour which it represents now that Germany has been defeated should perhaps be taken with a pinch of salt. Nevertheless, his statement that, thanks to Jean Decarnin's death, he now belongs to the France which he had 'so cursed and so desired' has a ring of sincerity that probably stems from the grief which he felt at the death of his friend. A further indication that he really is on the side of the angels in political matters is given by his admission that he still feels himself mysteriously linked to France, and weeps when his country suffers. The impossibility of discovering what Genet really means when he so frequently contradicts by his personal statements the aims which he says he is pursuing in his fiction can perhaps be linked to Sartre's contention that his object is always to destroy the reader's moral and intellectual self-confidence. 'The only way that Genet has of disposing the minds of others to form images is to catch them in the trap,' writes Sartre, and he argues elsewhere that Genet constructs what he calls *'tourniquets'* ('whirligigs') to trap the reader into the realisation that truth and objective reality do not exist. According to this interpretation, the passages in *Miracle of the Rose* and *Pompes Funèbres* in which Genet appears to be sharing the common-sense view of the world would be merely rhetorical devices and not actual confessions. They would, in addition, fit quite consistently into Genet's cult of evil by reinforcing the idea that this evil must be loved for what it is, and not because of the expression which it gives to an alternative form of goodness.

Logically, this last point is unimpeachable. If Genet's aim is to pursue evil in its absolute form, then the more stupid, inefficient and repulsive his criminals are, the better they serve his purpose. The more fully evil is shown to be self-defeating and contradictory, the more completely it is evil. Once again, however, the problem becomes different when Genet writes his books with a reader in mind, and when it is claimed that works such as *Pompes Funèbres* or *Our Lady of the Flowers* do disturb the honest reader's self-satisfaction. The main objection to Genet's novels, from this point of view, is that none of them is constructed with sufficient rigour to trap the reader into an intellectual maze from which there is no escape. *Pompes Funèbres*, in particular, even contradicts by its very plot the total reversal of all moral values which Genet presents as being its aim.

When the German army is facing defeat, and is represented only by the handful of soldiers whom Riton accompanies, or by those of their compatriots who seek refuge in the sewers of Paris, Riton does not act like a real traitor and change sides to save his skin. He remains loyal to Erik until the very end, and his reasons for killing him are so unexplained that his act could well be interpreted as an attempt to save his friend from falling into captivity. Just as Genet himself did the right thing by Jean Decarnin, and risked a prison sentence to protect his friend's name, so Riton does not desert his allies in their hour of adversity. In his *Playboy* interview, Genet remarked that 'if there were loyalty between two or three criminals, it would mean the beginning of a moral convention, hence of good', and he normally avoids describing such lapses in the portrait which he offers of the criminal world. The plot of *Pompes Funèbres*, however, shows that absolute evil is more difficult to attain in the world of politics.

As in the rest of Genet's fiction, the male characters in *Pompes Funèbres* all either begin or end as homosexual. At first, Erik is surprised when he feels sexually excited by *le bourreau de Berlin*, and tells himself that he isn't a queer. A moment's reflexion, however, is sufficient to convince him that if he feels like this he must be, and he makes no further struggle. For the first and only time in his novels, Genet attempts in *Pompes Funèbres* to offer some justification for homosexuality. He almost quotes *II Samuel, I, 26*, 'thy love for me was wonderful, passing the love of women', when speaking of his own love for Jean Decarnin, and he bases the whole plot of the book on the notion that only homosexual love is strong enough to bring him consolation in his bereavement. *Pompes Funèbres* also differs from Genet's first two novels in containing two female characters whose situation is studied in some detail: Jean's mother, and a housemaid called Juliette, whose illegitimate baby had been buried four months before Jean's death. His portrait of Jean's mother foreshadows his creation of Madame Lysiane in *Querelle of Brest* and Madame Irma in *The Balcony*, while the passages about Juliette contain a number of themes later developed in *The Maids*.

Like Madame Lysiane and Madame Irma, Jean's mother is a lady of mature charm, whom Genet describes as mourning her son '*à la manière des reines*', which for him means wearing white. She is living with Erik, and in his description of the efforts which she makes to retain the affection of her lover Genet shows both the '*malice pédérastique*' which informed his account of Mignon, and a talent for comedy that later reveals itself in some of the dialogues in *The Maids* and *The Balcony*. As she eats, Genet sees each of the movements that she makes, the care with which she rolls the spaghetti round her fork, her discreet swallowing, the speed with which she catches her napkin as it is about to slide off her knees, as forming 'an admirable love-song' composed in Erik's honour. In her relationship with Juliette, whom she has received into her home from charity, she anticipates the attitude which Solange and Claire consider a mistress cannot avoid having towards her maids. She maintains that 'a really good-quality servant is one that is really vulgar and low, more and more servile. That's why, when you tell them to be quiet, they shut their trap, so that you can't smell their guts rotting inside'. With her mouth full of food, she continues: 'Servants. Their bodies are all limp and flabby. They go on and are gone. They never laugh: they weep. Their whole life weeps and they soil our life by daring to intrude, bringing with them everything that ought to remain secret, shameful, and unavowed.'

At one point in the text, Genet states that the real father of the baby that Juliette is supposed to have had by Jean is a former adjutant from the regular army who is now a captain in the *Milice*. In the original edition, he describes how this officer salutes the flag every morning alone in his office, but this anticipation of the Lieutenant in *The Screens* is not developed to the point where the captain becomes as richly comic a creation. Indeed, there is very little about Juliette's life or her relationship with either Jean or the captain, and her main role in the novel is to provide a variation on the central theme of mourning. It is in keeping with the nightmarish quality of *Pompes Funèbres* that she should be raped in the cemetery by the grave-diggers who have just buried her child, but Genet's comments upon her passivity indicate that his sympathy is not here exclusively reserved for thieves and homosexuals.

> Her grief, he writes, made her insensitive to everything, to her very suffering itself. She felt at the end of her tether, that is to say on the point of taking off completely and leaving this earth behind her. And the grief that thus went beyond itself was due not only to the death of her baby girl, but was the sum total of all the misery she had felt as a woman, all her misery as a servant, all the human wretchedness that was overwhelming her today because a ceremony, based upon this very misery, had drawn together all the different sorrows which had earlier lain scattered within her.

There had been a similar passage in *Miracle of the Rose*, in which a meditation on friendship in prison had opened out into a vision of humanity consoling itself by human emotions for its permanent exile from paradise, but in his first two novels Genet is too preoccupied with his own problems to express sympathy for people unlike himself. What gives the passages dealing with Juliette their peculiar resonance is something comparable to what takes place in *Les Fleurs du Mal* when Baudelaire widens his emotional and intellectual horizon to take account of the fate which exiles other than poets suffer in the modern city. Although relatively few pages are devoted to her, it is the figure of Juliette which comes most convincingly to life in *Pompes Funèbres*, and the 'atmosphere of infinite sadness' which Jean-Marie Magnan sees her as carrying everywhere she goes contrasts most sharply and effectively with the 'rivers of green anger' that characterise Erik. The other characters, for the most part, move too exclusively in a purely dreamlike and disconnected world for the reader to maintain that degree of interest and belief in their actions which alone enables a novel to become, as Sartre would say, more than a lifeless collection of disparate signs.

It is true that Genet made no formal attempt to provide either *Our Lady* or *Miracle of the Rose* with a consistent plot. It is nevertheless possible to know more or less what is happening, and although the events which the novels describe may seem highly improbable, they are not impossible. Harcamone's apotheosis in *Miracle of the Rose* is frankly presented as a dream, and the rest of the action takes place in a world that is disconcertingly real. In the original edition, Genet went so far as to declare that 'all these names are accurate' and that 'these boys I am describing here were my friends'. 'I take my solemn oath upon it,' he continues, 'and this oath must be believed because poets believe in Heaven and fear it. I swear that from fifteen to seventeen I did live the wondrous life described here.' This realistic content does not of itself make *Miracle of the Rose* a better book than *Pompes Funèbres*, but it does give the novel the same kind of basic unity which Genet's concentration upon his own homosexuality gave to *Our Lady*. In *Pompes Funèbres*, there is no comparable framework, for the story of Erik and Riton is not powerful enough to sustain the various developments connected with it. Some of these are very good, as for example the description of how Riton was driven by hunger to join the *Milice*—as Genet himself says that he was driven to steal—and how, beforehand, he killed and ate a cat. Others offer apparently raw material for infinite psychological analysis, as when Genet describes how Erik tried to shoot all the images of himself which he could see in the looking-glass of the château where he was stationed before coming to Paris. Taken individually, the different passages often have considerable and sometimes overwhelming effect, although the scenes between Hitler and Paulo are totally impossible as well as intensely repulsive. But even the best passages do not fit together in any way that either gives unity to the book or effectively transposes the grief which Genet feels at the death of his friend into a powerful emotional symbol.

It may be, of course, that Genet should never be judged or criticised in this way. Sartre contends that he has 'reinvented literature', and adds that the average reader can expect to find neither pleasure, instruction nor information from his work. Genet remarks in *The Thief's Journal* that the idea of creating literary works of art makes him shrug his shoulders, and he clearly does not care whether he expresses his grief in a communicable form or not. For him, it is enough that he should give his ideas the permanence involved in their being written down, and he would certainly agree, as far as *Pompes Funèbres* is concerned, with the views attributed to the poet Mistral in Daudet's *Lettres de mon moulin*: that he does not need even a single reader in order to derive satisfaction from his art.

What is more significant than Genet's intentions, however, is the difference which undoubtedly separates *Pompes Funèbres* from his three other novels. Although the narrative in *Miracle of the Rose* may drag at times, the book has a definite unity, and *Querelle de Brest*, published immediately after *Pompes Funèbres*, has a relatively well-knit plot as well as a total consistency of atmosphere and theme. Genet is certainly so unique as a writer that he can be judged aesthetically only by the standard which he himself sets in his best work, and compared to *Our Lady of the Flowers*, *Pompes Funèbres* is a failure. This is less because of the inconsistencies in Genet's moral and political attitude, for these appear in all his work without really harming its total effect. It is essentially because there are not enough credible passages in the book to counter-balance both its general air of unreality and Genet's self-indulgent rhetoric. It undoubtedly has an appeal for those of his readers who, like Cocteau, place the highest value on the surrealistic and irrational aspects of his work. Those who hold that one of his greatest originalities as a writer lies in the balance which he keeps between his own intensely personal vision and an ironic awareness of its romantic falsehood, or in his view of homosexuality and crime as alternately fascinating and full of disappointment, will see *Pompes Funèbres* as his one experiment that did not succeed.

CHAPTER SIX

QUERELLE OF BREST

GENET's fourth novel differs from all his other prose works by the fact that he never intrudes in the narrative to talk openly about himself. He does not refer to his own past experiences, does not analyse his attitude towards society, and makes no attempt either to defy or endorse traditional moral values. If he does mention himself, it is in the first person plural, the editorial 'We', as he plays at being the self-conscious narrator unable to decide what his heroes will do next. This relative impersonality is also accompanied by what is, for Genet, a fairly coherent plot in which most of the events are connected realistically together and where only a few loose ends remain after the fate of the various characters has been decided. Each of these characters does, of course, reflect some aspect of Genet's own world view and private experience. When the hero, Georges Querelle, smiles at the thought that he is 'near to the shame from which there is no return, and in which we must find peace', there is a close resemblance to the theme of *Our Lady of the Flowers*, and when another of the characters, Gil Turko, feels 'a longing to surmount his crime by *willing* it deliberately' he offers an obvious parallel to Sartre's analysis of Genet's choice to be a thief. Nevertheless, this autobiographical content is neither obvious nor obtrusive. For example, after he had committed his first murder, Querelle is described as experiencing 'the feeling of being dead, that is to say, of inhabiting a profoundly remote region'. This passage is actually used by Sartre at the very beginning of *Saint Genet, actor and martyr* to illustrate Genet's lines in *Le Condamné à Mort* about '*L'enfant mélodieux mort en moi/Bien avant que ne me tranche la hache*' ('The melodious child dead in me/Long before the axe chops off my head'). However, the description fits so well into the general analysis which Genet offers of the life and motives of this particular character that its immediate relevance to Genet's own experience is in no way obvious. He consequently seems, in *Querelle of Brest*, to have reached the position where he can look back over his own experience and use it to create characters who enjoy rather more autonomy than Divine or Riton.

The plot of *Querelle of Brest* describes how Georges Querelle, a sailor in the French navy, kills a friend and accomplice called Vic, and manages to lay the blame for this crime on a young stone-mason, Gil Turko. Gil has, in fact, committed a murder, when in a moment of drunken frenzy he had stabbed an older workman, Théo, who had been making advances to him. By a happy coincidence, Querelle had picked up Gil's cigarette lighter from a café table a few days before killing Vic, and conveniently dropped it at the scene of his own crime. When, later in the book, Gil is hiding out in the ruins of the old military prison at Brest, Querelle befriends him and brings him food, clothes and money. He arranges for Gil to catch a train which will take him to Nantes, but also informs the police of what Gil is going to do. Gil is arrested, and presumably charged with both murders. Querelle gets off scot free, and leaves with his ship for a cruise in the Baltic.

Querelle is the only one of Genet's criminals who derives any profit from the crimes he commits, or whose betrayal of his confederates brings him any advantage. There is no indication that either Divers or Mignon gain anything by shopping their friends to the police, and neither of them shares Querelle's enviable ability for staying out of gaol. Querelle not only robs his victims and successfully hides his booty in various secret places throughout the world, but also runs a highly profitable side-line by smuggling opium into Brest. His immediate motive for killing Vic seems, indeed, to prevent his accomplice from ever revealing how the opium is brought ashore, and he afterwards continues the traffic with another helper, Roger, whom he meets through his association with Gil. Yet in spite of being a successful criminal, Querelle is in no way a cheerfully immoral pagan. After he has killed Vic, he immediately has a vision of his own arrest, and of his appearance before 'the imaginary Assizes which he made up for himself after each murder'. It is wrong, Genet maintains in this passage, to suggest that the criminal usually believes, at the moment of committing his crime, that he will not be caught. 'Incapable, in fact, of knowing whether or not he will be arrested,' he writes, 'the criminal lives in a state of uncertainty, of which he can rid himself only by denying his act, that is to say, by expiation, and further, by self-condemnation.' Querelle expiates his crime, and attains 'the comforting certainty that this execution would wash him clean of the murder', by becoming catamite to Norbert, the proprietor of the brothel 'La Féria', where much of the action in the novel takes place.

Genet's treatment of homosexuality in *Querelle of Brest* is more complex than in any other of his novels. For Querelle, it begins by being a means of expiating his crime, but later invades his whole personality. He becomes increasingly attracted to a police inspector called Mario Daugas, and eventually has a homosexual relationship with him. Before betraying Gil to the police, Querelle is also stated to be 'honestly and genuinely' in love with him, and in this particular relationship he represents a homosexual evolution whose two main stages are described separately in *Our Lady of the Flowers* and *Miracle of the Rose*. After being attracted to strong and supposedly virile males, as Divine is attracted to Mignon and Seck Gorgui, certain homosexuals move on to the stage where they find greater pleasure in younger boys, exactly as Genet describes himself as being drawn towards Bulkaen in *Miracle of the Rose*. At twenty-five, Querelle is just on the turn, half-way between Norbert, who is middle-aged, and Gil, who is only eighteen. He thus combines in himself the two stages which Genet has described in personal terms in his novels. Five years before the action of the novel takes place, Querelle felt only curiosity about what might happen to him when he was accosted by a wealthy Armenian in Beirut. It is because of the murder which he committed on that occasion that homosexuality has come to be associated in his mind with crime and expiation, and it is significant that his twin brother, Robert, should be furious when he discovers what is happening between Georges and Norbert. Although the similarity between the two brothers takes on its greatest significance in its relationship to what Sartre called Genet's *'dioscurisme fondamental'*, there is also a sense in which Robert is Georges Querelle's disapproving double, the man whose sexual normality feels insulted and endangered by the antics of one so close to him. At the end of the novel, Querelle eventually sleeps with Madame Lysiane, Norbert's wife and his brother's mistress, and feels very pleased with himself. The suggestion in this passage seems to be that Querelle has now succeeded both in escaping from his guilt and in growing out of a sexually infantile stage, and a remark which Genet makes elsewhere in the novel also seems to indicate that he now regards heterosexuality as essentially superior to homosexuality. By linking homosexuality with the feelings of guilt that Querelle has after his crime, he still seems very far from wishing to present it as admirable for its own sake. Nevertheless, it could be argued that it is because Querelle uses homosexuality to find release from his feelings of guilt that he manages to avoid capture by the police. Without this release, he might well be forced by his subconscious guilt feelings to give expression to that 'well-known inexcusable stupidity' of criminals which so often stems from a need for punishment and which leads to their arrest.

One of the aspects of homosexuality that Genet most emphasised in the relationship between Divine and Mignon was the feminising effect which homosexuality has on the most apparently virile of men. In *Querelle of Brest*, he explains this by saying that the very absence of women in the homosexual world obliges the two partners 'to discover whatever feminine streak there may be in their make-up, to invent the woman in them', and this is one of the remarks which acknowledge that homosexuality is an inferior and derivative form of sexual activity. Genet's recognition that this is so is also clear from what he says earlier in the same paragraph: that homosexual feelings can never 'be said to approach anything like genuine love between man and woman, or between two beings, one of whom is feminine'. Admittedly, Genet seems to contradict himself later in the book when he talks about 'the deep, tender, generous friendship which a homosexual alone can offer', but the whole atmosphere of the novel seems to belie this statement. Indeed, as both *Our Lady of the Flowers* and *Miracle of the Rose* showed very clearly, the one feature which characterises all Genet's homosexuals is infidelity. Moreover, this rather isolated approbation for homosexuality occurs in a passage devoted to Lieutenant Seblon, Querelle's commanding officer, who is essentially a frustrated rather than a practising homosexual. It may consequently represent an ideal which rapidly disappears once acts replace longings.

None of the characters in Genet's first three novels seemed to have any moral or aesthetic objections to homosexuality either in principle or in practice. Neither were anyone's homosexual longings seriously frustrated, for even though Genet never actually slept with Bulkaen, he found full consolation with Divers. In *Querelle of Brest*, however, Genet extends his range to describe both a frustrated homosexual, Seblon, and a person who, initially at least, feels an intense dislike for homosexuality, the young Gilbert Turko. Lieutenant Seblon is one of Genet's most successful creations, with the contrast between his stiff, over-formal ways and his private musings over Querelle's beauty, his decision to join the Navy because no one ever asked you why you were not married but also because he longed, alternately, to be 'some very precious object to be guarded by the soldiery' and 'a sort of spirit animating these muscular masses', and the rage which he feels, on entering a public lavatory, that 'so noble an edifice should be besmirched with crude political slogans'. There is no way of telling whether Genet himself thought that this last notation was funny or not. He omitted it from the 1953 Gallimard edition, together with the long and brilliant description of Querelle's first murder, and like certain omissions from the revised text of *The Maids*, this is an example of how uninterested he is in conventional literary effects. What he offers in Lieutenant Seblon is an analysis of the homosexual who is prevented, by natural timidity, rank and social position, from giving full expression to his sexual tastes. These hidden tastes explain why Seblon's brother officers, although finding him 'severe and slightly puritanical', also glimpse his true nature through the elegant and slightly precious way he talks. His curtness of manner stems from the need which he feels to hide this core of femininity which is 'at any time capable of spreading to every feature, overflowing into his eyes or to the tips of his fingers', and the hopeless longing which he has for Querelle is extremely well rendered. Genet's range as a novelist is, of course, highly limited and particular, for like the Baron de Charlus he tends grossly to overestimate the population of his native city. Yet in spite of his total inability to imagine men who are not homosexuals, he does offer variety within his own particular range. In *Querelle of Brest*, for example, he presents not only the frustrations of Lieutenant Seblon but also a perceptive account of homosexual problems within a genuinely working-class community.

With the exception of Lieutenant Seblon, none of the characters in Genet's fiction belongs to the middle class, though Madame Lysiane, as will be seen, makes every effort to be genteel. It is, indeed, only in *Querelle of Brest* that what his characters actually do for a living becomes relevant to their sexual behaviour, and that he ventures to describe the working-class world which, as Sartre remarks, simultaneously fascinates, terrifies and disgusts him. Gil is a building worker, and shares the contempt for homosexuals which is the official attitude of his class. Nevertheless, both he and his companions are acutely aware of their existence, and are continually making jokes about homosexuality. Because Gil feels unsure of himself when Théo begins to make advances to him, he also embodies another aspect of the homosexual experience: the reluctance of the normal man to be drawn into a kind of activity which, with his conscious mind, he finds repugnant. Genet's vision of this reluctance is, of course, limited by his inability to believe that the untempted heterosexual exists, but once his presuppositions are accepted, Gil's behaviour is not difficult to understand. He murders Théo precisely because the older man represents an aspect of his personality which he wishes to deny, and the homosexuality which he had tried to repress comes openly to the surface when he meets Querelle. It had earlier been implicit in his relationship with the fifteen-year-old Roger, his girl friend Paulette's younger brother, who had inspired him with emotions which he mistook for purely heterosexual longings. It comes out fully only after he has committed his first murder, and in this respect his development runs parallel to that of Querelle: both men deny their homosexuality until they have killed, but then almost hasten to acknowledge it. Querelle becomes genuinely attached to Norbert—'nobody can go on playing what he fondly imagines is no more than a sexy game every day of his life and not end up by taking to it,' comments Genet— and Gil becomes equally involved with Querelle. It is consistent with Genet's proclaimed attitude to society that murder should be so intimately linked with homosexuality, and the criticism of homosexuality which this implies is almost certainly unintentional. Nevertheless, the effect which homosexuality has on the society which Genet describes in *Querelle of Brest* is uniformly pernicious, and there is no question of his presenting it as a normally desirable form of activity.

The harm which homosexuality does is most visible in Genet's portrait of the working-class world. Théo, for example, is a skilled bricklayer and a good workman,

'Before placing it on its bed of cement,' writes Genet, 'he pressed his hands lovingly over each stone, turning it over, choosing the best-looking surface and always fitting the rougher side of each ashlar facing inwards, so that the finer face was exposed and destined for the façade.' Nevertheless, he is known to have a violent temper, and to be quite capable of 'getting up in the middle of the night and coming on padded feet to cut his victor's throat with a razor' if anyone dares to fight him. Gil is consequently unable to reply to Théo's constant provocative advances with the bout of fisticuffs that is his only normal weapon, and it is this impotence which eventually drives him to murder. Genet succeeds in making the reader sympathise with Gil in his dilemma, and the description of the physical and psychological atmosphere on the building site is one of the best features of the novel. Soldiers and sailors, he remarks, never have the feeling that they have really been working, and there is an interesting contrast running right through the book between the French navy, 'whose chief occupation seems to be to decorate rather than defend the coast of France', and the world of the builders and stone-masons where, in the evening, 'a grey mantle of impalpable dust had settled imperceptibly, giving a uniform colour to the whole yard, empty and lifeless, now that the commotion of the day's work was over'. At one point, Gil follows the same psychological pattern as Divine when, infuriated by Théo's constant taunts, he tries to reach the depths of shame by flaunting a homosexuality which he does not even admit to possessing. Nevertheless, he also belongs to a more immediately recognizable world, as when his embarrassment on waking up to another day of persecution is accompanied by a violent desire to urinate, which he dare not satisfy because of the taunts which he knows will greet him as he crosses the yard. Again in accordance with the social milieu to which he belongs, he finds consolation and a temporary escape by the humble task of cleaning his bicycle. This occupation, writes Genet, 'brought out the best in Gil.

Each operation was carried through with scrupulously neat perfection, whether with a greasy duster or a monkey-wrench. Every action was good to watch. Squatting on his heels or bending over the free-wheel to set it spinning, Gil was transfigured. He radiated joy by the very perfection and delicacy of every movement he made.' It is this joy which is destroyed by the intrusion of homosexuality into his world, and it may well be that, in his treatment of Gil, Genet is obeying two contradictory psychological impulses. On the one hand, he is describing himself as he might have been if, as Sartre says, he had originally been placed as a foster-child with industrial workers and not with peasants, and thus learned 'that one also *is* what one *does*'; and, on the other, he is using the plot of the novel to punish Gil for enjoying at least the beginnings of a self-respect and pride in his work which he himself was never given the opportunity to develop.

In *Querelle of Brest*, Genet not only extends his range to cover different types of homosexuality. He also, for the first time in his work, devotes considerable attention to analysing a woman's sexual feelings. Madame Lysiane, Norbert's wife and the proprietress of 'La Féria,' is fascinated by the close resemblance between Georges and Robert Querelle, so much so that it becomes the major obsession in her life. She even reaches the point of imagining that Roger, Gil's friend, is the child born of a union between the two brothers, and this idea fits in with the basic reason why the resemblance so haunts her. In one of her outbursts to Robert, she accuses the two brothers of 'living in each other's body', and continues:

> And, of course, there's no place for me. For me to come in between the two of you would be to make myself a sight too small. You'll throw me over. I'm too fat. Oh yes, that's what it is, I'm too fat...

In Genet's world, dominated as it is by homosexual concepts and standards, there are indeed grounds for the excluded female to feel such jealousy, and later on in the same scene Madame Lysiane is 'overcome with terrible confusion as the vision of two febrile muscular bodies came forcibly yet inescapably before her eyes, and, facing them, the softly crumbling mass of her own too fat body'. In so far as the idea of homosexuality is attractive on aesthetic grounds, it is because of the hardness and leanness of men's bodies, a quality which Genet particularly succeeds in evoking in his description of Querelle. Norbert also completes this relegation of soft, feminine curves to second place in the hierarchy of sexual attractiveness by claiming that homosexuality can enable men to do without women altogether, though neither he nor Querelle carries this attitude to the point of declaring themselves homosexual in every way. Indeed, Querelle still insists that it is 'not queer' because he 'still likes girls', and in this respect follows the example of Mignon-les-petits-pieds who slaps one of his mistresses for daring to suggest that he is *une tapette* because of his relationship with Divine. Where Genet gives an original twist to the somewhat banal notion of the jealousy which women feel for homosexuals is in the link which he establishes, within his own private mythology, between the Georges-Robert relationship and the other real or imaginary brothers in the rest of his work. In *Miracle of the Rose*, Rey and Rigaux are so much alike as to be indistinguishable from each other, and in *Pompes Funèbres* Paulo is Jean Decarnin's half-brother. In *Miracle of the Rose*, Genet comments explicitly on what he calls 'the mystery of the double', and writes about the 'fraternal double sovereignty' which characterised Family C at Mettray, because it alone had two 'elder brothers'. This, he says, disturbed him 'as much as the governing of the Russian empire by two child Czars, as much as the double death of Rigaux and Rey and the ceremony, savouring more of a marriage than of a burial, which unites them for heaven'. This fascination remains unexplained in Genet's earlier novels, and Madame Lysiane's attitude is only partly explained by the jealousy which she feels at being excluded from the perfect male couple. However, she is not the only person to be impressed by the similarity between Georges and Robert, for when Roger is watching the two brothers fighting, he reflects that they are so alike that it does not matter who wins. The original title of the novel was to have been *Les Mystères de Brest*, and the contrast between the physical similarity of the two brothers and the wide psychological difference which separates them adds an interesting problem in heredity to the other mysteries which it offers. Why Genet should have this interest in twin brothers is not immediately obvious from his published work; his use of it in *Querelle of Brest* gives the novel a curious but not unattractive air of having more meanings than normal analysis can elucidate.

In addition to her absorption with the similarity between Georges and Robert, which becomes less intense after she has slept with Georges and discovered that at least he differs from his brother by the dimensions of his sexual parts, Madame Lysiane also provides the focal point for a number of other themes in Genet's work. Her attitude towards both brothers even has its maternal side, and in this respect she provides yet another example of Genet's preoccupation with motherhood that showed itself in his vision of Mettray as his mother and in his creation of Ernestine. When she feels, as things begin to turn out badly for her, that the awkward and angular nature of reality is wounding 'the whiteness and warmth of her milk-nourished soul', Madame Lysiane also reflects one of Genet's own favourite ways of apprehending experience. Thus he describes the punishments at Mettray as 'prickly with painful angles', Bulkaen's personality as 'spiked with sharp angles', and he notes that when a soldier called Plaustener is robbed of his money, he 'loses his sharp angles'. Perhaps more important than this continuity in Genet's use of images is the humour with which Madame Lysiane is presented to the reader. Genet obviously feels very much at home in depicting mature women—Madame Lysiane is forty-five—and analysing their social pretensions. In the same way that Jean's mother, in *Pompes Funèbres*, tried to show her refinement in the way she ate, so Madame Lysiane refrains from smoking, for that would lower the tone of the house, and holds herself scrupulously above the perversions in which her girls are allowed to indulge. Indeed, she has so impressed Robert with how refined she is, that when she first begins to talk about his resemblance to his brother, Robert simply thinks that she is 'making allusions to the very delicate emotions which only a woman as "posh" as she could feel'. It is only later, in a long scene between Madame Lysiane and her lover, that the full intensity of her feelings begins to appear, and that Genet presents her with almost as much sympathy as irony.

The scene occurs after Madame Lysiane and Robert have been making love, and she is consequently deprived of the protection which her corsets and highly formal clothes normally provide. Indeed, as she stands in her bare feet, she realises how difficult it is for her to be majestic without the moral and physical support of her high heels, and comes to understand 'that anger can be expressed in the real tragic manner only when properly supported by the theatrical buskin'. There is also an interesting realistic touch when the lovers get back into bed and Madame Lysiane's ice-cold feet prevent them 'from sinking down into the wild intoxication from whence there is no emerging'. Nevertheless, the tone of the passage gradually becomes more serious as their love-making once more evokes, in Madame Lysiane's mind, the resemblance between Robert and Georges. When dawn comes, and 'the pale light of day "undoes" the room, as we say that a woman undoes her hair, or that a face is undone, a sure sign of great misfortune or nausea', Madame Lysiane's feeling of solitude becomes so intense that she craves for death. The woman who had earlier been described as 'lingering lovingly over all the most alluring, sugary and comfortable parts of her body' (*'tout ce que sa personne avait de sucré, de distingué et de confortable'*) then ceases to be an object for Genet's pederastic malice and shares in the suffering and anguish which form the real basis for the vision which creates all his characters.

For much of the time, however, Madame Lysiane is treated with a certain humour and detachment, just as her successor, Madame Irma, is in *The Balcony*. At one point, Genet sets yet another problem to his translators when he describes her as one of the women known in the past as '*accidentées, agenouillées, croqueuses, dégrafrées, filles de plâtre, gerses, instantanées Louis XV, luisantes, lumineuses, mousseuses, numérotées, suspendues, troncs des pauvres, universelles* . . .', and he makes an interesting socio-linguistic observation when he remarks that she always speaks of being '*allongée*' ('stretched out') and never '*couchée*' ('in bed'). The mention of homosexuality in her brothel would, Genet remarks, 'have been like calling the name of Satan in the choir of a cathedral', and she refused to recognise that the peculiar tastes exhibited by certain of her clients in any way reflected pederasty. She has, nonetheless, an essential tolerance towards sexual perverts, whom she treats as 'charming invalids'. Like Madame Irma's *maison d'illusions*, 'La Féria' caters for all tastes, and Madame Lysiane positively approves of fads and fancies. Without them, she tells her girls, the ugly would never know the delights of love.

Another way in which *Querelle of Brest* anticipates *The Balcony* is in the attention which it pays to the idea of the Policeman as an almost mythical figure. The police do not begin to figure largely in Genet's work until *Pompes Funèbres*, where he remarks that the *Milice* was 'at that ideal point where thief and policeman meet and mingle', and receive only one scornful mention in *Our Lady of the Flowers*. In *Querelle of Brest* and *The Thief's Journal*, however, they begin to take on the importance which culminates in the apotheosis of the Chief of Police in *The Balcony*, and which gives Genet's work its most immediate social relevance to the world of the nineteen-thirties and nineteen-forties. If *The Thief's Journal* is a genuinely autobiographical work, in the sense that it describes events and situations which really existed, Genet did at one time see a great deal of a police inspector called Bernardini, who seems to have served as one of the models for Mario, the inspector in *Querelle of Brest*. Genet felt so attracted to Bernardini that he used to follow him dog-like through Marseilles and was rewarded when Bernardini stopped two other policemen from beating him up. Without Genet realising it, Bernardini had noticed that he was being followed, and after his intervention on Genet's behalf the two became friends. Genet betrayed some of his accomplices to Bernardini, and he may well have used this experience in making the intimate relationship between policemen, criminals and police informers play an important part in the plot and atmosphere of *Querelle of Brest*. Mario employs a young boy called Dédé to spy on the criminals in Brest, and at one point effects a curious reversal of their normal rôles. When Querelle tells him about Gil's intended escape, it is Mario who gives the information to Dédé for transmission to his colleagues. This obviously improves Dédé's position, for at the end of the novel, he is described as reigning triumphantly over a *Monoprix*, sure of himself in his yellow gloves, free to be mean or generous as he pleases with the criminals he catches. Mignon, at the end of *Our Lady of the Flowers*, is arrested for shop-lifting in a *Monoprix*, and this recurrence of the French Woolworth's in two of Genet's novels may well reflect a personal experience on the author's part.

Mario's principal function in *Querelle of Brest* is, however, to illustrate two ideas: the omnipotence of the police, and the frequency with which men find psychological reassurance by identifying themselves with a large and powerful organisation. When Querelle, at the beginning of the novel, has felt inferior to Mario and Norbert because of their enviable, granitic solidity, he seeks to 'fortify himself with the full might of the Fighting Navy', and places himself under its protection when he reaffirms his threatened virility by insulting an innocent passer-by. When Mario feels afraid of the vengeance which 'Tony the docker' is said to be preparing to wreak upon him, he 're-entrenches himself behind the prestige of the Police, which can justify every kind of behaviour'. Later on in the book, he has so identified himself with the Police, and allowed himself to be possessed by its spirit, that he cannot prevent himself from making an arrest even when he does not particularly want to do so. Here Genet is presenting for the first time the theme of social masquerade which he exploits more fully in *The Balcony*, where all the principal male characters are obsessed with the idea of identifying themselves with a particular social function. Genet's own attitude towards the police seems to be one where a masochistic fetishism finds satisfaction in emblems and institutions rather than in actual physical objects, and he describes in *The Thief's Journal* how he used to feel sexually excited by the invisible presence of the inspector's badge which Bernardini carried in his pocket. He remarks in *Pompes Funèbres* that the police are always too powerful to allow the existence of criminal gangs, and it is a mark of Roger's naivety in *Querelle of Brest* that he should believe in the existence of such gangs and in their readiness to help him. The fact that Genet should so revere the Police, at least in his formal statements about them, is another indication of his intention to be evil rather than do harm, for their power is the strongest gurantee that the society he both defies and wishes to perpetuate will remain untouched.

He does, it is true, consciously make fun of the police from time to time, and there is an interesting passage in which he criticises the stereotyped concept which they have of homosexuality. Although they show 'almost pathctic precipitation' in fastening upon the idea of homosexuality when they wish to explain a crime, they still persist in seeing homosexuals as girlishly pretty and essentially feminine in appearance. They thus share the same illusion as Gil's fellow workmen, and this when all the events in *Querelle of Brest* reveal how mistaken they are. It is the most vigorous and tough-looking characters—Querelle, Mario and Norbert—who turn out to be homosexuals, and Genet is doubtless drawing on personal experience in making this point. Yet even though the police are occasionally comical —Mario takes a childish pleasure in the fact that he actually has his own office—Genet never reaches the stage of using this humour for serious criticism. He still chooses to see himself as the defeated rather than the successful criminal.

One of Genet's attempts to explain in more rational terms the general fascination which the police exercise involves the question of why they 'have such a strong resemblance to those they hunt down'. It is, he suggests, because the police themselves, like the criminals they pursue, represent society's unconscious and unacknowledged desires, which are to its ordinary life what people's dreams are to their waking moments. This idea of the subconscious as potentially evil also recurs in Genet's discussion of his attitude towards his own characters, and is perhaps the most interesting aesthetic and moral concept in *Querelle of Brest*. He remarks in *The Thief's Journal* that Saint Vincent de Paul should have 'been willing to commit the galley slave's crime instead of merely taking his place in irons', and earlier in the same book actually applies the same idea to Christ. '"Taking upon himself the sins of the world",' he writes, 'means exactly this: experiencing potentially and in their effects all sins; it means having subscribed to evil. Every creator must thus shoulder—the expression seems feeble—must make his own, to the point of knowing it to be his substance, circulating in his arteries, the evil given by him, which his heroes choose freely.' The idea of the connivance of the creator in the sins of his heroes first occurs in *Querelle of Brest* when Genet, using the editorial 'We', notes that Querelle, 'already flesh of our flesh and bone of our bone', was 'beginning to grow, to develop his personality within our deeper conscience and derive sustenance from the best in us'. Although Genet despairs of ever being able to be 'in any sense part of him'— in the same way that his self-consciousness, in *Miracle of the*

Rose, prevents him from having Botchako's enviable solidity and ferocity—he knows that he must take on himself some of the guilt for the crimes which he has made Querelle commit. This basically very moral way of presenting the relationship between an author and his world clearly made a deep impression on Jean Cocteau, who wrote in *La Difficulté d'Etre* that Genet was prepared to 'endorse the case which a higher justice might bring against his characters'. In other words, because Querelle had, in Genet's own phrase, 'sprung unarmed' from a dark region of his own personality, Genet recognises that he himself harboured all the evil which Querelle made manifest; and because Genet had already, before writing *Querelle of Brest*, admitted all his most shameful secrets both to himself and to his readers, he was in a position to make a confession applicable to all expressions of evil in literature: that if only the evil can imagine evil, no writer with imagination enough to create a convincing villain can ever enjoy a sense of inner virtue. From the truism that every author depicts himself in each one of his characters, and endows them with his own capacity for life, Genet extracts the truth that we all nourish, within ourselves, the most appalling crimes.

Interesting though *Querelle of Brest* is as a novel, Genet nevertheless communicates this particular insight through an incidental remark rather than through the overall construction and atmosphere. Within the book itself, everyone finds Querelle extraordinarily attractive, with the result that the horror which his crimes might evoke tends to fade into the background. Since almost all the men in the novel turn out to be homosexuals, and since Genet states on the first page that it is 'addressed to inverts', it is not surprising that Querelle should have this effect. All the nice girls, as the song says, like a sailor. The moral implications of Genet's remark about taking on the sins of his characters are thus not integrated in any way into the plot, and the predominant atmosphere of his novel does indeed tend to be one of connivance in the activities of the irresistible Querelle.

There is a similar indifference to the reactions and values of the common reader, this time on an aesthetic level, in Genet's final carelessness about his plot, for there are several incidents which remain totally unexplained at the end of the novel. What, as usual, remain so fascinating are the number of verbal felicities which the text contains and which serve to counterbalance the inconsistencies and contradictions of his overall vision.

The most outstanding of these good passages form part of Genet's treatment of homosexuality, and are therefore linked to the basic existential choice which Sartre regards as lying at the root of his achievement as a writer. Indeed, if one accepts Sartre's remark that homosexuality is a way out which a person invents in order to escape from a particular situation, all the insights into homosexuality which Genet offers in his work stem directly from the patterns of experience analysed in *Saint Genet, actor and martyr*. Thus, by the link which he establishes in *Querelle of Brest* between homosexuality and murder, Genet insists in the strongest possible manner on its life-denying qualities, and the fundamental sterility which it involves is wholly consistent with the negative attitude towards society which he originally adopted. However, the presentation of homosexuality in *Querelle of Brest* seems to involve a general psychological perspicacity and a use of language for its own sake rather than any direct or subconscious effort on Genet's part to explore and understand his own experience. The cause and effect relationship between his existential choice and literary excellence thus becomes particularly difficult to establish for this particular novel, since he moves so far from the directly personal problems which he analyses elsewhere that they no longer seem relevant. One passage which is especially interesting in this respect occurs in a long digression describing Querelle's first murder, and actually omitted from the 1953 Gallimard edition. In company with another sailor, Jonas, Querelle is approached in Beirut by an Armenian called Joachim, and eventually goes back with him alone to his flat. There Querelle strangles the man, and Genet gives the following description of his thoughts during the murder:

> 'Enfin, si un pédé c'était comme cela, un être aussi léger, aussi fragil, aussi aérien, aussi transparent, aussi délicat, aussi brisé, aussi clair, aussi bavard, aussi mélodieux, aussi tendre, on pouvait le tuer, étant fait pour être tué comme un cristal de Venise n'attend que la main large du guerrier qui l'écrasera sans même se couper (sauf peut-être la coupure insidieuse, hypocrite, d'une aiguille de verre aigue et brillante, et qui restera dans la chair). Si c'est cela un pédé, ce n'est pas un homme. Ça ne pèse pas lourd. C'est un petit chat, un bouvreuil, un faon, un orvet, une libellule dont la fragilité même est provocatrice et précisément exagérée afin qu'elle attire inévitablement la mort. En plus, ça s'appelle Joachim.'

('And then, as a final contention, if this were a typical queer—a creature so crushable, soft and delicate, a thing so fragile, light and airy, so clear and transparent, a being so melodiously gifted with tender, honey-sweet words—then one was almost justified in killing it since it was made to be killed, in the same way as Venetian glass simply cries out to feel the weight of the fist of a horny-handed warrior who will smash it to smithereens without so much as a scratch being inflicted, unless by some mischance a sharp and glittering splinter insidiously, hypocritically, slits the skin and lodges deep within the flesh. If it was a queer, it was certainly not a man, and nowhere near a man's weight. It was something in the nature of a kitten, a fawn, a goldfish, a blind-worm, or a dragonfly; something so provocatively and precisely exaggerated in its fragility that it must inevitably invite death. And, what is more, it went by the name of Joachim.')

The fact that Genet should have omitted this passage from the version published in his *Oeuvres Complètes* is again an indication of how indifferent he can be to some of his best effects. Although not a passage in which he attains the essentially mystical kind of poetry which is his declared aim as a writer, it does transpose into appropriately decadent and over-elaborate poetic language those associations of delicacy and sensitivity with which homosexuality has always been credited. It is an excellent way both of expressing these associations and of suggesting how false they are, for the people who turn out to be homosexuals in Genet's world are heavily-built, tough-looking and apparently insensitive males. What Querelle thus kills in Joachim is a perfectly expressed but completely fallacious vision of what homosexuals are like, and his action in killing is a totally ineffective way of denying the homosexuality that later invades his own personality. He murders Joachim in order to destroy his own homosexuality, only to find that as a very result of this and other murders he is forced into homosexual acts to expiate his crimes.

There are, however, other phrases in the novel which show that Genet's skill with words is not necessarily linked even with what might be interpreted as a highly transposed version of his own experience. Querelle's smile is '*ambigu, semblant plutôt s'adresser à celui qui l'émet qu'à celui qui le reçoit*' ('ambiguous, intended for the giver rather than the receiver') and there is a most unexpectedly humane comment on the nature of love in the very middle of an extremely detailed description of Querelle's sexual activity with Norbert. Genet writes that he was 'hugging Querelle with the same apparent passion as a female animal clings to the dead body of her little one—the attitude by which we understand what love is: the knowledge and understanding of separation from one particular being, of what it means to be divided, and knowing that we are looking at ourselves through our own eyes'. Reluctant though Genet may be to adopt the standards of what he calls elsewhere the 'supposedly rational disposition of our epoch', he is almost as skilful as Proust in using scientific comparisons to express certain ideas. In *The Thief's Journal*, he speaks of the 'still, silent males' having 'the violence of electronic corpuscles gravitating about a sun of energy: love', and in *Querelle of Brest* he has an equally

interesting if less obsessively sexual image to express the
effect which anxiety has on the character of Gil Turko.
'Gil gave himself away by his anxiety,' he writes, 'for it
betrayed the smallest fluctuation in his character and made
him vibrate, in much the same way as does the needle of a
gramophone passing over the rough surface of a record and
transforming the roughness into waves of musical frequency.' Like other authors of erotic books, Genet sometimes has a preciosity of style which makes his universe
seem even more decadent than it actually is. More frequently, however, this preciosity bears witness to a sensibility that remained curiously unblunted by the brutal and
degrading experiences through which he passed. Sartre
remarks in this respect that, while Oscar Wilde was broken
by Reading Gaol, Genet took the harsh reality itself as raw
material for his 'goldsmith's skill'. An immediate if very
minor example of his acute visual awareness can be found in
his description of sailors' full-dress puttees—'*de loin
impeccables comme les voiles mais, comme elles, imparfaitement
blanchies*' ('imperfectly whitened full-dress gaiters that look
as deceptively clean as white sails seen from a distance')—
and there are many other comparable notations. In *Querelle
of Brest*, the application of this unbroken sensibility to a
world of sailors, pimps and policemen is all the more
satisfying from a purely literary point of view because Genet
is dealing with problems that are not blatantly his own.
Most important, he does not preach, and is not constantly
badgering the reader to change attitude between one page
and the next. If Sartre's contention that 'ten years of
literature are as good as a psycho-analytical cure' is a valid
comment on Genet's progress as a writer, the apparently
greater poise which he shows in *Querelle of Brest* is an
indication that, by 1947, he was beginning to emerge from
the fixation on his own past which Sartre also presented as
his main psychological characteristic.

Genet's apparent lack of interest in writing further novels
like *Querelle of Brest* is, in this respect, highly significant.

He remarks at several points in the text that the characters in his novel are beginning to bore him, and that he is in a hurry to be finished with the book. Once he had explained himself to himself in his first three novels, he seems to have lost enthusiasm for prose works. Having shown in *Querelle of Brest* that he was capable of casting his obsessions into a semi-objective form, and even of going beyond them to create characters who gave the illusion of enjoying an independent existence, he remained interested in only two things: writing plays, and providing one final explanation of his attitude towards the world. This is his main pre-occupation in *The Thief's Journal*, the last and most intellectualised of all his prose works.

CHAPTER SEVEN

THE THIEF'S JOURNAL

PARTLY because of this intellectualisation, *The Thief's Journal* is Genet's best known and most immediately accessible prose work. It was the first to be openly published in France, has appeared in England in Penguin Modern Classics, and was included, in François Truffaut's film *Fahrenheit 451*, in a pile of major European literary masterpieces about to be destroyed by fire in the name of social stability. It is shorter than any of the novels, requires less imaginative effort from the reader, and appears to offer a convenient summary both of Genet's main ideas and of the most interesting period of his life. He himself states that its three basic subjects are 'theft, treason and homosexuality', and it provides a detailed account of the various humiliations which he chose to endure in his wanderings through Spain, Jugoslavia and the Low Countries during the nineteen-thirties. There is also extended discussion of sainthood, and at one point Genet provides Sartre with the starting point for a central passage analysing his relevance to the present day when he writes that he is an 'impossible nullity'. Compared to *Our Lady of the Flowers* and *Querelle of Brest*, however, *The Thief's Journal* is a fairly conventional literary work. Although Genet speaks at one point about persisting in 'the rigour of composition', the book actually goes back to one of the earliest and least rigorous of all European literary genres: the picaresque novel. Appropriately enough in this respect, much of the action is set in Spain, and Genet's own character, like that of the traditional picaresque hero, does not evolve. Yet whereas the predominant characteristic of Gil Blas was a sturdy common-sense, Genet describes his misadventures from the standpoint of a poet and a

metaphysician. This is visible even when he talks about
the activity which gives the book its title and which, since
homosexuality is not a criminal offence in Europe, led to his
various prison sentences: theft.

Thus he gives practically no details about how or what he
stole, and although he speaks with considerable enthusiasm
about his relationship with a professional cracksman called
Guy, his book offers few tips to the apprentice burglar. He
does not elaborate on his interesting if controversial
remark in *Miracle of the Rose* that it is quieter to walk on one's
heels than on tip-toe, and provides no examples to illustrate
what he calls the heroic aspects of robbery. The act of
stealing so excites Genet's thieves that some have to defecate immediately they have stolen, but this is not because of
the physical dangers which theft involves. It is because they
feel acutely aware of the moral challenge they are offering
society, and the most detailed account which Genet provides
of theft in *The Thief's Journal* concentrates upon the feelings
which he had while breaking into people's homes. In this,
he provides an interesting gloss on G. K. Chesterton's
essentially common-sense view that the burglar has an
intense respect for the idea of private property, and merely
wishes to alter its distribution. What interests Genet is the
'long shudder' which runs down his back when he realises
that he is going to steal, and the feeling that he is 'steeped in
the idea of property', at the very moment when he is
'looting' it. His choice of words is extremely significant
here, for he talks not about a transference of property, as a
Chestertonian burglar might, but about its destruction. The
word '*saccager*', that he uses in the French text, definitely
implies this, and takes on its full meaning in the light of an
analysis of theft in *Saint Genet, actor and martyr*. Let us
imagine, says Sartre, a Chinese miniature originally brought
back from the Far East by its present owner's grandfather.
It is stolen by a thief, who immediately converts it into a pile
of dirty bank-notes, which disappear as he spends them
on drink, women, gambling and fancy clothes. Whatever

his intention, the thief has converted a very specific object, with innumerable family associations, to nothing. It is because he destroys property, and thus defies the moral principles inculcated in him as a child, that Genet feels such awe and terror when he is stealing. It is perhaps because the theft of objects from houses causes him such intense anxiety that he gives so few details about it, and he is much more forthcoming about the money which he stole from some of his homosexual clients. Indeed, the anecdotes which make up the central story-line in *The Thief's Journal* are far more concerned with Genet's homosexual friends or with his life as a beggar than they are with the actual title of the book.

At the beginning of *The Thief's Journal*, Genet is already living as a beggar in Spain, sharing his food and pleasures with a vermin-ridden outcast called Salvador. He then makes the acquaintance of a more enterprising youth called Pépé, who calmly asks Genet to wait outside a public lavatory while he goes inside to masturbate in order to calm his nerves before an important card game. In spite of this apparently traditional precaution, Pépé loses, and kills another player who tries to snatch the money. Before escaping, he hands this money over to Genet, who runs off to join another of his friends, Stilitano, the original one-armed bandit. The last we hear of Salvador is when Genet has one of his rare attacks of generosity and sends him money to comfort him in gaol. In this respect, Genet treats him very much better than he does Pépé. Instead of sending him money when the latter is in Monjuich gaol, Genet treats himself to a sumptuous lunch, rejoicing in the thought that his friend is now languishing in prison and reflecting that by this particularly nasty action he has finally 'freed himself from moral preoccupations'.

Salvador's replacement by Stilitano is a definite improvement as far as the interest of *The Thief's Journal* is concerned. Sartre describes Stilitano as 'cowardly, empty and feminine', and in this respect he is typical of all the 'splendid males'

whom Genet presents with such irony in his work. Like
Divine, however, Stilitano has a kind of genius for transforming humiliation into victory by the same technique of
carrying a situation to the point where he triumphs through
the total abolition of conventional standards. Thus, on one
occasion, he is walking with Genet through Barcelona, when
he mistakes a group of 'real' men for a bunch of homosexuals
whom he can jeer at with impunity. He starts on his insults,
only to be greeted with a serious challenge to fight. He
escapes from this situation by holding out the stump of his
amputated arm and saying: 'After all, fellows, you're not
going to fight with a cripple.' Genet calls this 'vile hamming',
but also writes that it so ennobles Stilitano in his eyes that
'the absence of the hand was as real and effective as a royal
attribute, as the hand of justice', and this apparent contradiction throws an interesting light on his attitude towards
Stilitano and towards the reactions which he knows that his
reader will have. What he is saying is, in fact, that he knows
Stilitano is an absolute bounder, and admires him all the
more for it. A similar duality recurs when he talks about
Stilitano's clothes, remarking that they achieve 'a harmony
in bad taste' which he describes as 'the height of elegance'.
Stilitano, he writes, 'had unfalteringly chosen a pair of
green and tan crocodile shoes, a brown suit, a white silk
shirt, a pink tie, a multicoloured scarf, and a green hat',
and as he walks along by his side Genet can feel his own
body moving in sympathy as Stilitano's crocodile leather
shoes 'creak with the ponderous body of that monarch of
the slums' ('*monarque faubourien*'). The fact that Genet keeps
a completely straight face when he talks about Stilitano only
adds to the humour of his presentation, and in this respect
The Thief's Journal gains from being a more straightforward
and less obviously tormented work of art than *Our Lady of
the Flowers*. In his first novel, he still gave the impression of
being at least partly taken in by the Mignons and Notre-
Dames of his world, and to be laughing at them only
because his obsessions and sexual preferences could not

quite overcome his intelligence. In *The Thief's Journal*, at least as far as Stilitano is concerned, he is totally liberated from the prestige of the *mac*, and therefore all the funnier when he writes about him.

Cyril Connolly was so impressed with Stilitano that he claimed, in his review of the English translation of *The Thief's Journal*, that the interest of the book 'wanes, like that of a school story after the dare-devil has been sacked' when Genet loses Stilitano and leaves Spain. This is not quite fair to the book, for Stilitano does turn up again later in Antwerp, where he is doing a little honest pimping (his woman, a luscious blonde called Sylvia, hugs Genet's arm very tightly to show how glad she is to meet one of Stilitano's friends, and almost makes poor Genet feel sick), and even manages to steal a police motor cycle. When he does finally disappear, his place is filled very effectively by the two figures of Armand and Bernardini, who reflect an aspect of Genet's personality which had already expressed itself in the creation of Norbert and Mario Daugas in *Querelle of Brest*: the longing for solid, massive, brutal men, by whom he will be at one and the same time both dominated and reassured. Psychologically, this longing bears witness to a curious mixture in Genet's personality between a basic masochism and an intense longing for a father figure, and contrasts in every way with his attitude towards Stilitano and Mignon. His aim as far as these two characters are concerned is, as Sartre emphasises, to underline how deceptive their masculine appearance really is, and there is a brilliant passage in *Saint Genet, actor and martyr* which links this '*malice pédérastique*' to the common homosexual practice of *fellatio*. In his creation of Armand and Mario, Genet's aim seems to be different: to invent, within a sexual relationship, the security which he had never known as a child. Like the Mother in *The Screens*, Armand has an attitude of total permissiveness towards other people's actions, and this also gives him a place in Genet's imaginary reconstitution of a family: neither Armand nor Saïd's mother would have abandoned Genet at birth in anticipatory punishment for the crimes they knew he was going to commit.

It is not, however, as raw material for psychological analysis that *The Thief's Journal* offers its greatest interest, and there are two important objections to interpreting any of Genet's books in this way. Such an approach presupposes that authors do express through their work a childhood crisis which still dominates their creative process even when they are in their late thirties; and it offers no guide to the aesthetic value of what they write. From a more exclusively literary point of view, *The Thief's Journal* offers three main areas of interest: it describes an experience of physical and psychological humiliation; it gives an account of life among beggars, thieves and homosexuals in the nineteen-thirties; and it explains how the political and social structure of society appears to a man totally excluded from it. Intellectually, it raises the important question of whether, in his later work, Genet began to interpret his experience in the light of Sartre's ideas rather than of his own original feelings.

Genet's account of his life in the nineteen-thirties insists on the theme of humiliation in two ways: in the details which he gives about begging for food, cleaning out police station lavatories, and serving as a kind of whipping boy to Stilitano and Armand; and in the images which he uses to evoke the kind of experience he was trying to achieve. It is his images which are most consistently interesting, for after his description of Divine's life and of his own experiences at Mettray, even the most harrowing account of life in a Jugoslavian prison sounds a little flat. When, however, he compares his feelings of exile and humiliation to life on the planet Uranus, where the atmosphere is 'so heavy that the ferns there are creepers; the animals drag along, crushed by the weight of gases', he shows that his achievement as a writer depends not on what he actually did but on his ability to transmute his personal vision into effective terms. Stellar or planetary images clearly attract Genet, for he twice evokes the light still reaching us here on earth from a dead star to express the emotion which he feels for his dead friends. When he speaks of Uranus, it is to evoke a 'forlorn planet' where, amidst hideous reptiles, he will 'pursue an eternal, miserable death in a darkness where leaves will be black, the waters of the marshes thick and cold'. There, like his hero Querelle, he will 'recognise with increasing lucidity the unclean fraternity of smiling alligators', and experience the same 'monstrous participation in the realms of great muddy rivers and deep jungles'. When Genet uses this kind of imagery to speak both of his imaginary characters and of himself, he goes beyond the private mythology which expresses itself in the theme of the double in *Querelle of Brest* or in the snake worship and pyromania that recur in his film *Mademoiselle*. Instead, he creates in literary terms a universe like that of Hieronymus Bosch, in which man's horror of himself takes the form of an identification with the most repulsive and inhuman animal shapes. When, in Spain, he was *'un pou avec la conscience de l'être'* ('a louse and conscious of being one'), he was so far separated from the world of normal emotions and experiences that he did almost lose his humanity. It is this experience which, recorded in parts of *The Thief's Journal*, gives the book its greatest originality.

In contrast, Genet's treatment of homosexuality in *The Thief's Journal* is less complex than in any other of his works. He does not create characters like Divine or Querelle, but concentrates either on describing his own relationship with Salvador, Stilitano or Armand, or on reporting how the Barcelona homosexuals behaved. As in his account of Stilitano's clothes, it is difficult to believe that he is not being deliberately amusing when he tells how Theresa the Great used to take her knitting and a sandwich when waiting for clients at one of Barcelona's most celebrated public urinals, or when he describes how the Barcelona homosexuals, the 'Carolinas', went in 'shawls, mantillas, silk dresses and fitted jackets' to place a 'bunch of red roses tied together with a crape veil' on the site of one of the dirtiest but most beloved urinals that had been destroyed after the riots of 1933. He provides further light on his creation of Divine when he writes that the Carolinas' 'shrill voices, their cries, their extravagant gestures' seemed to him to have 'no other aim than to try to pierce the shell of the world's contempt', and his insistence on the contempt which homosexuals expect to receive from other people suggests that he chose this type of sexuality because it fitted perfectly into his aim of exiling himself from society and being despised. It is in every way a mistake to look to him for support in any rational or liberal attitude.

In spite of his refusal to question conventional bourgeois values, Genet is nevertheless quite ready to satirise the attitude which ordinary members of society take towards its outcasts. At one point in *The Thief's Journal*, for example, a group of French tourists visit Barcelona and take photographs of the community to which Genet belonged. He describes them as carrying on 'an audible dialogue, the terms of which were exact and rigorous, almost technical', and in which they discussed, 'without thinking that they might be wounding the beggars', the different aesthetic effects which their appearance created.

> 'There's a perfect harmony between the tonalities of the sky and the slightly greenish shades of the rags.'
> '. . . something out of Goya . . .'
> 'It's very interesting to watch that group on the left. There are things of Gustave Doré in which the composition . . .'
> 'They're happier than we are.'
> 'There's something more sordid about them than those in the shanty-town, do you remember, in Casablanca? There's no denying that the Moroccan costume gives a *simple* beggar a dignity which no European can ever have.'
> 'We're seeing them when they're all frozen. They have to be seen when the weather is right.'
> 'On the contrary, the originality of the poses . . .'

Genet claims to have felt uncomfortable, on this occasion, less for his own sake than for that of Lucien, his 'little

fisherman from Le Suquet' to whom he later dedicated one
of his poems. He nevertheless projects on to Lucien some of
the obsessions that went to the creation of Divine when he
writes of his being 'dizzily swept to the depths of the name-
less' by the way in which the tourists directed 'the cruel
lenses of their cameras' towards him. Genet undoubtedly
portrays the tourists with critical hostility, in the same way
that he attacks society for requiring beggars to produce what
he calls the 'humiliating "anthropometric card"' to prove
their identity. Nevertheless, there is both bad faith and
intellectual inconsistency in his criticism. He did, after all,
choose to behave in this way, and derived what can only be
called, in view of his aspirations to sainthood through
humiliation, spiritual benefit from experiences which the
scornful attitude of society alone made possible.

The Thief's Journal is the only one of Genet's prose works
to show any awareness of the political situation in Europe
either before or after the Second World War. In his earlier
works, he had been concerned with war only in so far as it
satisfied his two main interests of homosexuality and treason.
In Our Lady of the Flowers, war in general was 'the red blood
that flows from the artilleryman's ears . . . the lightfoot
soldier of the snows crucified on skis, a spahi on his horse of
cloud that has pulled up at the edge of Eternity', but like the
specific war which Genet evokes from time to time in this
book, it is interesting only because of the associations which
it has with sex. The political atmosphere of the nineteen-
thirties is evoked only very indirectly in Querelle of Brest
when Genet appears to be criticising the policy of appease-
ment by writing of Gil having 'cette face crucifiée des nations
qui refusent la lutte' ('the crucified countenance of nations
who prefer not to join in the struggle'), and in Pompes
Funèbres the occupation of France is significant only for the
opportunities it provided for treason. It is true that The
Thief's Journal in no way sets out to deal directly with
politics. The reference which Genet makes to the threat of
war which hung over Europe while he was actually writing

his book in the nineteen-forties is brief indeed, for he merely notes that warlike preparations involve 'no longer the high-sounding declarations of statesmen but the menacing exactness of technicians'. Nevertheless, this evocation of the pre-Krushchev phase of the Cold War is extremely effective, and for all his supposed lack of interest in what was happening in the higher reaches of society, he had also felt the political agitation which accompanied the growth of Fascism and the events leading to the Second World War. In the same way that he had had the impression, in Hitler's Germany, that he was in 'a camp organised by bandits', and would be breaking no law if he stole, he had also been aware of the atmosphere which preceded the outbreak of the Civil War in Spain. 'Under all the tinsel and idiotic gilding,' he writes, he could see 'the angular and muscular force which, suddenly taut and erect (*bandant soudain*), was to bring the whole thing down a few years later'.

It might be argued, of course, that such statements do not really reflect how Genet actually felt in the nineteen-thirties. After all, he was writing *The Thief's Journal* some ten to fifteen years after the events which it describes had taken place, and he may well have projected on to his past experience some of the political ideas picked up from his new friends on the intellectual Left. Nevertheless, his general account of how he saw society before the Second World War has a ring of accuracy and sincerity which suggest that he may well be describing real feelings. Thus he remarks that all he noticed of the complex social order around him was its 'perfect coherence'. 'I was astounded,' he continues, 'by so rigorous an edifice whose details were united against me. Nothing in the world was irrelevant: the stars on a general's sleeve, the stock-market quotations, the olive harvest, the style of the judiciary, the wheat exchange, flower-beds . . . This order, fearful and feared, had only one meaning: my exile.' What makes this disclaimer of detailed social awareness so interesting is the development of

Genet's later career as a dramatist, for after his first two plays, he openly concentrates on political themes. *The Balcony*, in particular, deals with one of the most important events in the nineteen-thirties: the transference of power, in Stalin's Russia as well as in Franco's Spain and Hitler's Germany, from working-class revolutionaries to efficient police forces. What *The Thief's Journal* seems to indicate is that part of Genet's original inspiration for this play stems from three aspects of his own personal experience: his encounter with the 'oppressively perfect' police system of the Central European states; the erotic attraction which he felt for policemen, which gave them virtually a mythical status in his eyes; and his diffused, unintellectualised awareness of what was happening in the nineteen-thirties. For all his sexual sophistication, his view of the world seems at that period to have been that of a child: an undifferentiated awareness of an incomprehensibly complex authoritarian structure. But in the same way that a child is often more sensitive than an adult to the general atmosphere around him, so Genet may well have had a similarly intense vision of something which he could not express until much later in his life. It is perhaps this, among a number of other factors, which accounts for the excellence of his third play.

The Thief's Journal is dedicated to Sartre and Simone de Beauvoir, and reads at times like a rationalisation in Sartrean terms of the more instinctive attitude which Genet had expressed in his earlier novels. The distance which Genet realised he had travelled since *Our Lady of the Flowers* is indicated by a comment which he makes in *The Thief's Journal* on the composition of his first book in La Santé prison. He began to write, he says, not because he wanted to relieve or communicate his emotions, but because he hoped, 'by expressing them in a form that they themselves imposed', to construct a moral order whose nature he himself did not yet know. Writing was thus, in the first instance, a means of self-exploration and self-knowledge, and an attempt to discover just what attitude he did have towards the laws which had condemned him and which he had chosen to defy. Once he began, in the early nineteen-forties, to live outside the criminal community, and to associate with intellectuals like Cocteau and Sartre, he seems to have been encouraged to rationalise this attitude much more systematically, and to understand why, as he remarks in *Querelle of Brest*, he had throughout his youth looked at the world through lowered eyebrows. In dedicating *The Thief's Journal* to Sartre and Simone de Beauvoir, he seems to be approving in advance of the basic theme in *Saint Genet, actor and martyr*. Sartre's study began appearing in *Les Temps Modernes* in 1950, some eighteen months after the publication in book form of *The Thief's Journal*, but since extracts from *The Thief's Journal* were published in July 1946, the question of a direct textual influence of Sartre's essay on this book must be ruled out. Nevertheless, Genet must have known from his many conversations with Sartre what attitude his friend was likely to take, and Sartre himself had indicated his approval of Genet's basic choice as early as 1947, when he dedicated his essay on Baudelaire to him. In returning the compliment, Genet was to some extent underwriting what he certainly realised would be the starting point for Sartre's essay, however devastating he may have found the whole essay when he finally saw himself stripped naked.

Genet had, of course, spoken in his earlier works of what he calls in *The Thief's Journal* his 'identification with the handsomest and most unfortunate criminals'. *Pompes Funèbres*, in particular, is full of autobiographical remarks about his choice of evil and disappointment in it. It is nevertheless in *The Thief's Journal* that he talks about clarifying the meaning of his choice to be a thief, and presents it as a 'moral adventure' in which he preferred to commit crimes in France because he wanted to accuse himself in his own language. It is in this book that he insists upon his desire to be guilty and condemned, and describes how, when he felt tempted to rebel against the perfect coherence of the rest of society, he was held back by 'the ingrained habit of living with my head down and in accordance with an ethic contrary to the one which governs the world'. It is also here that he speaks of the way in which prisons were constructed for him and 'have their foundations' within him, and thus either anticipates or echoes Sartre's view that he was the creature not only of his own choice but also of the predestination by which society selects its criminals and outcasts at birth. Indeed, *The Thief's Journal* does more than provide almost suspiciously perfect evidence for Sartre's views. It even reflects some of the ambiguities and obscurities of *Saint Genet, actor and martyr*, for like Sartre himself Genet seems constantly uncertain as to whether his fundamental choice was admirable and justified or not. In his essay, Sartre oscillates between the common-sense view that Genet 'is making a great to-do about a few acts of solitary or mutual masturbation' and the more romantic view that Genet's work 're-establishes the poetic truth of crime', and this duality recurs in *The Thief's Journal* as it does in the earlier novels. Similarly, both Genet and Sartre appear undecided as to whether *The Thief's Journal* is carefully constructed or not. At one point, Genet speaks of 'persisting in the rigour of composition' while nevertheless stating elsewhere that he is presenting his memories *'en vrac'* ('loose, or in bulk'), and Sartre refers to the 'rigorous, classical unity' of Genet's works nine pages after he has gone out of his way to say how carelessly they are put together.

While in this particular respect there is obviously no question of an influence of Sartre on Genet, there are other texts by Genet which had definitely expressed a neo-Sartrian attitude towards existence some time before *The Thief's Journal* was published. When Genet notes in *Pompes Funèbres* that *'nous souffrons de ne pouvoir fixer notre chagrin'*, the reflexions on the impossibility of actually holding an emotion there, and examining it as if it were an object, seem to come directly from *L'Etre et le Néant*. Similarly, when he remarks of Juliette that *'une bonne ne fait pas de projets pour sa fille'*, it is as though he were offering an example to illustrate the thesis which Sartre put forward in *Matérialisme et Révolution* in 1946: that only members of the bourgeoisie bring children into the world because they have a specific role for them in mind. Gil Turko's fear in *Querelle of Brest* that his parents have no real affection for him because his birth was the result of an inefficient douching—*'Je suis né d'une giclée qui n'a pas réussi'*—also parallels Sartre's views on the essential contingency of conception and physical birth. He notes in *Saint Genet, actor and martyr* that 'Genet's origin is a *blunder* (there would not have been a Genet if someone had used a contraceptive)', and he is equally unromantic in his own autobiography when he describes his father as 'shedding the few drops of sperm that go to make a man'. In Genet's plays, with their consistent attack upon the values and institutions of bourgeois society, the resemblance between his own ideas and those of the man who has done most to make him famous becomes even more marked.

PART THREE
THE PLAYS

CHAPTER EIGHT
DEATHWATCH

ALTHOUGH *Haute Surveillance* (*Deathwatch*) was the second of Genet's plays to be produced in Paris, there are good reasons for accepting the statement made on the cover of the English translation that it was 'his earliest play'. It was published in review form in 1947, shortly before the first production of *Les Bonnes* (*The Maids*) in April of the same year, and is very clearly linked by its setting, theme, images and ideas to the romantic vision of the criminal world expressed in much of his poetry and parts of his novels. Technically, it is the least original of his plays, and at times rather obviously imitates Sartre's *Huis Clos* (*In Camera*). Three people are shut up in an enclosed space, and their relationship is dominated by the attempt which one of them makes to compel the others to think of him in a certain way. It is the only one of Genet's plays to have been directed by the author himself, and, although adapted for the cinema*, has not so far received a full professional production in either London or New York. Its principal intellectual interest lies in the expression which it gives to the parallel between Genet's ideas and an over-simplified version of the Jansenist concept of Grace and Predestination. He sees the 'genuine' criminal as victim of an inescapable fatality which he has done nothing to deserve, just as the Elect are granted salvation irrespective of their deeds, and do not attain it by good works. In the same way that no man, by taking thought, can add one cubit to his stature, so no criminal, by acting with malice aforethought, can acquire what Genet

155

F

calls in *Our Lady of the Flowers*, '*le signe sacré des monstres*' ('the sacred sign of the monster'). Although not openly autobiographical to quite the same extent as his novels, *Deathwatch* also provides, through this insistence upon the theme of fatality, an indirect comment on the problem which Sartre discussed in *Saint Genet, actor and martyr*: was Genet the predestined victim of a society which had chosen him as a criminal before he was even born, or was his behaviour the result of a conscious choice?

The plot of *Deathwatch* concerns three criminals, Yeux-Verts, Maurice and Lefranc, who are all locked up in the same cell. The phrase *haute surveillance*, which Genet finally chose as title to replace the original *Préséances*, is a technical term used to designate the close watch kept over criminals sentenced to death and awaiting execution. If the play were intended to be taken realistically, this title would raise certain problems, since only one of the criminals, Yeux-Verts, is a murderer, and does not yet appear to have been tried. Lefranc is a petty thief, who is due to be released from prison within a few days, and the crime for which the young Maurice has been incarcerated is not specified. Neither is any particular watch kept over the criminals, and the only sign which the prison authorities give of their existence is a handsome and obliging warder, who brings Yeux-Verts greetings and cigarettes from another criminal called Boule de Neige, a Negro who enjoys even more prestige among his fellow inmates than Yeux-Verts himself. However, the stage directions state that the entire play 'unfolds as in a dream', and Genet is clearly uninterested in realism. *Deathwatch* differs sharply from the rest of his plays by its total lack of conscious humour, and there are none of those sudden intrusions of reality or common-sense which break the tension and provide laughter in *The Maids* and *The Balcony*. Nevertheless, it would require only the slightest shift of emphasis to make the play a satirical comedy in which the humour sprang from an ironic application of theological concepts to the criminal world, and it may have been Genet's determination to avoid this which led him to direct the play himself when it received its first and only professional production in Paris in February 1949.

The starting-point for the main argument in *Deathwatch* can be found in *Miracle of the Rose*, in a passage where Genet discusses the effect which the 1939–1945 war is having upon prison life. By filling the prisons with people who are not professional criminals, but merely ordinary citizens who happen to have committed political offences or been involved with the black market, the war has softened their atmosphere while at the same time making them more desolate. Genet continues, in one of his rare puns that are immediately translatable, '*Rien n'est plus plus répugnant qu'un innocent en prison. Il n'a rien fait pour mériter la tôle (ce sont ses propres termes). La Fatalité s'est trompée.*' ('Nothing is more repugnant than an innocent man in prison. He has done nothing to deserve gaol (these are his own words). Destiny has made an error.') The use of the word *mériter* anticipates the inversion of theological concepts in *Deathwatch*, and like the English word *deserve* it looks in two directions: outside Jansenism or Calvinism, men deserve and receive punishment for crimes or rewards for good behaviour. The plot of *Deathwatch*, however, is intended to show that no one can either earn or deserve, by his actions alone, the utter damnation that weighs down on certain predestined criminals.

By a somewhat crude piece of symbolism, the 'real' criminal, Yeux-Verts, is illiterate, whereas the would-be criminal, Lefranc, can read and write. He has, in fact, been writing to Yeux-Verts' woman, and is suspected by the latter of not reading him everything in her replies. He protests violently, and even promises to kill Yeux-Verts' woman if she really has been unfaithful. This leads Yeux-Verts to describe his own crime, which he presents as being totally without motive, 'a gift from God or the devil', and an action he had never wanted to commit. Indeed, in one of the most impressive dramatic moments of the play, he describes how he made every effort to avoid his crime, tried to be 'a dog, a cat, a horse, a tiger, a table, a stone', and even threw himself into a frenzied dance in an attempt to go backwards in time to the moment before he had killed. His attempt to avoid his fate is totally different from Lefranc's attitude, for the latter is obsessed by the thought of becoming a great criminal and enjoying the same kind of prestige as Yeux-Verts or Boule de Neige. He keeps photographs of famous criminals such as Weidmann, Soklay, Vaché and Ange Soleil hidden in his mattress, and even claims to have begun his career with the notorious Serge de Lenz.* Partly in a fit of anger, but principally because he wishes to acquire the sacred aura which hangs round The Murderer, he strangles young Maurice. Yeux-Verts, however, refuses to see him as his equal, precisely because his crime had the specific motive of making him a criminal. Yeux-Verts had killed because he had no choice, Boule de Neige 'in order to kill and rob', and neither of them was striving after damnation for its own sake. The paradox of salvation is that it comes only to those who do not deliberately seek it, and the person who acts morally in order to acquire spiritual merit falls immediately into the sin of spiritual pride. In *Death-watch*, Genet applies this fundamental Christian idea rather cleverly to damnation.

In addition to being able to read and write, Lefranc also has a full theoretical knowledge *'de tout ce qui est vrai signe de la poisse'* ('all the real signs of bad luck'). He knows about all the most important and significant tattoo marks, but has not dared actually to have them inscribed in his own flesh. They are merely drawn on with coloured ink, and this extra piece of symbolism again emphasises how far away from genuine damnation he is. Genet obviously disapproves of Lefranc, just as an admirer of the aristocracy would be hostile to a *parvenu*. Nevertheless, there is nothing moral in this disapproval, and he himself entertained feelings for Harcamone in *Miracle of the Rose* which foreshadow Lefranc's admiration for Yeux-Verts. Lefranc also repeats another of

Genet's own experiences when he shares his bread ration
with Maurice, for this is exactly what Genet had done for
Bulkaen, and in his one comment on the play Sartre suggests
that Lefranc's crime is motivated primarily by homosexuality.
'Lefranc, a girl-queen,' he writes in *Saint Genet*, 'strangles
Maurice, a future hero of crime.' Genet seems to have
transferred a good deal of his own personality to Lefranc,
and even puts the same kind of language into his mouth
which he had used in *Miracle of the Rose*. There, Harcamone
had been *'aussi terne dans sa vie libre qu'éblouissant dans les
pénitences'* ('as dull in his free life as he was dazzling in
prison'), and Lefranc says of Boule de Neige that he 'shoots
lightning' and 'lights up the whole two thousand cells'.
There is, however, an obvious difference between Genet and
Lefranc in that the former always seems to have recognised
his limitations whereas the latter did not. It is in this respect
that *Deathwatch* perhaps becomes relevant to Genet's own
life.

Biographically, the play seems to suggest that because
Genet's own criminal career never soared beyond petty
theft, it had its origin in a deliberate choice comparable to
that of Lefranc. Had he really been the victim of predestination, he would have been like Harcamone or Yeux-Verts,
and his remark in *Miracle of the Rose* that 'the poetry of the
great birds of prey' would always escape him takes on an
added significance in the light of his first play. In *Deathwatch*
he is at one and the same time both sticking to the highly
romantic concept of crime that he had expressed in his early
poems, and declaring his own unfitness for it. There is
nothing here of the rotting teeth and stinking breath
described in parts of *Miracle of the Rose*, and he obviously
intended the play to be an idealised and almost mythical
account of the criminal world. In his programme note, he
declared that it was his 'deepest wish' that 'each prison and
each cell should correspond in reality to the idea presented
this evening in the theatre', and this repetition of his
favourite though inaccessible daydream certainly created a

valid universe for at least two Paris critics. Marc Beigbeder, for example, maintained that Genet 'made his villains talk as Racine did his kings', and 'gilded the forces inspiring them with the same fatal, passionate and mystic grandeur'. J.-J. Rinieri, editor of the review *La Nef* in which the text of *Haute Surveillance* had first been published, also argued that Genet should be placed on the same level as the greatest writers, and he specifically mentioned Racine, Baudelaire and Proust. Like Beigbeder, he saw the play as a genuine metaphysical drama in which man discovers his true identity by following out his destiny, and obviously gave great importance to Genet's other statements in his programme note. There, Genet had summarised the plot as showing 'an almost fabulous assassin dominating another, who has less glamour (*de moindre éclat*), and who in turn dazzles a thief', and continued: 'This prestige draws its power from the very origin of seduction, the evil within which a criminal hierarchy takes shape.' For Rinieri, this prestige did come over in the play, and he claimed that Genet had succeeded in recreating 'the authenticity of the vocation for evil, the hidden world of criminals, and the dazzling glory which the heroes of this chivalric order of crime bestow upon one another'. Georges Bataille, the editor of another well-known review, *Critique*, was even more enthusiastically on Genet's side when he claimed that 'there is no tragedy without sacred characters given divine status by horror' and continued: 'But the young delinquents of *Deathwatch*, sick with the infamous glory conferred by crime, jealous of the misfortune without which no atrocious charm exists, are, in their prison, the only people who reach the level at which the kings and gods of ancient Greece placed tragedy.' At least in intention, Genet seems to have been very far from making *Deathwatch* an expression of the difficulties which he encountered in trying to make the reality of crime conform to the romantic image which he had of it. No other play except *The Screens* presents quite so absolute and uncompromising a challenge to normal moral values.

It is doubtless this fact which provoked the very violent attacks directed against *Deathwatch* by critics such as Jean-Jacques Gautier, François Mauriac, and Gabriel Marcel. Rather predictably, the Communist paper *L'Humanité* used Genet to illustrate the general thesis that 'societies have the writers they deserve', and to argue that Western capitalism had, in France, shown its true nature by giving birth to an author who had been 'a common criminal' and had chosen, in one of his books, 'to celebrate the "artistic" virtues of the SS'. Yet while the general tone of *Deathwatch* is certainly immoral by any conceivable civilised standards, its actual message is not one which, if rightly understood, would lead people to commit crimes. What Genet is saying is that the real criminal, the one who enjoys prestige among his fellows, cannot be imitated. Lefranc's final solitude and failure could even be looked upon as a warning to anyone who, like him, was tempted by the glamour of becoming a real criminal into consciously choosing to commit crimes. Even apart from this, however, *Deathwatch* would be unlikely to influence anyone's behaviour or attitude. If a work of art is to persuade, it must first of all convince the reader or spectator that it is a valid and relatively accurate account of human experience. This is something which *Deathwatch* signally fails to do. Each of the characters embodies an abstract idea so peculiar as to fall much more within the realm of pathology than in that of psychological realism, and Genet's instructions that it should be played 'as in a dream' are an indication that he does not really expect anyone to believe in the events it depicts. Georges Bataille may contend that '*la voix populaire*' supports Rimbaud and Genet in seeing the criminal as 'adorned with a sacred halo', but he forgets that real criminals see murder as highly unprofessional. It may be, as Genet argues in *Pompes Funèbres*, that criminals attain their real prestige only when they are in prison, and in this respect *Deathwatch* could throw light on an aspect of criminal psychology which professional investigators might miss. But the reasons which he gives for this prestige are so linked to his own preoccupation with fatality as to be virtually incommunicable outside the context of his own work.

The fact that *Deathwatch* has not been produced again in Paris since 1949 is an indication that a certain automatic censorship operates in the field of immoral as well as of moral literature. Paradoxically, it is only aesthetically successful works of art that can ever seriously threaten established moral values, and *Deathwatch* does not come into that category. When he wrote it, Genet had not yet reached the point where he could cast his ideas into communicable form, and it is significant that he succeeds in doing this only after deciding, in his subsequent plays, to put on stage characters whose preoccupations seem well removed from his own. *Deathwatch* is certainly interesting from an intellectual point of view, and there is something pleasing in the neatness with which Genet has stood Christian concepts on their head. However, he has not yet begun to fulfil the ambition which he set out in a very late essay, *Le Funambule*, and which Jean-Marie Magnan sees as his major concern: to disappear completely behind his work. If he never does so completely, at least he begins, in *The Maids*, to cast his personal obsessions into a rather more comprehensible form. He said in an interview in 1949 that the two plays had been written round about the same time, and that he had simply 'changed cells' in moving from one to the other. He was, he said, now writing a third play, which would also deal with the same theme. 'A man never has more than one major problem to solve', he concluded, and his first two plays do both deal with people who want to achieve the notoriety of the great criminal. *The Maids*, however, placed this ambition in a much more psychologically convincing context.

CHAPTER NINE

THE MAIDS

LIKE *Deathwatch*, *The Maids* is a short play, and the action does indeed take place in an enclosed space. Two maids, the sisters Claire and Solange Lemercier, have invented a secret game in which they take it in turns to dress up as their mistress and speak as they think she feels. The maid who is not playing the part of the mistress has to surrender her own identity to the point of taking on her sister's name, so that when Claire is being Madame, Solange has to pretend to be Claire. This enables Claire to act out the feelings of intense hatred which she has towards her mistress and towards herself, for Claire-Madame insults Claire-Servant until Claire-Servant—in the person of Solange—rises up against her mistress and tries to kill her. However, the game never actually reaches the point where the murder takes place, because the sisters spend so much time on the preliminary insults that they never manage to reach the climactic moment. They always set an alarm-clock to warn them of the probable time of their mistress's return, and this rings before the one playing the part of the maid manages to kill the one playing the part of the mistress.

It is only gradually that the spectator realises the nature and function of this game, for Solange and Claire are already playing it when the curtain rises. It is through what they say after the alarm-clock has brought them back to reality that the spectator comes to understand, retrospectively, why Solange suddenly interrupted one of Claire-Madame's speeches in order to remind her to call her Claire and not Solange, and to realise that this is a frequently repeated ritual. On the particular evening when the spectator is privileged to attend, something new has happened.

Claire has sent a letter denouncing Madame's lover to the police, but while the maids are tidying up the traces of their game in preparation for Madame's return, he telephones from a nearby bar to say that he has been released for lack of more definite evidence. The fear that their attempt to have him, as Madame dramatically says on her return, '*in-car-cé-ré*', will be discovered, makes it urgent for Solange and Claire to take some definite action. They decide to poison Madame, and Claire puts ten pills of phenobarbital in Madame's tea. However, she fails to make her drink it, and after learning of her lover's release, Madame departs triumphantly in a taxi to meet him at the bar. The two sisters are left alone again, and after a long speech in which Solange dwells lovingly on the idea of committing a crime, Claire once again assumes the rôle of Madame. She then forces Solange to make her drink the poisoned tea, and thus makes sure that they will both escape from the servile world. She herself will die, and Solange will be found in such circumstances that she will be accused of murdering her. Claire sacrifices her own life in order that Solange may attain the glory and prestige of being a murderess, and Solange's final speech proclaims that they have now achieved their final deliverance:

> 'Madame steps into the car. Monsieur is whispering sweet nothings in her ear. She would like to smile, but she is dead. She rings the bell. The porter yawns. He opens the door. Madame goes up the stairs. She enters her flat—but, Madame is dead. The two maids are alive: they've just risen up, free, from Madame's icy form. All the maids were present at her side—not they themselves, but rather the hellish agony of their names. All that remains of them to float about Madame's airy corpse is the delicate perfume of the holy maidens which they were in secret. We are beautiful, joyous, drunk and free.'

Genet is said to have taken as his starting-point in *The Maids* the famous case of the two sisters, Léa and Christine Papin, who killed their mistress, Madame Lancelin, and her daughter Geneviève at Le Mans in 1933. If he did so, he changed the events almost completely in the process.

Madame Lancelin belonged to an extremely respectable middle-class family, whereas the Madame of *The Maids* is, Genet states in one of his prefaces, '*un peu cocotte et un peu bourgeoise*'. Like Jean Decarnin's mother in *Pompes Funèbres*, who also kept a maid, she clearly lives on the fringes of polite society, and her desire to follow Monsieur 'to Devil's Island, to Siberia' if he is convicted of a serious crime, shows that she is as ready to romanticise prison life as Genet or Lefranc. The Papin sisters slaughtered Madame Lancelin and her daughter with great ferocity, whereas for all Solange's rhetoric, it is quite clear that when Madame returns with her lover to the apartment, she will merely have the annoyance of finding that one of her maids has either been murdered or committed suicide. Like *The Balcony*, *The Maids* is a study of unsuccessful rebellion. A basic theme of the play is that, as Solange puts it, '*la crasse n'aime pas la crasse*' ('Filth does not love filth'), and she repeats the same idea when she says '*s'aimer dans la servitude, ce n'est pas s'aimer*' ('when slaves love one another, it's not love'). The insults which the maid playing the part of Madame heaps upon the whole race of servants—'I loathe servants. A vile and odious breed, I loathe them. They are not of the human race. Servants ooze. They're a foul effluvium drifting through our rooms and hallways, seeping into us, entering our mouths, corrupting us'—underline the hatred and contempt which Claire and Solange feel not for Madame but for themselves. Because they are not proud of their condition, they cannot use it as a basis for effective rebellion. As Malraux observes in *La Condition Humaine*, and as Sartre has often argued in his political essays, revolutions are possible only when the victims of oppression can look upon their present condition as a possible source of future dignity. In classical times, the slave who became a Christian saw in the virtues of poverty and humility the very image of his own condition; in the eighteenth century, the French bourgeois greeted the idea of natural equality as a concept whereby his own exclusion from the aristocracy was a sign of natural worth; and, in modern times, both Marxism and revolutionary nationalism have transformed the very poverty of the underprivileged into the symbol of political purity. By the time he wrote *The Maids*, Genet may well have come into contact with ideas of this kind either through books or through his personal contacts with left-wing intellectuals. In 1946, Sartre's *Matérialisme et Révolution*, published in the same number of *Les Temps Modernes* as the extracts from the *Journal du Voleur*, had put forward just such a thesis, and *The Maids* reads in many ways like an ironic commentary upon it. It is highly probable, however, that Genet had no such political ideas in mind when he wrote his play. As in *Deathwatch*, he was casting his personal obsessions into dramatic form, and it may well be sheer accident that this time he found a theme so rich in broader connotations.

One of Sartre's basic contentions, in *Saint Genet, actor and martyr*, is that Genet always remained deeply attached, on an emotional level, to the society and system of values which originally condemned him. 'In his worst deviations,' he writes, 'he will remain faithful to the morality of his childhood. He will flout it, he will perhaps hate it, he will try to drag it with him through the mud, but the "original crisis" has burned it into him as with a red-hot iron. Whatever happens from now on, whatever he may do, whatever way he may invent, one thing remains forbidden to him: *self-acceptance*'. Genet himself expresses his respect for established morality in slightly ironical terms when he writes, at the beginning of *Miracle of the Rose*, that he stole '*pour être bon*' ('to be kind'). He wanted, he said, to become rich 'in order to be kind, so as to feel the gentleness, the restfulness that kindness accords (rich and kind, not in order to give, but so that my nature, being kind, would be pacified)'. This kindness is the quality which Solange and Claire most envy in Madame, but Solange recognises how unattainable it is for them when she says that it is easy 'to be kind, and smiling, and sweet—ah! that sweetness of hers!—when you're beautiful and rich. But what if you're only a maid? (*'Mais être bonne quand on est bonne!'*) The best you can do is give yourself airs while you're doing the cleaning or washing up.' It is perhaps Madame's kindness that Solange resents most strongly, and when Claire tells her that 'Madame is kind. She adores us', Solange replies: 'She loves us the way she loves her armchair. Not even *that* much! Like her bidet, rather, like her pink enamel lavatory seat.' Nevertheless, like Genet's criminals, Solange and Claire have no alternative value to offer. They would like to possess Madame's qualities themselves, and although their fury at being unable to do so may express itself in dreams of murder, they finally punish only themselves. Theirs is the problem of the oppressed who have no values to which to turn, for however much they may envy her kindness, they really despise Madame. Their only refuge lies in the criminal dreams which, like Genet, they nourish without being able to transform them into reality. The most appropriate preface to *The Maids*, from this point of view, would consist of extracts from those parts of *Miracle of the Rose* or *Pompes Funèbres* in which Genet proclaims his disillusionment with the criminal world without ever taking the apparently logical step of accepting traditional values.

It is not until *The Blacks* and *The Screens* that Genet's sympathy for oppressed races begins to offer values which challenge the emptiness of official society and compensate for the parallel failures of criminal revolt and working-class revolution reflected in *Deathwatch*, *The Maids* and *The Balcony*. Sartre argued that Genet expressed the fundamental ethical dilemma of his readers because 'he exaggerates our dishonesty to the point of making it intolerable to us' and 'makes our guilt appear in broad daylight'. In more directly sociological terms, *The Maids* can be seen as reflecting another, more exclusively political aspect of European society in the nineteen-forties: the failure of the socialist revolution forecast so confidently as one of the results of the Second World War. The ruling classes, as represented by

Madame, are corrupt and decadent. She is a silly, vapid woman, with none of the confidence in the rights and values of her own class that used to make Madame Lancelin put on white gloves to check that Léa and Christine Papin had dusted her furniture properly. Like all the figures in Genet's work who represent authority or the established order, she is an absurd caricature. But the revolutionaries, as embodied in Claire and Solange, are no real challenge to her. They succeed in hurting only themselves, just as the European proletariat bled itself white in the fight between Fascism and Communism in the nineteen-thirties and nineteen-forties.

There are a number of verbal similarities between *The Maids* and Genet's first two novels which indicate that he was carrying the atmosphere of his early work into his second play. In *Our Lady of the Flowers*, for example, he describes prisoners wishing one another a Happy New Year 'as humbly as servants must do among themselves in the pantry', and in *Miracle of the Rose* he describes servants as the 'unwholesome exhalations' of their masters. The same expression recurs when Claire accuses Solange of acting as a mirror which throws back her own image at her 'like a bad smell', and the readiness with which the two sisters exchange insults and threats recalls the treason-ridden atmosphere of Mettray or Fontevrault. The difference between *The Maids* and Genet's novels, however, lies in the fact that the pattern of failure delineated in his play has a far more obvious historical applicability. It needs the talent and acute moral awareness of a Sartre to see the novels as exemplifying the demand between 'the exigencies of an ethic *inherited* from individual property and a collectivistic ethic in the process of formation'. The expression which *The Maids* and *The Balcony* give to the contradictions of revolutionary politics in the nineteen-forties is much more obvious. Robert Kemp, reviewing the first play in *Le Monde*, remarked that the capitalist class appeared 'almost pure' by the side of a proletariat 'poisoned by its own inferiority'. It was, it is true, by coincidence rather than intention that

Genet transposed into his second play the resentful impotence which characterised the European proletariat after
socialism had been defeated by Fascism in Spain and betrayed by Stalinism in Europe. He was, as usual, talking
about himself. But it was with an extraordinary clarity that
he expressed, in the attitude of Claire and Solange towards
Madame, the mingled love and fury which frustrated
revolutionaries must have felt towards the decadent
capitalism that offered them condescending protection on its
own terms.

The political meaning that can be read into *The Maids*
does not, of course, explain why the play has enjoyed so
marked a success in the theatre and why it is, from an
aesthetic point of view, one of Genet's most successful
works. It does not make quite so immediate an appeal as
The Balcony, and is certainly more difficult to understand.
The spectator needs his wits very much about him if he is
to follow just what is happening in the first five minutes, and
Genet makes no concessions to the convention that a play-
wright should offer an exposition scene to enable his
audience to take their bearings. Once the initial difficulty is
overcome, however, the play tells a good story and tells it
well. Solange and Claire are not mere embodiments of
abstract ideas, as were Yeux-Verts or Lefranc, but create the
illusion of being real people whose suffering the spectator can
share. This is not, of course, something which Genet would
ever admit was part of his aim as a dramatist. In a preface
to an edition of the play in 1954, he stated that his intention
was to write a kind of 'theatre within the theatre'. He hoped,
he continued, that this would enable him to achieve 'the
abolition of characters—who normally exist only because of
a psychological convention—and their replacement by signs
which, though as far removed as possible from what they
really mean, are nevertheless linked to this meaning and thus
succeed in joining together both author and spectator'. It is
a little difficult to see quite what Genet means by this, and
certainly impossible to claim that Solange and Claire have

the same kind of reality as the characters of Maupassant or Augier. They nevertheless evoke the spectator's sympathy— as did Juliette, in *Pompes Funèbres*—because their destitution is so absolute and they suffer so intensely from it. Perhaps Genet's most extraordinary achievement as a writer is that he should, in *The Maids*, make his audience feel sorry for characters whom it would have been so easy to present merely as psychological case histories. The reasons for this achievement lie in the many different dramatic qualities which *The Maids* possesses, as well as in the fascinating social and historical questions which it raises.

Thus even Jean-Jacques Gautier, while disapproving of what he considered the extreme decadence of Genet's themes, recognised that *The Maids* is a very well-constructed play. However uninterested Genet may be in traditional stage effects, he creates a perfect moment of dramatic irony when Madame, flustered by the news about Monsieur and by Claire's insistence that she needs a good drink of tea to calm her, exclaims: 'You're trying to kill me with your tea, your flowers, and your suggestions', and there are other incidental felicities which fit perfectly into the plot. At one moment, for example, when Madame is dramatising her grief at Monsieur's arrest to the point of abandoning her elegant life and following him to Siberia, she offers to give all her finest dresses to Solange and Claire. And, so that they will appreciate their good fortune, she points out to them that no one ever does this for her. When she wants new dresses, she has to buy them. It is again a sign of Genet's indifference to his best traditional effects that he should have omitted this particular remark from certain editions of his play, and its original inclusion is based upon one of the rare incidents in which Sartre shows him as having a critical attitude towards society. A lady once told Genet that her maid ought to be very happy, since she gave her all her old dresses. 'Excellent', Genet replied. 'Does she give you hers?'. Whatever general political meaning it may have, *The Maids* is first and foremost a play about servants, and the number of defensive jokes which critics made about it both in France and else-where showed that Genet was still touching a very sensitive middle-class nerve. Thus Maxime Belliard, reviewing the play in *France-Libre* in April 1947, wrote somewhat un-graciously that its only quality was to console people for no longer being able to afford servants, and Austin Clarke, analysing an excellent production given in English at Trinity College in 1958, showed an even clearer nostalgia for the good old days. 'It is clear,' he wrote in the *Irish Times*, 'that M. Genet has deliberately ignored the servant problem, which is so acute in France as in other countries, and has borrowed from a past age, when maids were base-ment prisoners. Obviously, Claire and Solange could demand, in a real world, high wages, or get employment in the nearest cigarette or clothing factory.' The very fact that *The Maids* could evoke comments such as these is an indica-tion that, for all Genet's avowed lack of interest in his ostensible subject, the play is not quite so empty of social comment as he intended. He wrote in his preface to the 1963 edition of *The Maids* that it was not intended to be *'un plaidoyer sur le sort des domestiques'*, and continued: *'Je suppose qu'il existe un syndicat des gens de maison—cela ne nous regarde pas'* ('I suppose servants have their trade union—it's no business of ours'). The original production was set in the early nineteen-hundreds, but the servant problem is obvi-ously a permanent feature of bourgeois society. Precisely because it is not tied down to a narrow concept of social realism, Genet's treatment of it is sufficiently close to familiar reality to be relevant to what his audience knows, and yet far enough removed for its implications to be very wide indeed.

In theory if not always in practice, feudalism offered a satisfactory answer to the problem of the relationship between masters and servants. In return for their services, the feudal overlord offered his servants and tenants protec-tion and security. However hard he had to work, the servant could not simply be dismissed because he was no longer needed. If his lord obeyed the spirit of the system, he had something of the security of a child within the family. It was when social relationships began to be based on a cash for services basis that the position of the servant became contradictory, because the master, while considering that his responsibilities were fulfilled if he paid their wages, continued to require from his servants the same kind of devotion which had seemed acceptable only within the earlier, more personal relationship. The idea that Jack is as good as his master, and enjoys the same right to have his feelings respected, forms the subject-matter of *Le Mariage de Figaro*, and underlines how untenable the official theory had become. But Figaro is a rationalist striving after independence, and does not need Almaviva's care and protection. Like the middle classes whose revolt he symbolises, his aim is to run his own life himself. Claire and Solange, on the other hand, are different. They long for a family, and for the security which it offers. This is why they stay with Madame and do not go off to work in the nearest cigarette factory. They are trying to keep the servant's part of the bargain within a feudal society that has totally disappeared. They cannot really face up to the fact that Madame cares absolutely nothing for them, and are terrified lest she should discover the traces which they leave of their game. Their relationship towards her is that of children towards a mother who threatens punishments without ever offering security. It is, in fact, virtually the same relationship which Genet himself had had towards his foster-parents.

The pages in which Sartre describes this relationship, at the very beginning of *Saint Genet, actor and martyr*, are among the best in his whole work. While never appealing specifically for the reader's emotional sympathy—just as Genet makes no such direct appeal in *The Maids*—he shows how Genet was, as a child, placed in a situation where adults treated him in totally irrelevant terms. They expected him to be grateful for what they were doing for him, while he felt nothing but the coldness of charity and the moral disapproval of adults willing to protect him only on certain conditions. This is an impossible situation in which to place a child, and however ungrateful his rebellion against them may have seemed in their terms, it is totally comprehensible in his. Again like Claire and Solange, however, he could not carry this rebellion through to the point where he really did something to his foster-parents. In the end, he hurt only himself, and like the game which Solange and Claire play together, or Claire's final suicide, his choice of evil merely had the result of leading him to Mettray and plunging him into a series of impossible emotional and intellectual contradictions. Like Solange and Claire, he was in a position of emotional dependence that prevented him from ever rebelling effectively. When he later cast this experience into a play about servants, he provided an excellent if unintentional expression of the paradoxical situation which they have in modern society.

What T. S. Eliot called 'the damp souls of housemaids' have never really found adequate literary expression. Flaubert's *Un Coeur Simple* is a study of alienation, but of an alienation voluntarily undergone. The most memorable servants in literature—Sam Weller, Figaro, Jeeves—have been quite able to cope with the problems of living a feudal relationship on middle-class terms. The books in which they have figured have been comedies, where the contradiction of one man performing personal services for another in return for an impersonal cash payment has been exploited for laughs. What Genet offers in *The Maids* is an examination of this contradiction in a melodramatic or even tragic mode, for Solange and Claire have the longing for an absolute and the refusal to settle for half which, in Arthur Miller's view, characterise the tragic hero. Their feelings of impotent resentment seem much more probable, both socially and psychologically, than Félicité's dog-like devotion or Jeeves's benevolent tyranny over the young master. The jokes about housemaids that used to fill the pages of *Punch*, and which crept back into the reviews of *The Maids*, are an indication that society has always suspected that such feelings existed, and yet refused to recognise them. The basic theme of these jokes about servants is always the same: the servant makes a claim for equality of treatment on what the cartoonist sees as the demonstrably false grounds that she is as good as her mistress. In *The Maids*, Genet takes the cartoonist's assumption as true, and follows out its tragic consequences: revolt based upon resentment leads to the defeat and destruction of the rebel precisely because resentment is a sign of inferiority. Claire and Solange punish themselves for the inferiority which Madame takes so calmly as one of the facts of life.

In a review of the play published in 1947, in the psycho-analytical journal *Psyché*, Henriette Brunot argued that *The Maids* did reflect a far more fundamental social and psychological problem than Genet's apparently unrealistic technique seemed to indicate.

> 'The wretchedness of female servants,' she wrote, 'does not lie in the actual work that they do. It stems much more from the fact that the psychological conditions in which they work are themselves emotionally disturbing. They have to share the life of the family, and yet remain outside, on the margin. They are never free, and consequently never adult. They live in a state of frustration, not being allowed to reply when spoken to, handling dresses and not putting them on, laying the table but not sitting down to the meal, breathing an atmosphere of luxury which they have no right to enjoy themselves.'

Had Genet expressed this problem in a directly realistic way, his play would have indeed become a plea for a more humane treatment of servants—or, indeed, for the disappearance of domestic service as an institution. As it was, however, his highly experimental and consciously theatrical technique raised the various social and psychological problems of his subject in the only way which can be theatrically valid: by inference, by suggestion, by implication. He did not set out to write a play about the failure of social revolution in mid-twentieth-century Europe, or about the contradictions of domestic service in a capitalist economy. As he implies in his preface to the 1963 edition of the play, he was seeking primarily to understand himself. 'I go to the theatre,' he wrote, 'in order to see myself (reconstituted in a single character, or with the help of a multiple character and in fictional form) such as I could not—or dare not—see myself or dream of myself as being, but such as I nevertheless know myself to be. The actors' function is thus to don the gestures and costumes which will enable them to show me to myself, and to show me naked, alone and in the joyfulness of solitude.' It is in *The Maids*, more than in any other of his works, that Genet's own personality, expressed without apparent regard for the preoccupations of the society in which he lived, links up most fully and spontaneously with them.

This would not happen if *The Maids* did not also have the quality of being an avant-garde play with a good plot, and an example of experimental theatre which puts on stage people with whom the audience can sympathise. The features which link it to the plays of Beckett or Ionesco, or the theories of Antonin Artaud, are fairly obvious: it is an experiment in theatricality, it presents man as the victim of illusions which prevent him from ever attaining reality, it deals with the failure to communicate, it attempts to create on the stage a ceremony that restores to the theatre some of its original mythical significance. When the curtain rises, Solange and Claire are already playing parts in a play within a play, and they continue, as Sartre points out, to remain cut off from reality during the whole of the action. When Claire finishes playing the part of Madame and Solange the part of Claire, they immediately have to prepare to play other roles in which they will appear, for Madame, faithful and obedient servants. When they are alone, they play at being mistress and servant; when they are with someone else, they have to play at being servants. Genet originally wanted to emphasise the artificiality of the action by having the two parts played by boys, and had he done so the play would have made the spectator turn yet another corner in the labyrinth. Because they are women living in another woman's house, Solange and Claire are denied the traditional feminine satisfactions of motherhood and home-making. Because Madame is also a kept woman, they will not be able even to enjoy the experience of motherhood vicariously, for she will obviously observe the traditional sterility of the prostitute. If all three parts are taken by men, this kind of sterility would be emphasised even further. Solange and Claire, according to Sartre, represent passive pederasts, and in this world where false men—homosexuals—play the part of false women—actresses—pretending alternately to be mistress and servants while succeeding in being neither, illusion becomes the only reality. There is no communication between Madame and her maids, and no real communication between Solange and Claire. Because neither of them ever really is what she appears to be, they can communicate only when they pretend and their communication has to cease when they return to reality. However, this reality is also one where they do nothing but play a different part, and their personality therefore remains forever elusive.

Genet's own view of the theatre insists less upon what a critic in *Le Monde* called 'the successive illusions to which human relations are reduced' than upon its links with religious ceremonies. The real theatre, he says in his preface to the 1954 edition of *The Maids*, is the Catholic mass: 'Under the most ordinary of appearances—a crust of bread—men devour a god.' *The Thief's Journal* bears ample witness to the fascination which the ceremonies of the Catholic Church exercised over him, and to the opportunities which it provided for him to satisfy his taste for sacrilege. When in a state of mortal sin, for example, he would take communion, and feel 'a sickening impression of mystery'. 'From this nausea,' he would then think, 'has arisen the magnificent structure of the laws in which I am caught.' As far as the theatre is concerned, however, his aim is to recreate something of the sacred fervour that accompanies religious ceremonies, especially those of a more primitive or magical type. And, as in *Pompes Funèbres*, he is obsessed by these ceremonies because of their association with the idea of death.

> 'I do not know what the theatre will be like in a Socialist world,' he wrote in his 1954 preface to *The Maids*, 'I have a better idea of what it would be among the Mau Mau, but in the Western world, more and more touched by death and turned towards it, it can do nothing but become more and more subtle in a "reflection" of play-acting by play-acting, of the shadow of a shadow which a ceremonious game could make exquisite and almost invisible. If we have chosen to dwell deliciously on the spectacle of our own death, we must rigorously pursue our funeral rites and order them correctly.'

The plot of *The Maids*, in the context of these remarks, is clearly intended to have a very far-reaching social significance. In Genet's view, it seems to be western society as a whole that dwells lovingly upon the idea of murder and ends up by committing suicide. It is perhaps not necessary to agree absolutely with this diagnosis to appreciate the highly ceremonial style in which *The Maids* should be, and generally is, performed. Solange and Claire, Genet remarks, speak as he would speak, on certain evenings, if he were a maid: in exalted, rhetorical, deliberately artificial language which expresses what they long to be within themselves rather than what they are for the outside world. Each man, says Malraux in *La Condition Humaine*, is for himself an incomparable monster whose dreams cannot normally be even avowed to himself, let alone communicated to his fellows. The declamatory language which the maids speak when they are alone is an expression of this monster which they are, but which can be expressed, both for themselves and for others, only through the deliberate movement away from realistic dialogue which the experimental theatre offers.

In his later plays, and especially in *The Blacks*, Genet returns to this idea of the theatre as ceremony, and particularly to the opportunity which it offers for the expression of violence. He also, in *The Balcony*, centres a whole play round the theme of play-acting and of pretence, and exploits even further the hall of mirrors device which had formed the basis for his *'Adame Miroir*, the ballet which Roland Petit danced to the music of Darius Milhaud in June 1946. Just as in *The Maids*, however, he also chooses themes which inevitably go beyond formalistic experiments, and which involve a kind of higher realism which reflects the patterns of experience of modern society. Whether he is always conscious of the implications which arise inevitably from his themes is impossible to say. The fact is that he always does choose subjects which have wide connotations, and he could scarcely complain if, in *The Maids*, his theme calls to mind the political experience of revolt, or the whole institution of domestic service. The general implications of *Deathwatch* were more narrow, and limited mainly to a particular aspect of religion. Perhaps this was because the play was based on an exclusively personal vision and not on any form of social reality, however transposed this might be. The thesis that certain criminals have a sacred aura because they are fatally destined to a life of spectacular crime is, like the Jansenist theories which it parodies, totally unverifiable by experience and largely irrelevant to the actual problem of crime in modern society. The same is not true of the ideas which Genet takes as his starting-point in his other plays, though this does not mean that the superiority of *The Maids* or *The Balcony* to *Deathwatch* stems from the wider social questions which the first two raise. *The Maids*, in particular, is better because it has a well-knit plot, because its characters are more than abstract ideas, because its dialogue is sometimes very witty and always directed to the immediate situation, and because the action follows inevitably from an initial situation which it effectively resolves. In its concision and economy, *The Maids* is that most curious of aesthetic phenomena: an experimental play which fulfils Boileau's requirements of unity, relevance and comprehensibility.

CHAPTER TEN

THE BALCONY

IN style and technique, Genet's third play stands halfway between the enclosed, claustrophobic world of *Deathwatch* and *The Maids*, and the world of open movement and extended action depicted in *The Blacks* and *The Screens*. It begins, like the first two plays, with the action taking place in a setting isolated from the outside world, but differs from *Deathwatch* and *The Maids* in that external events do influence what happens. Genet's first two plays, like Racine's tragedies, present situations which lead by their own inner logic to the catastrophe of the final dénouement. When the curtain goes up on *The Maids*, the anonymous letter has already been sent to the police and Monsieur is about to be released from prison for lack of evidence. The need for Claire to solve her own and Solange's problems by killing herself is implicit both in the danger that Madame will find out what has been happening, and in the stage which both sisters have reached in their game. The tension they have built up in their own relationship with each other is so great that something irredeemable has to take place, and nothing that happens outside can possibly affect this. In *The Balcony*, the situation is different. Were it not for the revolution, the various characters could continue to play their games in the enclosed and a-historical atmosphere provided for them by Madame Irma. But the revolution is there, and threatens at one moment to destroy their world of illusion completely. Until this revolution is finally defeated, its presence leads to a confrontation between illusion and reality which strikes a new note in Genet's work. And, for the first time, he seems to be making a conscious effort to treat the political events of his day without concentrating exclusively on treason and homosexuality.

The action of *The Balcony* takes place in an elaborately
equipped brothel, situated in a country that could be anywhere in Europe or South America. Like Madame Lysiane's
'La Féria,' Madame Irma's 'Grand Balcon' caters widely for
perversions. But whereas there was no particular pattern to
the tastes of the clients described in *Querelle of Brest*—an
official from Police Headquarters 'loved to have Carmen
refuse to give him jam'; a retired Admiral 'strutted about
naked gobbling like a turkey-cock, a feather stuck out of
his behind and pursued round the room by Elyane dressed
as a farmer's wife'; there was a clerk who 'liked to be rocked
to sleep'; another man 'liked to be chained to the foot of the
bed where he would howl like a dog'—the perversions that
occupy Genet's attention in *The Balcony* all centre round the
theme of social power and prestige. One man dresses up as a
Bishop, and delights in forgiving the sins of a beautiful
penitent. Another dons a Judge's robes, and revels in
judging the crimes of a petty thief, while a third, clad in the
full-dress uniform of a General, has a girl prance around him
as if she were his horse and remind him of the glorious
military conquests he has made. Other more conventional
sado-masochistic, fetichistic or infantile perversions are
mentioned in passing, but sex itself is not the major preoccupation of Madame Irma's clients. What Genet has done
in this play is take the slang term for a brothel, *une maison
d'illusions*, and use it to examine how people use sex to realise
the dreams of power and influence which predominate in
modern society. Yet although the play is, as he remarks in
his preface, 'a glorification of Images and Reflexions', the
actual driving force for the plot does not come from the
characters who come to 'Le Grand Balcon' in order to
enjoy the idealised image which it already offers of themselves. It comes from a man whose social *persona* has not yet
been consecrated by inclusion in the repertoire of the brothel,
but who nevertheless wields the only really effective power
in the outside world: the Chief of Police.

His most immediate connection with 'Le Grand Balcon'

stems from the fact that he has, in the past, been one of Madame Irma's lovers, and Genet advises his actors to make the brief moments where the two are alone together reveal 'a former tenderness'. At each of his visits, however, the Chief of Police is deeply hurt by the repeated if unintentional slight on his reputation and functions implied by the fact that nobody wants to come to the brothel in order to put on his uniform and act out his social rôle. His disappointment is quite understandable, for the police force which he commands is the only organisation to remain intact after the revolution, and he could therefore well be expected to enjoy considerable prestige. The Archbishop's palace, the Law Courts, the Military Headquarters, have all been destroyed, and the Queen herself is dead. But the popular imagination has not yet caught up with the real pattern of power within modern society, and the Chief of Police realises that he can bring the country fully under his control only by using the glamour and prestige still enjoyed by the Monarchy, the Church, the Army and the Law. He therefore decides to dress up Madame Irma as the Queen, and also succeeds, after considerable difficulty, in persuading the three men who normally play at being Bishop, Judge and General, to don their costumes for a more public purpose. They parade through the streets, are greeted enthusiastically by a tradition-loving populace, and the revolt is over. Its final defeat becomes obvious when its leader, Roger, turns up at the brothel with the request that he be allowed to dress up as the Chief of Police. He then proceeds to act out part of what is obviously the latter's private dream, and descends into an enormous tomb specially constructed for the Chief of Police. However, this is suddenly revealed as a ruse, for Roger whips out a knife and castrates himself. The Chief of Police immediately understands the import of this attempt to snatch victory out of defeat by the use of imitative magic, and manifests delighted reassurance at finding that he himself is still intact. His principal enemy has destroyed himself, and he can now go down into the tomb and sit there triumphantly. In all the brothels of the world, he proclaims, his image will now be intact and revered, the symbol that men have at last come to realise who the most important person in a modern state really is.

On a political level, the plot of *The Balcony* is extremely clear: a working-class revolution is defeated by a Chief of Police efficient enough to maintain his authority over his men, and intelligent enough to exploit the traditional establishment until his own power is recognised as absolute. Genet himself, protesting against what he considered was Peter Zadek's distortion of his play into a satire of the British monarchy, stated in an interview that he had originally set the action in Franco's Spain and added that the revolutionary who castrated himself 'represented all the Republicans when they acknowledged their defeat'. Roger's action is, indeed, as blatant a piece of symbolism as any in *Deathwatch*, for the establishment of a police state by Hitler in Germany, by Franco in Spain and by Stalin in Russia was either preceded or accompanied by a destruction of the power of the revolutionary working class.' In *The Balcony*, the Chief of Police adds a further element to this account of how a revolution can be made to fail when he speaks of the 'wild hope' that the people have had: 'In losing all hope they will lose everything,' he declares, until they finally come to lose themselves in him. Camus's *L'Homme Révolté* argues that the dictatorships of the mid-twentieth century proved acceptable because men were exhausted by an absolute revolt and disillusioned by its failure, and this remark by the Chief of Police suggests a very similar idea. It is not, of course, a particularly original one. Alexis de Tocqueville expressed it by quoting a phrase that was already four hundred years old when he wrote *L'Ancien Régime et la Révolution*: '*Par requierre de trop grande franchise et libertés chet-on en trop grand serviage*' ('By demanding too great and too extensive a liberty, men fall into too great a slavery'). There is also a parallel between the ending of *The Balcony* and that of Flaubert's *L'Education Sentimentale*, where the

ex-socialist Sénécal becomes a policeman and shoots the
idealistic Dussardier. What is curious is to find an author as
unconventional as Genet suggesting ideas so closely associated with conservative and even reactionary thinkers.
Lucien Goldmann, arguing in *Les Temps Modernes* in
favour of a sociological interpretation of Genet's play,
pointed to a fundamental difference between modern
dictatorships and the absolute monarchies of the past when
he compared the fame of a Himmler or a Beria with the
obscurity of Louis XIV's minister for police, La Reynie.
What *The Balcony* expressed, in his view, was a phenomenon
that modern writers had so far tended to ignore: '*l'accroisse-
ment de prestige des techniciens de la répression dans la conscience de
la grande masse*' ('the growth in prestige, among the masses,
of technicians of repression'). It was quite possible, he
suggested, that this aspect of social reality had found its way
into Genet's text '*implicitement et en dehors de toute volonté
consciente*' ('implicitly, and independently of any conscious
intention'), and both *Querelle of Brest* and *The Thief's Journal*
bear witness to a personal attitude of Genet towards
policemen that may alone have inspired this aspect of *The
Balcony*. Yet whatever Genet's original inspiration may have
been, it is certainly true that this play deals more directly and
more perceptively with the fundamental structure of modern
society than any of his other works. This is visible even in
relatively minor details, for another supposedly powerful
figure whom no one coming to the brothel wishes to imitate
is a colonial administrator. Empire-building never really
caught the popular imagination either in France or in Great
Britain, and it seems unlikely that this gap in what the
English translation of *The Balcony* calls The Nomenclature
will ever now be filled. In contrast, the position which the
Chief of Police finally obtains still seems relatively secure.
Lucien Goldmann also pointed to a number of other
features that, in his view, enable *The Balcony* to be interpreted
as an allegory of the power relationships existing within
modern capitalist society. Thus the Bishop, Judge and

General have no authority of their own. They can play at being powerful only when provided with a ready-made scenario by Madame Irma, or with a ready-made situation by the Chief of Police. They represent what Anthony Sampson called 'the divorce between prestige and power' which characterises much of modern British life, or what Marx would have seen as an example of imbalance between economic infrastructure and ideological superstructure. Genet also provides a fascinating vision of the pretensions which outmoded social institutions can still sometimes legitimately entertain when he shows the Bishop, Judge and General, after their triumphant procession through the streets, trying to assert their independence of the Chief of Police. They know that until someone comes to the brothel with a request to impersonate him, the social institutions which they represent will still be able to use their prestige as a bargaining counter in their relationship with the holders of real economic or military power. Genet's view of society in *The Balcony* is a curious mixture of Marx and Pascal. Like the first, he seems to be arguing that real power lies not in the official institutions of society but with those who have the financial or physical means to enforce their will: Madame Irma counting her money and organising the imaginary lives of her clients, the Chief of Police who goes as automatically to her in a moment of national crisis as reactionary dictators are reputed to run to Wall Street. But like Pascal, Genet also suggests that human nature is so in need of illusions that no social order can ever be based on reality. Madame Irma is afraid that if the revolutionaries win, they will bring the reign of her *maison d'illusions* to an end. The workers, she says, are 'without imagination. Prudish and probably chaste', and her words are an apt commentary on the puritanism that seems to have characterised all revolutionaries from Cromwell to Castro, and from Robespierre to Mao Tse Tung. However, the revolutionaries are not so far above the common run of humanity as she imagines, since they too need their emblem. They find it in Chantal, a girl only recently rescued from the brothel by Roger, and whose ability to inspire the troops with her songs is reminiscent of the rôle played by La Pasionaria in the Spanish Civil War. Chantal is shot dead at the very moment when Madame Irma, the Bishop, Judge and General appear on the Balcony itself, which, as the stage directions indicate, 'projects beyond the façade of the brothel', and the audience is later told that this killing had been arranged by the Bishop. From that point onwards, the revolution is doomed to failure as much by its inability to offer a rival image to those of the Church, Monarchy or Law, as by the superior fighting power of the police. It is almost as though Genet were agreeing with Pascal that men can act politically only if led by illusions, and the Chief of Police himself is inspired less by a desire for real power than by the hope of attaining the prestige symbolised by a place in the Nomenclature. By its associations with Pascal's ideas, *The Balcony* puts forward an essentially reactionary view of mankind, which seems to contradict the wider implications of Lucien Goldmann's contention that Genet had written 'the first great Brechtian play in French literature'. Moreover, the insistence throughout *The Balcony* that nothing whatsoever is real constitutes a major obstacle to interpreting it as a left-wing play in the full sense of the word. True, it deals critically with the failure of a left-wing rebellion; Roger, Genet implied in his remark about Spain, was wrong to act as he did. But nowhere is there any suggestion that right action in politics is possible. If everything is illusion, nothing really deserves to be taken seriously.

The theme of illusion reaches its climax at the very end of the action, when Madame Irma comes to the front of the stage to remind the audience that they have, after all, only been watching a play. 'You must now go home,' she tells them, 'where everything—you may be sure—will be even falser than here.' The insistence upon the unreality of what happens on stage is a truism in modern drama, but Genet gives it an extra twist by introducing it at the end of a play which itself shows people attempting to realise their identity through acting a series of rôles. In *The Maids*, Solange and Claire were perpetually condemned to playing a part in order to be what they were, and in *The Balcony* it is only when the Chief of Police can play at being himself in the Nomenclature that he really feels himself becoming the Chief of Police. This idea has analogies with some of the views which Sartre expresses in *L'Etre et le Néant*, but the importance of play-acting is too frequent a theme in the novels which Genet wrote before he met Sartre for there to be any serious question of a direct influence. In *Our Lady of the Flowers*, the criminals and homosexuals are all playing at being criminals and homosexuals, and the convicts in *Miracle of the Rose* draw their prestige less from what they are than from the success which they have in projecting a certain image of themselves. The characters in *The Balcony* are all intensely aware of the motives which inspire their actions, and the Bishop gives a lucid account of how superior to reality illusions are when he recalls how happy he and his fellows were when they pursued 'the quest for an absolute dignity' in the privacy of their rooms. 'In peace, in comfort, behind shutters, behind padded curtains, protected by attentive women, protected by a police force that protects brothels, we were able to be a general, judge and bishop to the point of perfection and to the point of rapture!' Reality does, it is true, offer other pleasures, but these are 'the bitter delights of action and responsibility'. The ideal, suggests the Bishop, is to dream and not to do.

When the Chief of Police first suggests that they should help him, the clients incarnating the Notables show considerable reluctance to be dragged from their dream world into the harshness and dangers of reality, and their misgivings are shown to have been justified by what happens to them. It is not that they suffer physically by going out among the people, for the crowds greet them with quite extraordinary enthusiasm. It is that once they have become, for the outside world, what formerly they only pretend to be in private, they are deprived of the solace afforded by imagination. The Bishop complains that he no longer looks forward to putting on his lace ornaments because they have 'become himself', the Judge laments that he is 'just a dignity represented by a robe', while the General sums up their whole problem by saying that he 'no longer dreams'. Were they to remain in reality what they had so enjoyed pretending to be in the past, they would have to go to another brothel, where the General would be, for example, a judge or a stonemason, and the Bishop a plumber, or a soldier in the Foreign Legion. 'Human kind,' wrote T. S. Eliot, 'cannot bear very much reality,' and *The Balcony* provides quite unexpected support for his view. It is partly to compensate themselves for the loss of their dreams that the Bishop, General and Judge make their attempt to exercise real power, and it is significant that everyone in the play is much more anxious to *be* than to *do*. While this may reflect something of Genet's own experience in trying to *be* evil, he greatly enlarges the appeal of *The Balcony* by making his characters want to be bishops, generals, judges or policemen and not merely famous criminals. Its treatment of the contrast between illusion and reality undoubtedly benefits from being placed in a wider context than a prison cell, and the jokes about sex and religion make it the most relevant of all Genet's works to the ideas and experience of the average reader or theatre-goer.

A central theme in Genet's novels was undoubtedly the gap between criminals as he had imagined them and criminals as he found them to be. This gap is even wider if the almost idyllic atmosphere of his poetry is compared to the much more disillusioned account of crime provided by his novels, but the humour which arises from the contrast in his fiction is almost certainly unintentional. The middle-class reader, secure in his own values, may find Mignon very funny, but there is little evidence in *Our Lady of the Flowers* to suggest that Genet is presenting him with deliberate comic intent. In *The Balcony*, on the other hand, there is no doubt that when he suddenly allows reality to intrude into the general atmosphere of illusion, he is doing so to raise a laugh. At one point, for example, Madame Irma is so carried away by the splendour of the illusions which she can offer that she launches into a magnificently rhetorical speech where she quite loses contact with reality. Carmen, the girl to whom she is speaking—and for whom, in what is apparently an established tradition, she nourishes markedly Lesbian feelings—suddenly interrupts her to say how well she speaks. *'J'ai poussé jusqu'au brevet'* ('I went through elementary school'), replies Madame Irma, and the audience is brought quickly back to earth. Her remark also echoes a detail in *Our Lady of the Flowers*, since Divine, Genet remarks, *'porte toujours sur elle le diplôme graisseux et gris de son certificat d'études supérieures'* ('always carries in her pocket her oily grey diploma for advanced study') and it may well be that this was yet another way in which Louis Culafroy repeated one of Genet's own habits. The interesting point is that Genet should have been able to take up this minor feature of his first fictional character and use it to such excellent and apparently impersonal dramatic effect. According to Jean Fayard's review of the play in *Le Figaro*, Marie Bell said the line in a voice worthy of Bérénice, and in a way it epitomises the complexity of the dramatic illusion in *The Balcony*: the characters cease to play one part only to begin another, and the humour lies in the different degrees of unreality that this fact suggests. Like all Genet's works, it expresses that side of his personality which Sartre emphasised when he called him a *comédien*. The difference is that the play-acting is now controlled and exploited to provide both laughter and social comment.

The play is indeed constructed around the contrast between reality and illusion, and a number of other incidents emphasise this in a humorous and perceptive way. The General, for example, hears a woman cry out for help in an adjoining room, and prepares to leap to her defence. However, Madame Irma tells him not to bother since he is

now in civilian clothes. The Bishop also takes the greatest
pleasure in forgiving the sins committed by his pretty
penitent, but insists that she should really confess to them.
'Our holiness,' he tells the girl, 'lies only in our being able to
forgive you your sins', and he obviously could not do this
unless he could persuade himself that she has sinned. When,
however, she suddenly asks him what he would do if her
sins were real, his mask immediately drops. 'You're mad,'
he exclaims, 'I hope you didn't really do all that . . . If your
sins were real, they would be crimes, and I should be in a
fine mess.' Like the man who said that he was a masochist
until it started to hurt, the Bishop can extend his fantasy
world only up to a certain point. Once reality breaks in,
the fantasies become unbearable. While he is playing his rôle,
however, the Bishop makes a remark which again emphasises
how many of Genet's own preoccupations are still dodging
about only slightly below the surface of this play. In the
brothel, the Bishop maintains, 'there is no possibility of
doing evil'. 'You live in evil,' he tells the girl, 'in the absence
of remorse. How could you do evil?' The brothel not only
reflects the real world because people spend all their time
there playing social roles; there too, as in life as we know it,
absolute evil is impossible. The insistence upon pretence is
also linked to another theme in Genet's novels, since like
them, *The Balcony* stresses the elusiveness of satisfactory
experience in the realm of sexual abnormality.

In an article published in *Encounter* in May 1959, Wayland
Young argued that *The Balcony* expressed more of the nature
and atmosphere of prostitution than any social survey could
hope to reproduce. Although there is a reference in the play
to '*les passes simples*', it is clear that very few of Madame
Irma's 'vi-si-tors. I don't even allow myself to refer to them
as clients' come to the brothel for straight sex. The emphasis
throughout is on perversions, and this very much reflects the
general picture which Wayland Young gave of prostitution
in London. All the sexual deviations which Genet mentions
in *The Balcony*, from the Judge or General with their major

power fantasies to 'the one you tie up, spank, whip and soothe, and then he snores', also have the same feature in common: they are attempts to use sex in order to obtain a particular psychological mode of being. The men who indulge in them are, apparently, referred to by prostitutes as *'cérébraux'*—people concerned with ideas rather than physical reality. Because such people are, to use a phrase coined by Gilbert Ryle to express a different kind of mistake, 'trying to gaff a salmon with an ace of spades', they will always remain unsuccessful and unsatisfied. One of the characteristics of de Sade's novels, and of sado-masochistic literature in general, is the accumulation of more and more complicated tortures in a frenzied attempt to attain a particular mental state: that of the person who feels either that he has absolute power or that he is a helpless victim. But since this psychological state has to be achieved through dwelling on physical events, there is a constantly frustrating discrepancy between the means employed and the results pursued. In the presence of genuine suffering, the reaction of the sadist or masochist who had not sublimated his sexual urges into other channels would be like that of the Bishop faced with a real sin: horrified indignation. When, at the very end of the play, the Chief of Police goes down into his tomb to wait two thousand years for his apotheosis, he adopts the only permanent solution which there is to the problem of aberrant sex: he goes mad. The Bishop, Judge and General will simply have to come back for more. They are not only incapable of transforming their illusions into reality; they do not even want this to happen.

The Balcony differs from Genet's novels by presenting sexual deviations with no shade of compassion or complicity. In *Our Lady of the Flowers*, Divine is pitiful as well as comic, and in *Querelle of Brest* there is Madame Lysiane's comforting: '*Heureusement qui y a les vicieux, Mesdemoiselles, ça permet aux mal foutus de connaître l'amour.*' ('Good thing there are perverts, girls. It lets the ugly know what love is like.') In showing Madame Irma's clients as funny, Genet is endorsing the conventional attitude in a way quite unique in his whole work. Discuss sexual perversions in any saloon bar, and the reaction will be the same: kinkies are comic. Perhaps Genet adopts this attitude towards his characters because they are all, for all their peculiarities, heterosexual. He may thus be replying to the implications of the English term 'queer' by pointing to a corresponding queerness in heterosexual behaviour, and there is no doubt that Genet carefully directs the laughter away from his own characteristics. Nevertheless, it is possible to see links between the experience of homosexuality described in Genet's novels and his account of heterosexual perversions in *The Balcony*. In the same way that Divine gradually infected Mignon and Notre-Dame with her own wild, feminine ways, or Mario and Querelle became more feminine through their sexual relationship with each other, so Madame Irma's visitors gradually impart their own taste for illusions to her girls. Carmen, for example, has so enjoyed being the Immaculate Conception of Lourdes 'for a bank clerk from the National Provincial' that she implores Madame Irma to allow her to play the part again. The world of homosexuality, as *Our Lady of the Flowers* showed, is also one of illusions, where men are attractive through a masculinity that has to be false if they are to have sexual relations with their male admirers. In transposing the need for illusions into the heterosexual world of Madame Irma's 'Grand Balcon', Genet is by no means taking an unjust revenge. It would be a brave heterosexual indeed who claimed that fantasy was totally absent from his own sex-life, and the following conversation is an indication of the extent to which Genet makes *The Balcony* into a fairly serious discussion of this particular problem.

Carmen: He's married, isn't he?

Irma: As a rule, I don't like to talk about the private life of my visitors. The 'Grand Balcony' has a world-wide reputation. It's the most artful, yet the most decent house of illusions . . .

Carmen: Decent?

Irma: Discreet. But I might as well be frank with you, you inquisitive girl. Most of them are married.

Carmen: And when they're with their wives, whom they love, do they keep a tiny, small-scale version of their revels in a brothel . . .

Irma: Carmen!

Carmen: Excuse me, Madame . . . in a house of illusions. I was saying: do they keep their revels in a house of illusions tucked away in the back of their heads in miniature form, far off? But present?

When *The Balcony* was virtually banned in Paris in 1957, it was suggested in *Combat* that the reason lay in Genet's audacity in showing a General and a Bishop in a brothel. This may well have been the case, and the Fourth Republic was, by that time, so ill-assured that it could afford to offend no possible pillar of the establishment. The ban must have given Genet great pleasure, for it showed him that blasphemy was still possible because the official view which society had of itself still coincided with his vision of it. He had spoken in *The Thief's Journal* of 'the supposedly rational disposition of our epoch', and it could certainly be argued that a truly rational society would not have been offended by *The Balcony*. For such a society, judges and generals would be no different from other civil servants. No sacred aura of the Law or of Military Glory would hang around them, and a Bishop would be merely a person paid and disguised to run a particular organisation and perpetuate alternately comforting and frightening myths. For the Genet who was still, even in *The Balcony*, living out what Sartre calls his 'original crisis', such figures were very different, and the reaction which he evoked from the French authorities in 1957 showed how acute an analysis of the irrationality of modern society his private obsessions could still enable him to make.

The banning of his play also indicated, however, not only that the France of the Fourth Republic was still trying to give its social myths a semi-sacred function, but also that its censors could not understand fairly conventional works of avant-garde literature. Genet was not showing a bishop going into a brothel, but a gas man* going into a brothel in order to play at being a bishop. An ingenious advocate could even have pointed out that this was less of an insult to the Church than a compliment to the prestige which it still enjoyed, and Genet's treatment of religion in *The Balcony* is not without certain perception. Perhaps by accident, the Bishop puts his finger on the contradictory situation of those clerics who seek preferment but also wish to observe the Christian virtues when he says: 'Never—I affirm it before God who sees me—I never desired the episcopal throne. To become bishop, to work my way up— by means of virtues and vices—would have been to turn away from the ultimate dignity of bishop. I shall explain: in order to become a bishop, I should have had to make a zealous effort not to be one, but to do what would have resulted in my being one.' From the context, he appears to be talking about the impossibility of anyone coinciding absolutely with his function, for he continues: 'Having become a bishop, in order to be one I should have had—in order to be one for myself, of course!—I should have had to be constantly aware of being one so as to perform my functions.' But whatever ideas Genet may have intended to suggest, it is the paradox of the ambitious cleric which he underlines most clearly, and this particular incident embodies his whole achievement in *The Balcony*: he talks about his own permanent concern with illusions, and does so in terms of ceremonies; but he also sheds light on a much wider variety of general topics than he evokes in any other work.

For a number of reasons, however, none of the productions which *The Balcony* has so far received has given equal importance to all the different themes which it presents. Invariably, the opening tableaux representing the Bishop, Judge and General have gone over very well, while the second half, with its insistence upon the failure of the revolution, has been less convincingly performed. T. C. Worsley, reviewing the 1957 London production, summed up a fairly general reaction when he wrote: 'A plunge into the visionary comedy of the first act is warmly recommended. But at the interval you may well reach for your respectable hat and coat and you would not miss much by obeying the prompting.' Kenneth Tynan, commenting on the same production, also showed how fully the political theme had been underplayed when he stated that 'a stranger asks permission to dress up as the Chief of Police'. This was not altogether Peter Zadek's fault, for his production was still based to a large extent upon the early version of the play which Genet had published in 1956.* In this, Roger's self-castration takes place off-stage and is reported to the audience by Carmen. Moreover, since she refers to him merely as *l'ancien plombier de Madame Irma* ('Madame Irma's former plumber'), the wider significance of his gesture inevitably disappears. Even in the revised version which Peter Brook finally managed to put on in Paris in May 1960, a number of cuts were made in the scenes dealing with the defeat of revolution, though these prevented neither Lucien Goldmann from writing his brilliant analysis of the play nor Bernard Dort from underlining how relevant it was to the immediate political atmosphere in France. 'For us who live under the Fifth Republic,' he wrote, 'in this republic with no republicans, in a régime which borrows its appearance and language from History in order better to deny it, the games at which Genet invites us to be present are far from gratuitous.'

Relatively few critics, however, have discussed the very obvious political ideas which the final text of *The Balcony* presents when read in its entirety in the study, and this lack of comment throws an interesting light upon the way in which an author's general reputation may, especially in the theatre, affect the interpretation given to one of his works. Because Genet has, for the most part, been associated with the essentially a-political 'theatre of the absurd', and because he has almost always chosen to emphasise this aspect of his work in his writings on the theatre, directors have fought shy of bringing out the full political significance which his work undoubtedly contains. They may have been right to do so, and there is also a strong temptation even for the sociologically minded critic to share David Grossvogel's interpretation of Genet's plays in terms of his homosexuality. 'The patterns of this drama,' Mr. Grossvogel wrote of The Maids, 'are like the sterile turgescence and detumescence of the homosexual act, conceived in loneliness and fraud and ending in deception. This is also the way in which each of Genet's plays is constructed.' For it is true that, with the exception of The Blacks, each of Genet's plays tells the story of a defeat, since even in The Screens there is no hope of an individual salvation for Saïd in the revolution which he has helped to make possible. The fact that Genet is so unremittingly pessimistic in things political should not, however, necessarily prevent his plays from being presented as comments on how modern society is evolving.

CHAPTER ELEVEN

THE BLACKS

Two features of *Les Nègres* (*The Blacks*) immediately distinguish it from Genet's first three plays: its production by Roger Blin, in September 1959, received Genet's enthusiastic approval; while continuing to exploit the themes of illusion and being-for-others, it recommends a specific political attitude. In the 1954 preface to *The Maids*, Genet had spoken scornfully of how it had been commissioned by *'un acteur célèbre en son temps'*, and his remark seems to imply that he was not enthusiastic about the way Jouvet had directed the play in 1947. His preface to the 1962 edition of *The Balcony* denounced all the productions which the play had so far received, and however much sympathy one may feel for a director who is required, simultaneously, to ensure that *The Balcony* be performed 'with the solemnity of a mass in a cathedral' and that it be 'vulgar, theatrical and in bad taste', some of the details which he gives of them make his indignation appear justified. His preface *'Pour jouer* Les Nègres', on the other hand, begins by paying Blin the highest compliments: *'Imiter Blin? Sa réussite était de l'ordre de la perfection, l'imiter équivaudrait à le dégrader. Sa mise en scène ne peut être qu'un exemple d'audace et de rigueur.'* ('Imitate Blin? His success belonged to the realm of perfection. To imitate it would be to degrade him. His production can only be an example of daring and rigour.') While most of the Paris critics agreed that Blin's production was excellent on the physical level, in that he made his actors move very well, the play nevertheless had the considerable disadvantage of being frequently inaudible. The actors chosen by him were amateurs, from different parts of Africa, and spoke French with strong regional accents. It is true that, dealing as it did with the colour problem, *The Blacks* necessarily offered a more exclusively visual experience than any of Genet's previous plays, and it is impossible to imagine it receiving as successful a production on the radio as *The Balcony* did in England in 1964. Nevertheless, the text is important, for it gives very clear indication of how Genet tried to assimilate his own experience to that of a race of men who, in their contacts with the West, have always been oppressed and exploited. It also puts forward a highly controversial and somewhat contradictory suggestion, again linked with Genet's own attitude, as to how this race can and should free itself.

Like *The Maids*, *The Blacks* is centred round a ceremony presented as a play within a play. Just as Claire and Solange played at being Madame and preparing to kill her, so one of the negroes in *The Blacks* plays at being a white woman who is murdered by another negro. The difference is that whereas the person to be killed in *The Maids* was, for all her vapid frivolity, at least a symbol of oppression, the victim in *The Blacks* is a harmless and unimportant white person. Genet was dealing with race hatred, and he had the courage to recommend, at least within the ceremony, that the negroes should behave with all the barbarity attributed to them by their worst enemies. The ceremony is, apparently, performed quite often, and on the particular occasion represented in the play, the negroes are said to have found their victim in a drunken old beggar woman whose coffin is set on a catafalque in the centre of the stage during the whole action. But just as, in *Our Lady of the Flowers*, 'un faux meurtre en faisait découvrir un vrai', and it was a mannequin which led the police to arrest Notre-Dame for the murder of Ragon, the coffin is really empty, and the real murder is taking place elsewhere. The oppressive aspect which the white races have always had for the black is represented by a group of masked figures who watch the ceremony from one of the wooden terraces set high above the stage. These figures consist of a queen, her valet, a colonial governor, a judge and a missionary, and express the image which, in Genet's view, Western society would like to perpetuate of itself.

Their function in the play is to judge and condemn the negroes taking part in the ceremony, and then to have their judgment nullified. When, at the end of the play, they come down on to the stage as a kind of punitive expedition, they are ambushed and massacred.

Nothing in this part of the play is real, however, for these five representatives of white civilisation then proceed to take off their grotesque masks and reveal themselves to be negroes just like the others. The whole ceremony, together with the arguments about whether or not the murder should be committed, the murder itself, and the defeat of the masked figures, is all illusion. The negroes have been playing at being negroes to entertain the white audience for whom, Genet remarks in his preface, the play was written. If ever, he added, it were played before a black audience, 'then a white person, male or female, should be invited every evening. The organiser of the show would welcome him formally, dress him in ceremonial costumes and lead him to his seat, preferably in the front row of the stalls. The actors will play for him. A spotlight should be focused upon this symbolic white throughout the performance.'

The presence of this white person is also essential to what might be called the second plot of *The Blacks*, which takes place off-stage and gives the play its real political meaning. One of the negroes, Ville de Saint-Nazaire—his name in the English translation is Newport News—is not wearing the full evening dress which the other actors put on for the ceremony. Because he has real work to do, he goes barefoot and is wearing a woollen sweater, and he appears on stage solely to report what is happening in the events to which he is contributing. It is only towards the end of the play that the audience realises what he has been doing, and thus understands the real, as distinct from the apparent, significance of the ceremony. Off-stage, a negro who has betrayed his people has been judged and executed. As Ville de Saint-Nazaire says, 'We shall have to get used to the responsibility of executing our own traitors', and he proclaims that, while this was happening, a congress was welcoming another negro who was now 'going off to organise and continue the fight'. The ceremony therefore has two essentially political aims: to divert the attention of the whites by entertaining them with images; and gradually to corrode, by satire and exaggeration, 'the idea they'd like us to have of them'. There must be a white spectator, for otherwise there would be no one to deceive, and the hatred of the blacks would have no object. There must also, Ville de Saint-Nazaire declares, be a physical struggle in which the negroes fight the whites 'in their actual persons', if they are to obtain the political independence which will alone enable them to enjoy human emotions. For in addition to being a play where treason is at last punished in the name of a political programme which Genet presents as desirable, *The Blacks* also presents a man and woman 'who really love each other'. These are Village, who has to play the rôle of the murderer in the ceremony, and Vertu, who at one time has been a prostitute. At the end of the play, their love becomes positively idyllic, for once Village has eventually recognised that he must love her as a black woman and without any reference to the values of the whites, the two lovers move across the stage to the minuet from Mozart's *Don Giovanni*.

Before this final release of tension takes place, the spectator is plunged into an atmosphere of hatred so intense that it seems to imply, as Bernard Poirot-Delpech remarked in *Le Monde*, that racial prejudices cannot and indeed should not be surmounted. The ceremony is conducted by a racial extremist, Archibald Absalom Wellington, who at one point gives the following advice to his fellow actors:

'I order you to be black to your very veins. Pump black blood through them. Let Africa circulate in them. Let Negroes negrify themselves. Let them persist to the point of madness in what they are condemned to be, in their ebony, in their smell, in their yellow eyes, in their cannibal tastes. Let them not be content with eating Whites, but let them cook each other as well. Let them invent recipes for shin-bones, knee-caps, calves, thick lips, everything. Let them invent unknown sauces. Let them invent hiccoughs,

belches and farts that'll give out a deleterious jazz. Let them invent
a criminal painting and dancing. Negroes, if they change towards
us, let it not be out of indulgence, but of terror.'

Like Sartre, Genet here seems to be finding in the revolt of
ex-colonial people against Western civilisation the solution
through violence of his own personal problems, and the plot
of this play has analogies with the view that Sartre expressed
in his preface to Franz Fanon's *Les Damnés de la Terre*:
'Shooting a European is like killing two birds with one
stone, getting rid of the oppressor and the oppressed at one
and the same time.' Just before Village re-enacts the murder
of the white woman whose body is supposed to be there in
front of them in the coffin, Bobo puts black shoe polish on
his face to make him even blacker. Again, it is a very obvious
symbol, though one fully in the logic of the concept of
négritude which the French existentialists have done so much
to popularise. It also has a parallel in Genet's own experience
for it shows the negroes exaggerating the features for which
they were originally excluded from the benefits of Western
society just as Genet chose to exaggerate his own wickedness in response to the accusation of thief originally levelled
against him. The difference is that in *The Blacks* he is
translating his own situation into a context where the
quality that originally earned reprobation can serve as a
basis for positive action. However much his white audience
may disapprove of what the negroes are doing, they are not
seeking evil purely for its own sake, but for political aims
that can be rationally formulated: independence, freedom,
self-respect.

When Claire, playing the part of Madame, declares in
The Maids that 'everything coming out of the kitchen is spit',
she may be giving voice to a contempt which mistresses feel
for their servants, in the same way that it may be true, as
Genet alleges elsewhere, that certain employers peep through
the key-hole to see what their maids are doing. Nevertheless,
these are not feelings or actions to which anyone in present-
day society would admit, and Genet is very much in the

position of the Freudian psycho-analyst who tries to persuade his patient that the subconscious emotions whose existence the latter so vigorously denies are really there. In *The Blacks*, the situation is rather different, for when the valet admires the negroes for their splendid spontaneity, when the governor comments upon their sexual vigour or when the missionary discusses their bush telegraph or liking for abstruse theological discussions, they are repeating well-established clichés. *The Balcony* also offered an analysis of society's subconscious attitudes, for the figures openly admired nowadays are those who embody rational and not semi-magical qualities: the scientist, the doctor, the engineer. Judges, bishops and generals stand at a fairly low premium, and to appreciate the force of Genet's play the spectator has to admit, temporarily, that he still holds them in the same ancient awe. No such suspension of disbelief is needed to see that Genet's analysis of the colour problem is basically accurate, and the objections to his play, as far as its ideas are concerned, arise essentially from the solution which he suggests. 'We are what they want us to be,' says Archibald. 'We shall therefore be it to the very end, absurdly,' and the whole message of the play is reminiscent of the programme of the Black Muslims. The disadvantages of such a programme are well-known, and Gabriel Marcel summarised them with some force in a violent attack which he published on *The Blacks* some time after its first performance. The criticism which seems most applicable to *The Blacks*, and which Marcel did not mention, is that an inverted form of Genet's play, written by a white racialist, would never be performed in a state based upon the principles of Malcolm X. Perhaps more than any other writer, Genet incarnates the paradox of the rebel in Western liberal society: the principal target for his attacks is the bourgeoisie, and it is the members of this class who buy his books; the main objects of his admiration are those states and political philosophies which would rapidly send him back to prison.

It is curious, in this respect, that one of the most violent criticisms of *The Blacks* should have been written by an author whose hostility towards the society in which he lives is almost as violent as that of Genet himself. After Gene Frankel's rather more audible production of the play had been running for two years at St. Mark's Playhouse, New York, Norman Mailer published a long denunciation of it in *The Village Voice*. While claiming that *The Blacks* was 'the truest and most explosive play anyone has yet written about the turn of the tide, and the guilt and horror in the white man's heart as he turns to face his judge', Mailer argued that the conflict between the black and white races was too serious a matter to be left to Genet's unrealistic and neo-Pirandellian approach. 'Black and white in mortal confrontation,' he wrote, 'are far more interesting than the play of shadows which Genet brings to it,' and he maintained that *The Blacks* would have been a much better and a more useful play if 'literal White had looked across the stage at literal Black'. For Mailer, Western society was sick with liberalism, and threatened by the peril that the economic security created by bureaucrats would 'extinguish the animal in us'. Genet, for him, was actually contributing to this 'liberal cancer' by pirouetting away from the real violence of his subject-matter into an empty, avant-garde formalism. How much better, how much more useful, how much closer to the real violence which society needs, concluded Mailer, would it have been if real white had been shown as confronting real black, and the play performed in Charleston, Atlanta, New Orleans or Savannah.

Several English critics made basically the same criticism in less extreme terms, and John Bowen, for example, wrote that *The Blacks* was 'not an adequate theatrical presentation of a conflict which is deep in the personal and political lives of Europeans, Africans and Americans too'. In so far as *The Blacks* is a purely formalistic exercise, presenting much the same interplay of images and illusions which characterises *The Balcony*, these criticisms are certainly justified. In a note describing how the play came to be written, Genet asks

'But what is a black? First of all, what's his colour?', and the implication of his question seems to be that black and white are both illusions. By its associations with the view that, since all men are brothers through their common humanity, there are no ineradicable differences between races or nations, this is a typically liberal concept, and Norman Mailer was, by his own curious but consistent standards, fully justified in rejecting it. It is impossible to argue, at one and the same time, that negroes should use their blackness as a basis for violent revolution, and that this blackness is not a quality at all but something which exists solely in the eyes of the whites.

It is by no means certain, however, that Genet is really saying this in *The Blacks*. When read in the study, the play does carry the very definite political message outlined earlier in this chapter, and Genet's negroes are very far from denying the reality of their blackness. They are taking part in a ceremony of recognition and self-assertion, not of self-questioning and Pirandellian doubts, and nothing which they say or do supports the implications of the question which Genet asks in his note to the play. The fact nevertheless remains that the only critic in either France or England who actually mentioned the 'real' plot of the play (the execution of the traitor off-stage) was Guy Leclerc, in *L'Humanité*. Most of the others, even Albert Ollivier in *Les Lettres Françaises*, shared Norman Mailer's view that the play tended to by-pass the real problem of racialism in its concern for the general question of identity. The fault may have been Genet's in suggesting through the device of the masked white characters that all racial differences might be illusory. It is nevertheless a valid criticism to say that, if an important theme of a play passes virtually unnoticed by almost all the critics, while nevertheless leaping to the eye as soon as the play is read, then there must also have been something wrong with the production.

Nevertheless, Roger Blin's presentation of *The Blacks* received Genet's whole-hearted approval, and although the ceremony may be hiding the 'real' action taking place in the wings, it nevertheless occupies the stage throughout the play and presents the most violent challenge to the spectator's imagination. If the references to the traitor who is executed in the wings were totally omitted, the overall impression of the play would not be greatly affected. These references seem, indeed, to have been added almost as an afterthought, and are by no means as central to the main action of the play as the repression of the revolution and the defeat of Roger are to the plot of *The Balcony*. From this point of view, *The Blacks* is certainly a less unified play than either *The Maids* or *The Balcony*. It has none of the tightness and economy of construction of the first, and little of the vigorous plot of the second. For all Genet's insistence that nothing is real, there is always something happening in *The Balcony*: clients, policemen, revolutionaries and whores come in with specific plans and definite proposals, and since the Chief of Police is so intensely concerned about his image, the political theme is completely integrated into its general insistence on the importance of imagination. In *The Blacks*, the ceremony tends to lose itself in meandering and inconclusive arguments. There is some magnificent rhetoric in the speech where Félicité evokes 'sulking Africa, wrought of iron, in the fire, Africa of the millions of royal slaves, deported Africa, drifting continent', and some quite funny but untranslatable puns involving the word *noir**. But perhaps because it is primarily a director's play, raw material to be shaped in the theatre into whatever form he may choose, it has none of the intellectual richness and consistency of *The Maids* and *The Balcony*.

CHAPTER TWELVE

THE SCREENS

Les Paravents (*The Screens*) is the only work by Genet whose title refers to its form and not its content. This unaccustomed emphasis seems particularly strange in view of the fact that its political theme is more clearly marked than in any other of his books, and may perhaps have been intended to warn critics against concentrating too much on its highly controversial subject-matter. It is said to have been completed by 1960 and initially to have been rejected by Genet's publisher because of the offence it was likely to cause, and even after it was published in 1961 it was widely considered to be quite impossible to stage. This was partly because of its excessive length, and a private performance of only the first half, given in the Dolmar Rehearsal Rooms in England in July 1964, lasted a full two and a half hours. The play contains one hundred and four different characters, and Genet's stage directions state that the same actor will have to perform several rôles. In fact, the cast list of the production which Jean-Louis Barrault finally presented at the Odéon-Théâtre de France in April 1966 contains the names of sixty-four actors, and there seems to have been no doubling of parts. The play consists of seventeen tableaux, and the change from one setting to another is effected by movable screens which the actors push about, and on which they rapidly sketch the smaller objects needed by any particular scene. This simple device for avoiding lengthy scene changes is what gives the play its title, but not its originality. After all, the idea of actors carrying their own décor has been a commonplace of the theatre for some time, and was used to really striking effect in only two scenes: the evocation of revolutionary violence in Tableau XIII, and the representation

205

of the world of the dead in Tableau XVI. Neither were the play's violence of language and frequent crudity of subject-matter particular novelties either in Genet's own work or in the avant-garde theatre in general. The really controversial aspect of *The Screens* was political, and lay in its treatment of the Algerian war. Barely four years after this war had ended, a play was presented at the National Theatre, at the taxpayer's expense, which depicted the French army as composed of incompetent and attitudinising homosexuals, and one hundred and thirty years of French presence in Algeria as a totally ludicrous experience. The Algerian rebels, it is true, fared little better, and Robert Abirached declared in the *Nouvelle Nouvelle Revue Française* that *The Screens* was 'as offensive for Algerians as for Europeans'. Nevertheless, they were at least shown to be on the winning side, though it was in his attitude towards their victory that Genet indicated, in contrast with *The Blacks*, how he had gone back to rejecting all forms of positive association with any kind of society.

Social

The main story in *The Screens* is a relatively simple one, and concerns a young Algerian called Saïd. When the play opens, he is travelling on foot to marry Leïla, the ugliest girl in the village, who is the only wife he can afford. He seems, in fact, to be marrying her simply through social convention, for he finds her so unattractive that he has to spend large sums of money at the local brothel. His marriage also brings him into so much general contempt that his fellow Arabs refuse to work with him, and he decides to leave Algeria and seek work in France. Either deliberately, because he wanted to steal, or accidentally, because he mistook its colour in the twilight, he takes the coat belonging to one of his fellow workmen, Taleb. When he is arrested and put into prison, Leïla steals in order to be with him, and together they both sink from degradation to degradation. His personal story, however, fades into the background as the revolution grows in importance, and he does not take the centre of the stage again until the very end of the play. What he does is to grow in symbolic stature as a result of the treatment which Genet gives to the Algerian war.

Although Saïd plays no direct part in the revolution, and even works against it by showing the French paratroops the path taken by the Arab patrols, he is nevertheless adopted as its flag by an important group of revolutionary activists. The women of the village maintain, throughout the play, that the revolution can triumph only through the use of violence and evil, and it is because of this insistence that they choose Saïd as their emblem. In this respect, they differ completely from the soldiers in the revolutionary army, whom they accuse of becoming indistinguishable from the French soldiers because of their concern for honour, military discipline and martial glory. The debate between the two sides of the revolution reaches its climax at the end of the play when Ommou, the old woman who perpetuates the tradition of revolutionary extremism, tells Saïd that this revolution has been able to triumph because it had him and Leïla to show it the way of evil. Saïd, however, rejects even this degree of integration with society. Not only does he refuse, on his return to the village, to go and stand by the side of one of the soldiers. He is also the only character in the play not to move into the world of the dead, where all is reconciliation and the political and racial differences which were so important in this life disappear. Almost his last words in the play are: '*A la vieille, aux soldats, à tous, je vous dis merde*' ('I have one thing to say to my old woman, to the soldiers, and to everyone: Up You'). If it is legitimate to interpret Genet's works as fragments of an intellectual and spiritual autobiography, *The Screens* falls into place as his final gesture of defiance. He is, apparently, going back on the identification which he seemed to announce in *The Blacks* between his own situation and that of the newly independent nations. Instead, he is reverting to the solitude and sterility of the man who chooses evil purely for its own sake.

In his programme note to the play, Jean-Louis Barrault

brought out the passive rather than the active significance of Saïd's character when he wrote: '*Conclusion: un ordre ancien, injuste, disparaît. Un ordre nouveau est né. Entre les deux, l'éternelle misère dont on ne s'occupe jamais, qui ne peut avoir recours que dans le Mal.*' ('Conclusion: an old, unjust order, disappears. A new order is born. Between the two, the eternal wretchedness which can have recourse only to Evil.') This is a more moral interpretation than the text of Genet's play can justify, for Saïd is not merely the symbol of all the oppressed and exploited whose interests seem equally neglected by colonial governments and triumphant revolutionaries. He is actively evil, apparently through sheer perversity, for he not only steals and betrays, but also puts out one of Leïla's eyes. Nevertheless, it is the active power of evil which the two women, Kadidja and Ommou, exalt in their advice to the revolutionaries, and which they admire in Saïd. In one of the most powerful scenes of the play, Kadidja utters even in the moment of her death a lyrical invocation to evil as the ultimate source of energy.

> I have not yet finished my work, and the moment has come when death and I must struggle together. Saïd, Leïla, my beloved! You too would tell each other, each evening, of the evil which you had done during the day. You had understood that only this could offer us any hope. Evil, miraculous evil, which still remains when everything else has collapsed, miraculous evil, you will help us. I implore you, I implore you, standing here, upright. Come, Evil, and fertilise my people.

As she lies dying, the Arabs who have thrown in their lot with the revolution dash in one after the other and draw pictures on the screens in order to represent the various atrocities they have committed in the cause of freedom: Lahoussine, the blood of a girl he has raped and killed; M'Hamed, a heart he has torn out; Kader, the hands he has cut off; Azouz, a fire he has started. But this is evil to some purpose, and recalls the message of *The Blacks* in the same way that Félicité's description of her race as '. . . Darkness in person. Not the darkness which is absence of light, but the kindly and terrible Mother who contains light and deeds' is a first version of Kadidja's speech. This aspect of *The Screens* may well be historically accurate. National liberation movements, especially in under-developed countries, commit atrocities to compensate for the technical inferiority of their troops compared to the well-equipped armies belonging to colonial powers, and Genet's account of the Algerian revolution has at least the merit of not blinking this problem. Like Sartre's remark that he 'always refused, during the Algerian war, to put the terrorism of the bomb-attack which was the only weapon at the disposal of the Algerians, on the same level as the actions and exactions of a richly-equipped army of 500,000 men occupying the whole of the country', Genet's presentation of the use which revolutions make of evil and violence is part of an honest account of what revolutions are like. It is also significant that, in *The Screens*, it should be the Algerian women who urge their menfolk on to commit these atrocities. They thus mirror the attitude of the young English ladies who would send their fiancé a white feather if he refused to take part in a nineteenth-century colonial war. The dissension between the women, representing the originally undisciplined upsurge of revolt, and the triumphant revolutionary army, with its cult of discipline and clean living, also reflects what happened in Algeria itself, and entitles the play to be considered as a historical drama. *The Screens* nevertheless differs significantly from *The Blacks* by the attitude which Genet, through the character of Saïd, takes towards these historical events. Like Sartre, he is morally and intellectually prepared to condone all forms of violence committed to bring about the political independence of ex-colonial peoples, and for him, as for Sartre, Gandhi might just as well have never lived. But he no longer sees this struggle as his own. His attitude is the ultimate in existential independence, for as soon as a cause looks as if it might win, even without compromise with bourgeois values, he turns his back on it.

There is, however, a very marked contrast between the

political or biographical considerations to which *The Screens* naturally gives rise and the predominantly unrealistic, a-historical and poetic atmosphere in which Genet wished it to be performed. Like *The Blacks*, the play was directed by Roger Blin, and once again Genet was extremely enthusiastic about the interpretation which his director succeeded in imposing upon the text. While the play was being rehearsed, he wrote Blin a number of letters commenting on the progress which his production was making, and offering his advice. In August 1966, just before *The Screens* had its second triumphant run at the Odéon-Théâtre de France, these letters were published, and probably figure among the most laudatory that a dramatist has ever written to the person responsible for directing one of his plays. 'In *The Blacks*,' wrote Genet, 'where the text was more boldly designed to produce its effects, I found your achievement less surprising. In any case, the success of this play was, I feel, as much my work as yours. The whole success of *The Screens* is your work. If I had thought that the play could be performed, I should have either made it more beautiful—or ruined it completely. Without changing anything in the play, you have taken hold of the difficulty and made it light and easy to handle. It is magnificent. You have my friendship and my admiration.'

There is no doubt that, of all Genet's plays, *The Screens* has proved the greatest success on the stage. Of course, Blin had every possible advantage: a subsidised theatre, with all its technical resources for lighting and stage effects; the best actors in France, including Jean-Louis Barrault, Madeleine Renaud and Maria Casarès; one of the best-known designers, André Acquart, for the costumes and décors; and apparently unlimited financial resources. But he managed to control these advantages while at the same time overcoming the difficulties of Genet's text, and he brought out both the central movement of the play and its various changes of tone. In particular, his control of physical groupings of the actors was excellent, and the photographs included in the *Lettres à Roger Blin* show how well he succeeded in organising the increasing complexity of the various tableaux. Maria Casarès, as the Mother, was superb, and the decision to have Saïd as the only character not elaborately made up brought out all the real torments involved in his pursuit of evil and solitude. Yet in spite of all this—and, indeed, precisely because of the very good timing in the humorous passages—Blin's production did not quite achieve what Genet's letters to him imply is the real essence of the theatre: the abolition of rational communication and its replacement by what Genet, in his very first letter, calls '*une déflagration poétique*'. The final aim of the production, continued Genet, was to create the feeling that the actors and producer 'have worked for the dead and have succeeded'.

The *Lettres à Roger Blin* have the same insistence as Genet's 1954 preface to *The Maids* on the need for the theatre to provide a semi-religious experience and not an expression of ideas or an account of social reality. 'My play is not an apology for treason,' he writes. 'It takes place in the realm where ethics are replaced by theatrical aesthetics ('*où la morale est remplacée par une esthétique de la scène*'), and he recommends Blin to bring all the actors '*vers un théâtre plus hiératique*' ('towards a more hieratic theatre'). Ideally, he continues, he would like to have the lights full on both in the theatre itself and on stage during the whole of the performance. This would lead both actors and spectators to be caught in the same 'conflagration', and prevent them from 'half-hiding from themselves' ('*que nulle par l'on réussisse à s'à demi-dissimuler*'). He clearly expects a very great deal from his actors and his audience, and writes that each actor, however minor his part, should follow the play attentively every night—as Maria Casarès apparently did—instead of spending his time watching the television in the actors' common-room. The letters give the impression that the spectator who succeeded in experiencing genuinely religious fervour in the theatre would emerge from *The Screens* more than purged. He would be exhausted for weeks.

When discussing the designs for the costumes, Genet describes his play as *'cette histoire de cinglés'* ('tale about the mad'), and recommends that André Acquart should find his inspiration for the costumes among the patients in a lunatic asylum. He describes Ommou, who carries on the tradition of violent revolution after Kadidja's death, as a mad woman, and some of the lines which she has to say do carry paradox to the point of total incommunicability. 'Certain truths,' she proclaims, 'cannot be applied, for otherwise they would die. They must live by the song they have become. Long live song!' Genet's overall aim is clearly to make the theatre go back to its Dionysiac stage, and cease to be a primarily verbal exploration of the human condition. Like certain other avant-garde playwrights, he is trying to transform a theatre that has been, in the West, traditionally based upon the idea of communication, into a theatre which fascinates and overwhelms the spectator by the vision which it provides of the incommunicable mysteries of poetry. What he was seeking, he tells Blin, was not *'un spectacle, même beau selon l'habituelle beauté'*, ('not a play, even a beautiful one by conventional standards') but *'un acte poétique'*. And, as the rest of his letters to Blin made clear, his concept of poetry had not really changed since he defined it, in *Our Lady of the Flowers*, as something which 'always pulls the ground away from under your feet and sucks you into the bosom of a wonderful night'.

Overwhelming as *The Screens* was when performed on stage, it did not quite do this. To begin with, the subject matter had too many political connotations. Had Genet set the play in ancient Babylon, he might perhaps have avoided them. As it was, the memory of the real Algeria was always there. Secondly, his actors simply did not have the wide variety of skills which his ideas required. In one of his letters, for example, he complained that the little spray-guns which the actors had been given to sketch their atrocities on the screens were ugly and ridiculous. This was true, but there was no other method available. Had the actors done as he wished, and drawn these atrocities on the screens with chalk, the speed at which they were required to perform would undoubtedly have made them go right through the paper. As it was, they used the spray-guns, and the spectators were brought back to earth by a strong smell of peardrops which gradually spread all over the theatre. This is not to say that *The Screens* always failed to convey those ideas which obviously meant most to Genet himself. The Mallarmean vision of '*ce peu profond ruisseau calomnié la mort*' was very effectively suggested by the scene in which the characters discovered how simple it was to die by bursting through the fragile paper of the screens. The theme of death is prominent in each one of Genet's books, from Divine's funeral in *Our Lady of the Flowers* to the descent of the Chief of Police into his tomb in *The Balcony*, from the execution of Harcamone in *Miracle of the Rose* to Claire's suicide in *The Maids*, and from the murders in *Deathwatch* or *Querelle of Brest* to the false corpse and real execution in *The Blacks*. In *The Screens*, death is present in the very first scenes when the Mother, because of Saïd's crimes, is rejected by the other women of the village as a mourner at the funeral of Si Slimane, the militant revolutionary leader who has just been killed. She goes to see Madani, an old man with the gift of communicating directly with the dead, and whose own voice gradually disappears as he is filled with the presence of Si Slimane. Jean-Louis Barrault's performance in the rôle provided another of the scenes in which Genet's highly original vision of death came over on the stage, and the theatre was then filled with something of the barbaric awe which he was trying to create.

A number of equally effective and noteworthy scenes, however, were much less directly associated with the aesthetic of the theatre as poetic rapture which was outlined in Genet's letters to Roger Blin. Several episodes, for example, are set in the local brothel, and Madeleine Renaud gave a magnificent performance as the senior whore, Warda, whom Saïd had booked as a consolation since the day before his marriage. With twenty-four years' experience, she is endeavouring to reduce herself to the purest essence of whoredom, and her progress is symbolised by the immensely complicated, hieratic costume she wears, as well as by the way she picks her teeth with a large hat-pin. In one respect, Warda is a 'poetic' character through the exaggerated formalism of her dress and her attempt to attain perfection through her art. But in other respects, she and the rest of the whores provide a certain amount of fairly realistic comment on society. Thus a client has insulted Malika, a younger whore, by asking her to undress. This, apparently, is an exclusively Western custom, for in Arab countries prostitution still retains enough of its originally sacred function for the whores to keep their vestments on. The conversation about this strange demand leads to a second piece of social comment when Mustapha, an Arab recently back from France, remarks that the French were 'very upset when they saw us with their whores'. 'Did they let you do anything else?' asks Warda, and her question immediately evokes the whole inferior position of the Arab workers in France. Later in the play, the brothel serves to measure the different stages of the revolution, for the prostitutes become socially acceptable in the first movement of national unity and idealism, only to be reduced to their former despised status when the new authorities take over the reorganisation of the country and establish a regular tariff. The prostitutes, in fact, stand half way between the semi-private vision which Genet expounds in his *Lettres à Roger Blin* and the more immediately accessible historical or political ideas which *The Screens* also offers. Two other groups of characters, the official figures representing French civilisation, and a platoon of paratroops, provide effects even further removed from Genet's official aesthetic.

As in *The Balcony* and *The Blacks*, these official figures are caricatures of the most formal and outdated aspects of Western society. In *The Screens*, they wear costumes reminiscent of the 1840 conquest of Algeria, and Genet explained that this was because he saw the history of Algeria as one continuous moment. Scarcely had the Bey of Algiers struck the French consul with a fan, he declares, than the first cannon-shot was fired and '800,000 *pieds-noirs* were inventing Tixier-Vignancour'. In Blin's production, the principal function of the Academician, the Officer, the General, the Banker and the Vamp was to make the audience laugh. To do this, he merely needed to follow Genet's text, for the following dialogue was performed in its entirety:

> *The Banker:* The sands of the desert are not only wide but thick.
>
> *The Academician:* 'The sands of the desert.' That's a fine expression.
>
> *The General* (arm outstretched): Let us carry our conquests and our fame for ever further south. And further southward still, our territories in the Sahara. One day, it will be our Beauce.
>
> *The Academician:* And Chartres standing out far off upon the horizon. I can see its stained-glass windows glinting in the sunlight. And processions of young Muslim pilgrims reading Péguy in the original. (A sudden glint in his eye.) Ah, General, the young Muslim between fifteen and seventeen! (He clicks his tongue greedily.)
>
> *The Soldier* (looking the General straight in the eye): Be on your guard! You begin with a liking for a young Muslim of fifteen. Three months later, you understand him. Then, you support his demands. And in the end, you betray your own race. (A silence.) That is how it all began.

Laughter was similarly evoked in another scene by the Vamp, who replied to a compliment from one of her admirers in a phrase whose meaning and elegance would be equally untranslatable on the English stage: *'C'est ainsi que doit parler dans notre monde un jeune homme quand il bande pour moi.'* In addition to providing laughter, the *notables* also serve to underline, by the emptiness of the ideologies which they represent, the comparative vigour of the revolutionaries. Once again, Genet had his humour well under control, and was using it for a specific purpose. Nevertheless, the link between these particular scenes and the ideals set out in his *Lettres à Roger Blin* was tenuous indeed.

The same is true of his treatment, through the character of the Lieutenant, of the French army in Algeria. This contains some very direct historical comment, for at one point the Lieutenant asks one of his soldiers if he is French. The soldier indicates that he is surprised by the question, and the Lieutenant repeats it by asking if he is an Arab. The ironic reference to *L'Algérie Française* is obvious, and when one of the European land-owners complains that the Army is being too gentle with the Arabs, he too is serving as a mouthpiece for historical comment. The split between the extremist *colons* and the soldiers sent out from France remained an important feature throughout the Algerian rebellion, and it was only sections of the Army which lent support to the more violent settlers. In Genet's play, there are no Frenchman among these Europeans, who consist of an Englishman called Sir Harold and a Dutchman called Monsieur Blankensee. Genet's intention was clearly to satirise general colonial concepts and not specifically French ones. Sir Harold, for example, remarks that if an Arab steals from him, he is not really changing his nature, and tells his native workers that they have come on to his land 'to labour and to learn friendship'. Crude though the satire is, it has its starting-point in the reality of colonialism, and it is significant in several ways that the only aspect of European culture which Genet is able to present convincingly should be its treatment of conquered races.

The Lieutenant also has another idea to represent: that he is, as Genet wrote to Roger Blin, '*le double, lumineux selon l'Occident, de Saïd, ou, si vous voulez, son contraire en tout. L'homme solaire s'opposant au saturnien, même si les solaires nous font chier—et, dans ce cas, c'est nous qui les ferons chier. C'est une belle donzelle en uniforme.*' ('Saïd's twin, seen by the West as a glowing example, or, if you prefer, his opposite in everything. The solar as against the saturnine man, even if men of light give us the shits—and, in this case, we are going to make them shit. He's a lovely girl in uniform.') The

Lieutenant did, in fact, wear a dazzling white uniform, but his appeals to his men to shine with the beauty of war—which he described as *'une partouze du tonnerre'* ('the greatest sexual free-for-all')—became highly ironic as the men grew more and more dishevelled in their defeat. Curiously enough, Genet made only the briefest mention of the tortures for which the French paratroops in Algeria were notorious, and was clearly much more interested, for once in his work, in showing homosexuality sublimated into an apparently non-sexual attitude: the cult of military glory. Because the Lieutenant, in the best traditions of sublimation, seems totally unaware of his queerdom, he is one of the most magnificently comic of all Genet's homosexual creations, worthy to take his place in French literature by the side of the Baron de Charlus or the Abbé Carlos Herrera, alias Jacques Collin, alias Vautrin.

It was, however, less the life of the Lieutenant which led to what the critics called *'le scandale des Paravents'* than the manner of his death. The Lieutenant is shot, and his men, unable to offer him the scent of burning candles, the blessèd box-wood, *'le testament déchiré, une chambre mortuaire posée là, comme un nuage dans un tableau de Murillo'* ('his will torn across, and a death chamber placed there like a cloud in a Murillo painting'), decide to give him, by breaking wind over his face, the one memory of France that they can still provide. Farting clearly exercises a kind of fourth-form fascination on Genet, and recurs in a number of contexts in his novels. Querelle breaks wind in the direction of Lieutenant Seblon, the prison chaplain in *Pompes Funèbres* is *'atteint d'aérophagie'*, and when Riton farts in the presence of the German soldiers he thinks that, as foreigners, they may not understand. In *The Screens*, it seems to have been this particular scene that provoked the riots which broke up certain performances, and compelled Jean-Louis Barrault to offer free seats to the huskier members of the left-wing student community so that they could act as a *service d'ordre*. In his letters to Roger Blin, Genet insisted on retaining this scene, and justified it by a variant on Montaigne's remark that '*les dames chient et les rois aussi*'. He did not actually make the defence which could have followed logically from a scene in *The Thief's Journal* and which would consist of saying that acts express reverence by their intention rather than by their nature. As far as the public and critics were concerned, the scene provided a focal point for all the protests made against the play, and Georges Portal summed up these protests when he wrote, in *Ecrits de Paris*: '*Mais ceci, comme disait le vieux poète, est la conséquence de cela. Il fallait commencer par ne pas abandonner l'Algérie*' ('But this, as the old poet said, is the consequence of that. We ought to have started by refusing to give up Algeria'). De Gaulle, it was alleged in *Combat*, had allowed *The Screens* to be performed while at the same time banning the film of Diderot's *La Religieuse* because the Church had lent him its support during his attempts to end the Algerian war while sections of the Army had proved disloyal. To such subtle considerations did Genet's apparent concern for a totally poetic theatre lead in the French press.

Had *The Screens* conformed to the aesthetic sketched out in the *Lettres à Roger Blin*, it would neither have caused a scandal nor been a particularly interesting play. Genet is always a better writer than his formal aesthetic would theoretically allow, and the interest of *The Screens*, like that of his other novels and plays, goes far beyond the neo-surrealistic, Cocteau-esque quaintness that his various definitions of poetry present as his aim. It is not that his theories play no part in his achievement, for this stems from the tension between his acute awareness of things as they are and this highly idiosyncratic, poetic vision. Presented as realism or even as conscious farce, *The Balcony* or *The Screens* would be theatrical disasters. As experiments in a kind of poetic realism, where nothing is as it seems and yet still expresses what it is, they are extraordinary examples of an author communicating on his terms because he succeeds, for the time the play lasts, in imposing them on his audience.

But this imposition is possible only because his subject-matter mirrors the concerns of his readers at the same time as his attitude towards it constitutes a complete defiance of their values.

Acknowledgements

I SHOULD like to thank Anthony Blond and Faber and Faber for permission to quote from the English translations which they have published of Genet's work, and W. H. Allen for permission to quote from *Saint Genet, actor and martyr*. I am also most grateful to Mr. Blond and to Faber and Faber for allowing me to consult their press cuttings on Genet.

In preparing this study, I received invaluable help from the staff of a number of libraries: The *Bibliothèque Nationale* and the *Bibliothèque de l'Arsenal* in Paris, the British Museum Reading Room in London, and the Brotherton Library of the University of Leeds. Mrs. Claire Warwick and Mr. Derek Turton helped me to verify certain points when I could not get to Paris, and Mr. William Johnson provided information about the production of Genet's plays in America. Mrs. Lorraine Winter showed exemplary care and patience in preparing the typescript for the press. Needless to say, I myself am alone responsible for any omissions and inaccuracies, and should be most grateful to any reader who can provide corrections or offer further information on any of the points raised in this book.

Productions of Genet's Plays

Les Bonnes (The Maids).

1. *Théâtre de l'Athénée.* Double bill with Giraudoux's *L'Apollon du Bellac.* April 19, 1947 to October 10, 1947, with a break for the *clôture annuelle* from July 2 to September 24.
   Directed by Louis Jouvet. Solange: Monique Mélinard; Claire: Yvette Etievant; Madame: Yolande Laffon.

2. *Théâtre de la Huchette.* Double bill with Chekhov's *Matinée d'un homme de lettres.* January 14, 1954 to April 6, 1954.
   Directed by Tania Balachova. Solange: Tania Balachova; Claire: Tatiana Moukhine or Anne Reiberg; Madame: Alberte Tailhade.

3. *Odéon-Théâtre de France.* Double bill with Ionesco's *Amédée ou comment s'en débarrasser.* Part of a series of productions to illustrate *Le théâtre nouveau,* which lasted from May 5, 1961 to July 3, 1961.
   Directed by Aldo Bruzzichelli and Jean-Marie Serreau. Solange: Reine Courtois; Claire: Tatiana Moukhine; Madame: Yvonne Clech.

4. *Gaité-Montparnasse.* Double bill with Ionesco's *Le Tableau.* From June 26, 1963 to July 26, 1963. Followed by 30 *représentations exceptionnelles* at the *Théâtre de l'Oeuvre* from August 22, 1963.
   Directed by Jean-Marie Serreau. Solange: Danielle van Berchyche. Claire: Morena Casamance. Madame: Toto Bissaminthe.

London.

1. In French. *Mercury Theatre, Notting Hill Gate.* October 29, 1952. Then at the *Royal Court* on November 11, 1952.
   Directed by Peter Zadek. Solange: Selma Vaz Diaz. Claire: Olive Gregg. Madame: Oriel Ross. In the Royal Court performances, the part of Madame was played by Betty Stockfield.

2. In English. *New Lindsey Theatre Club,* June 5, 1956.
   Directed by Peter Zadek. Solange: Selma Vaz Diaz. Claire: Hazel Penwarden. Madame: Betty Stockfield.

3. Broadcast on BBC Third Programme, June 4, 1963.
   Solange: Brenda Bruce. Claire: Sian Phillips. Madame: June Tobin.

Haute Surveillance (Deathwatch).

1. *Théâtre des Mathurins.* Double bill with Feydeau's *Léonie est en avance ou le Mal Joli.* February 26, 1949 to April 5, 1949.

Directed by the author. Yeux-Verts: Tony Taffin. Lefranc: Robert Hossein. Maurice: Claude Romain. Le Surveillant: Jean-Marc Lambert.

2. *Arts Theatre, London.* One performance, on the evening of Sunday June 25, 1961.
Directed by Ronald Hayman. Green Eyes: Jon Rollason. Lefranc: Philip Locke. Maurice: David Andrews. Guard: Walter Hall.

3. Filmed independently and presented at the San Francisco Film Festival in 1965.
Directed by Vic Morrow from an adaptation by Vic Morrow and Barbara Turner. Green Eyes: Michael Forest. Lefranc: Leonard Nimoy. Maurice: Paul Mazursky.

Le Balcon (The Balcony).

1. *Arts Theatre, London.* April 22, 1957.
Directed by Peter Zadek. Madame Irma: Selma Vaz Diaz.

2. *Théâtre du Gymnase.* May 18, 1960. For a series of 50 performances.
Directed by Peter Brook. Madame Irma: Marie Bell.

3. *Circle in the Square Theatre,* New York. February 28, 1960 to December 31, 1961.
Directed by José Quintero.

4. *Théâtre des Nations,* Paris. Four performances, on 6, 7, 8, 9 of July, 1961, by the Volkstheater of Vienna.
Directed by Léon Epp.

5. Broadcast on BBC Third Programme, November 20, 1964.

6. Filmed by British Lion, 1963. X certificate.
Directed by Joseph Strick from the screenplay by Bed Maddow. Madame Irma: Shelley Winters.

Les Nègres (The Blacks).

1. *Théâtre de Lutèce,* October 28, 1959 to April 4, 1960. Revived at the *Renaissance—Véra Korène,* December 16, 1960 to January 15, 1961.
Directed by Roger Blin and performed by the Compagnie des Griots. Décor and costumes: André Acquart.

2. *St. Mark's Playhouse,* New York. May 4, 1961 to September 27, 1964.
Directed: Gene Frankel. Sets: Kim Swados. Costumes: Pat Zipprodt.

3. *Royal Court Theatre*, London, May 30, 1961. 40 performances. Directed by Roger Blin. Décor and costumes by André Acquart.

Les Paravents (The Screens).

1. *Schlosspark State Theatre*, West Berlin, June 1961.
2. *Donmar Rehearsal Rooms*, May 4, 1964. The first twelve scenes performed by members of the Royal Shakespeare Company Experimental Theatre Group. Directed by Peter Brook in collaboration with Charles Mankowitz.
3. *Odéon-Théâtre de France.* Twenty performances between April 16 to May 7, 1966, followed by 20 performances from September 16, 1966 to October 1966. Directed by Roger Blin. Costumes and décor by André Acquart. Saïd: Amidou. La Mère: Maria Casarès. Warda: Madeleine Renaud. Si Slimane (Madani: La Bouche): Jean-Louis Barrault.

Bibliography of editions of Genet's work used in preparing this study

A. PROSE WORKS PUBLISHED IN UNRESTRICTED EDITIONS

1. *Oeuvres Complètes*. Volume II, Gallimard, 1951. 402 pages. Contains: *Notre-Dame-des-Fleurs, Le Condamné à mort, Miracle de la Rose* and *Un Chant d'amour*. Volume III, Gallimard, 1953. 350 pages. Contains *Pompes Funèbres, Le Pêcheur du Suquet* and *Querelle de Brest*. (Volume I of Genet's *Oeuvres Complètes* consists of Jean-Paul Sartre's *Saint Genet, comédien et martyr*, Gallimard, Paris, 1952. 573 pages. This was translated into English by Bernard Frechtman and published under the title of *Saint Genet, actor and martyr* by W. H. Allen and Company, London, 1964. 625 pages.)

2. *Journal du Voleur*. Gallimard, 1949. 286 pages.

3. *Lettres à Roger Blin*. Gallimard, 1966. 69 pages, 36 photographs.

B. PROSE WORKS PUBLISHED PRIVATELY OR IN LIMITED EDITIONS

1. *Notre Dame des Fleurs*.[1] *Au dépens d'un amateur*. Monte Carlo. No date. 265 pages. *Justification du tirage: Il a été tiré de cet ouvrage trois cent cinquante exemplaires numérotés de 1 à 350, qui constituent l'édition originale. Ce tirage est réservé uniquement aux souscripteurs.'*

2. *Notre Dame des Fleurs*. Barbezat, Lyon, 1948. 411 pages. *Justification du tirage: 'Achevé d'imprimer le trente août mil neuf cent quarante-huit*

Notre Dame des Fleurs
de
Jean Genet

composé en caractères romain Bodoni de corps douze, a été tiré sur la presse à bras de Marc Barbezat, à Lyon, 8 rue Godefroy, à un nombre limité d'exemplaires in-seize Jésus sur papier pur fil Lana filigrané "L'Arbalète", réservés aux souscripteurs.'

---

[1] The printing *'Notre-Dame-des-Fleurs'* does not appear until the 1951 Gallimard edition. The first edition reads *Notre Dame des Fleurs*. The 1951 Gallimard edition also offers the printing *Notre-Dame des Fleurs* on the cover.

3. *Our Lady of the Flowers.* Translated by Bernard Frechtman. Morihien, Paris 1949. 394 pages. Printed for the Editions Morihien, Paris, April 30, 1949, by the Imprimerie Union. There have been issued five hundred copies of *Our Lady of the Flowers*, twenty-five of which are on Rives paper. All copies are reserved for subscribers.

4. *Notre-Dame-des-Fleurs.* L'Arbalète 1966. 109 pages. *Mis en page par Marc Barbezat à Décines (Isère), a été imprimé en mars 1966 à Lyon sur bouffant Alfa pour L'Arbalète.* (This edition gives precisely the same text as the privately printed French editions listed above but was put openly on sale in Paris.)

5. *Miracle de la Rose.* Barbezat, Lyon, 1946. 537 pages. *Justification du tirage:* '*Achevé d'imprimer le 30 mars mil neuf cent quarante-six,* Miracle de la Rose *de Jean Genet, composé en caractères romain Bodoni de corps dix-huit, a été tiré sur la presse à bras de Marc Barbezat, à Lyon, 8 rue Godefroy, à quatre cent soixante quinze exemplaires in-quarto coquillle sur pur fil Rives filigrané L'* "*Arbalète*", *et numérotés de 1 à 475 tous réservés aux souscripteurs.*'

6. *Miracle de la Rose.* Barbezat, Lyon, 1956. 484 pages. *Justification du tirage:* '*Achevé d'imprimer le vingt janvier mil neuf cent cinquante-six la seconde édition du*

Miracle de la Rose

de Jean Genet dont l'édition originale parut en mil neuf cent quarante-six à l'Arbalète. Composée en caractères Bodoni corps 12 a été tiré à Décines Isère sur la presse de Marc Barbezat sur pur fil Lana in-seize Jésus filigrané "L'Arbalète" à deux cents exemplaires de presse et deux mille exemplaires réservés aux souscripteurs numérotés de 1 à 2000'. (This edition follows the standard Gallimard text, not the original).

7. Jean Genêt (sic.) *Pompes Funèbres.* '*A Bikini aux dépens de quelques amateurs MCMXLVII.*' 311 pages. *Justification du tirage: Il a été tiré de cet ouvrage quatre cent soixante-dix exemplaires justifiés comme suit: vingt exemplaires sur murier d'Annam, numérotés de 1 à 20 et quatre cent cinquante exemplaires sur vélin pur fil de Lana, à la forme, de 21 à 470; en outre, vingt-cinq exemplaires réservés dont cinq sur vélin pur fil de Lana, à la forme, de VI à XXV.*'

8. *Querelle de Brest.* 1947. 250 pages. *Justification du tirage:* '*Achevé d'imprimer en décembre 1947 et tiré à mille cent cinquante exemplaires.*'

9. *Journal du Voleur. Aux dépens d'un ami.* 310 pages. *Justification du tirage:* '*Il été tiré de cet ouvrage dix exemplaires sur vélin teinté à la forme des paperies d'Arches, numérotés de I à X; quatre cents exemplaires sur vélin à la forme des papetries de Lana, numérotés de 1 à 400.*' (Slightly different from the openly published Gallimard edition.)

10. *L'Enfant Criminel et 'Adame Miroir.* Paul Morihien, 1949. 51 pages.

11. *L'Atelier d'Alberto Giacometti, Les Bonnes, l'Enfant Criminel, Le Funambule.* Barbezat, 1958.

12. *L'Atelier d'Alberto Giacometti.* Barbezat, 1963. Not paginated. 33 photographs.

C. TEXTS OF PLAYS

1. *Haute Surveillance.* Gallimard, 1949. 135 pages.

2. *Haute Surveillance.* Gallimard, 1965. 97 pages. *Edition définitive.*

3. *Les Bonnes.* Preceded by *Comment jouer 'Les Bonnes'.* Barbezat, 1963. 93 pages.

4. *Les Bonnes. Pièce en un acte. Les deux versions précédées d'une Lettre de l'auteur.* Jean-Jacques Pauvert. À Sceaux, 1954. 149 pages. Edition limited to 2000 copies. Contains the text performed at the *Théâtre de l'Athénée* in 1946 and the text performed at the *Théâtre de la Huchette* in 1954.

5. *Le Balcon.* Barbezat, 1962. 205 pages. The *justification du tirage* for this volume reads: '*Achevée d'imprimer le dix mars mil neuf cent soixante-deux sur les presses d'Audin à Lyon d'après Marc Barbezat en Bodoni. Les lettres de la couverture d'Alberto Giacometti. L'édition troisième et définitive en 9 tableaux du balcon de Jean Genet a été tirée sur bouffant Alfa pour l'Arbalète de Marc Barbezat Editeur à Décines (Isère).*' There were, in fact, earlier editions of *Le Balcon* in 1956 and 1960.

6. *Les Nègres. (Clownerie.) Pour jouer 'Les Nègres'.* Barbezat, 1963. The *justification du tirage* runs: '*La troisième édition des* Nègres *de Jean Genet précédée de "Pour jouer* Les Nègres" *illustrée de 33 photo-graphies prises au Théâtre de Lutèce par Ernest Scheidegger et mise en page Marc Barbezat a été imprimée sur bouffant Alfa en août MCMLXIII sur les presses d'Audin à Lyon pour l'Arbalète de Marc Barbezat à Décines (Isère).*' As in the case of *Le Balcon,* two earlier editions of *Les Nègres* had appeared, in 1958 and 1960.

7. *Les Paravents.* Barbezat, 1961. 260 pages.

D. WORKS BY GENET AVAILABLE IN ENGLISH TRANSLATION

1. *Our Lady of the Flowers.* Translated by Bernard Frechtman. Anthony Blond, 1964. 318 pages. With a preface by Jean-Paul Sartre. Published as a Panther book in 1966.

2. *Miracle of the Rose.* Translated by Bernard Frechtman. Anthony Blond, 1965. 291 pages.

3. *The Thief's Journal.* Translated by Bernard Frechtman. Anthony Blond, 1965. 240 pages. Published in Penguin Modern Classics, 1967.

4. *Querelle of Brest.* Translated by Gregory Streatham. Anthony Blond, 1966. 320 pages.

5. *The Maids.* Translated by Bernard Frechtman. Faber and Faber, 1957. 43 pages.

6. *The Balcony.* Translated by Bernard Frechtman. Faber and Faber, 1958. 112 pages. Revised edition, 1966. 112 pages.

7. *The Blacks.* Translated by Bernard Frechtman. Faber and Faber, 1960. 96 pages.

8. *Deathwatch.* Translated by Bernard Frechtman. Faber and Faber, 1961. 40 pages.

9. *The Screens.* Translated by Bernard Frechtman. Faber and Faber, 1963. 176 pages.

E. POETRY

A number of different editions of Genet's poetry have been published. In 1966, a volume entitled *Poèmes* was published by Marc Barbezat, and includes all the individual poems listed as appearing elsewhere.

F. CRITICAL STUDIES

In addition to Sartre's essay, the following critical studies of Genet's work have been published:

1. Joseph H. McMahon. *The Imagination of Jean Genet.* Yale Romanic Studies, 1963. 263 pages. Contains a critical bibliography.

2. Claude Bonnefoy. *Genet. Classiques du XXᵉ siècle.* Editions universitaires, 1965. 126 pages.

3. Jean-Marie Magnan. *Pour un blason de Jean Genet.* Number 148 in the series *Poètes d'aujourd'hui.* Seghers, 1966. 187 pages.

4. T. F. Driver. *Jean Genet.* Columbia Essays on Modern Writers. 1966. 48 pages.

5. R. N. Coe. *The Vision of Jean Genet.* Peter Owen, 1968. This study also contains an excellent critical bibliography.

Notes and References

The following abbreviations are used:

SG—*Saint Genet, comédien et martyr.*
NDF—*Notre-Dame-des-Fleurs.*
MR—*Miracle of the Rose.*
PF—*Pompes Funèbres.*
QB—*Querelle de Brest.*
JV—*Journal du Voleur.*
HS—*Haute Surveillance.*
Par.—*Les Paravents.*
Tr.—Translated by.

Unless otherwise stated, all quotations are from the standard Gallimard edition and from the translations of Genet's work published by Anthony Blond and Faber and Faber.
Saint Genet, actor and martyr is quoted in the translation published by W. H. Allen.

CHAPTER I

Page 3. Genet's birth—JV 46. Tr. 38. Joseph H. McMahon writes on page 1 of his *The Imagination of Jean Genet* that there are 'various editions and critical articles attributing different birth-dates to this enigmatic man'. However, he does not say what these birth-dates are or where they are mentioned.

The dream—JV 219, Tr. 184.

Foster-mother stealing—JV 238, Tr. 200. Sartre is probably referring to this episode when he writes ironically (SG 18, Tr. 11): 'Moreover, his foster-mother wasn't shy about filching. She was an "honest woman", of course, and remained honest while stealing. Honesty is an eternal essence which is not dimmed by accidental lapses.'

Page 4. What were described as extracts from the *Journal du Voleur* appeared in No. 10 of *Les Temps Modernes*, July 1946, pp. 33–56. The passage translated here is on page 41, and it is perhaps also significant that it had already been omitted by the time these same extracts appeared in translation in No. 4 of *Transition* (January 1949, pp. 66–75).

Page 5. Stole to eat—JV 13, Tr. 10.

Playboy—the interview with Genet is in Vol. 11, no. 4, April 1964, pp. 25–55. According to Jean-Marie Magnan, *Pour un blason de Jean Genet*, the interview was given on the insistence of Simone de Beauvoir.

Sartre on the Negro—see *Orphée noir*, *Les Temps Modernes*, October 1948, page 582. On SG 192, Tr. 203, Sartre specifically compares Genet's situation to that of the Jew.

Genet's dignity—SG 60, Tr. 55; deeply admire—SG 55, Tr. 49.

To give up stealing—*Les Temps Modernes*, July 1946, page 50.

Not interested in how taste for theft originated—*Les Temps Modernes*, July 1946, page 41.

Page 6. Little pilferer—SG 68, Tr. 64.

Simple-minded, theological—SG 56, Tr. 51.

Sartre, original event—SG 12, Tr. 5.

Genet's entry to Mettray—MR 233, Tr. 66.

Page 7. Placed under psychiatric observation—SG 239, Tr. 254.

Gouging out an eye—MR 341, Tr. 216. Also referred to in NDF 152, Tr. 283; *Nègres*, 72, Tr. 40; Par. 201; QB 286, Tr. 200.

Laziness and daydreaming—JV 47, Tr. 39.

The details about the foundation of Mettray are taken from two brochures, both of which are in the British Museum reading room. The first is entitled *Fondation de la Colonie Agricole de jeunes détenus* (Benjamin Dupont, Paris, 1839), and the second *Notice sur la Colonie Agricole de Mettray* (Paris, 1861). The modern reference to Mettray is taken from page 351 of Walter C. Reckless, *Criminal Behaviour*, McGraw-Hill, 1940. Alexis Danan's articles appeared in *Paris-Soir* in October and November 1934 under the general title of *Bagnes d'enfants*. On November 23rd, Mettray was described as 'a private institution—of tortures', and Danan alleged that one member of the staff was himself a former convict. He also pointed out that the work which the boys did in the fields made a handsome profit for the share-holders.

Courteilles a baron—MR 322, Tr. 190. Genet spells the name Courteille.

Page 8. Dates for Genet at Mettray—thus if he was 15 years seventeen days old, and was born on December 19, 1910, he entered the *colonie* in January 1926. MR 369, Tr. 254 says that he spent three Julys at Mettray. On JV 48, Tr. 39, he says that he ran away in order to enlist. Genet meeting Danan—details of this are given on page 457 of the 1946 edition of MR but omitted from the Gallimard edition.

The collection of letters from former inmates at Mettray was entitled *Maisons de supplices* and published by Denoël and Steele, Paris, 1936.

Mettray a paradise—MR 220, Tr. 49. Mentioning the same
names—page 457 of the 1946 edition of MR and page 168 of *Maisons
de supplices* both speak of a physical training instructor called Guépin.
Idiotic vandals—MR 308, Tr. 170.

Page 9. Jean Cau's portrait of Genet was published in *L'Express* on
5/11/59. Genet himself refers to stealing the luggage belonging to a
Negro officer in JV 48, Tr. 39. Page 157 of *Par.* (Tr. 105) where the
sergeant tells the lieutenant that he feels stupid when standing to
attention, may refer to the incident related by Jean Cau.
Marseilles—JV 175, Tr. 147.
Hitler's Germany—JV 131, Tr. 110–111.

Page 10. Meeting Guy—JV 60, Tr. 50.
Good, honest robbery—MR 206, Tr. 28.
Aged 26—SG 373, Tr. 402.
Aged 23—JV 190, Tr. 160.
Never caught *en flagrant délit*—JV 100, Tr. 84.
Police too powerful—PF 129.

Professional criminologists—thus Paul Reiwald, in his *Society and
its Criminals* (International Universities Press, Inc., New York, 1950)
states on page 138 that in all the analyses so far made of criminals
'we encounter the same description of a pitiful type, for the most part
psychopathic and lacking in real energy', and W. H. J. Sprott,
writing in *The Listener* on May 12, 1966 on *The Social Background of
delinquency*, remarks that 'studies of persistent offenders have revealed
that they are not, on the whole, competent, hardened professional
criminals, but a hopeless, inadequate lot, who drift through life,
committing petty offences, spending a large proportion of their lives
in prison, where they become even more inadequate to cope with
life'. A survey in Wakefield prison in 1948, reported in *The British
Journal of Delinquency* No. 1, page 23, came to the conclusion that
'really intelligent men are rare' in prison, and this is certainly the
impression given by Genet's novels. In *The Bookseller* for February
23, 1957, Mr. Denis Howell was reported as saying that a full critical
analysis of the relevance of Genet's work to the social problems of
crime, written by a Mr. John Croft of the Home Office, had been
published in *The British Journal of Delinquency*. I have been unable to
find such an article, and should be most grateful for any further
information. See also *Hansard*, Vol. 565, pp. 166–176.

Page 11. Professional song writer—SG 395, Tr. 426.
Taught him rules of versification—Bonnefoy, *Jean Genet*, Editions
Universitaires, 1965, page 93.
First poetry booed—SG 399–400. Tr. 431–432.
Le Condamné à mort—a copy of this poem is in the *Bibliothèque*

Nationale, and the publication date reads Fresnes—September 1942. It is printed on rather poor paper, with many misprints, and has a note saying that the corrections are in Genet's own hand. It follows the same text as *Oeuvres Complètes,* Vol. II, pp. 179–196. There is no indication of who printed or published it.

Maurice Pilorge—see *L'Oeuvre* 5/2/39, '*Maurice Pilorge a payé sa dette avec un sourire.*' His execution had had to be delayed for twenty-four hours because the public executioner, Anatole Deibler, died of a heart attack in the Métro on February 3rd. Again according to *L'Oeuvre,* Deibler had executed 400 people during his long period of office. *Détective,* on March 30, 1939, said that his victims numbered 299, and that he had held office since 1899. *L'Oeuvre* did not confirm all the details which Genet gives about Pilorge—NDF 10, Tr. 61 'he killed his lover, Escudero, to rob him of something under one thousand francs'—but it does point out (7/2/39) that he was sentenced to five years' imprisonment for another crime two days after he had been executed. The amount of space devoted to Pilorge and other criminals in *L'Oeuvre* illustrates the kind of fame which the popular press undoubtedly did give to criminals in the Third Republic. At the beginning of NDF, Genet speaks of the enthusiasm with which criminals circulated such newspapers, and cut out the photographs of the more notorious characters.

Page 12. Composition of NDF—SG 415, Tr. 447 and the *Playboy* interview. At the end of the novel, Genet says he wrote it in Fresnes prison, but on p. 59, Tr. 125, and JV 81, Tr. 152 at La Santé.

Cocteau, *La Difficulté d'Etre,* Morihien, 1947, footnote to page 267. I have not been able to find any references in the French newspapers of the time to the comments which this intervention by Cocteau on Genet's behalf is said to have evoked. Cocteau says that '*Les journaux d'Occupation en firent de gorges chaudes*', but mentions none of these newspapers by name. The article in *Poésie* 43, no. 15, July-September 1943, pages 74–75, says that Cocteau's intervention was reported in *Comoedia. Poésie* also referred to a rumour that Genet had submitted 'a remarkable essay, which unfortunately could not be published because of its cynicism,' to a Paris publisher.

Page 13. Simone de Beauvoir—*La Force de l'Age,* Gallimard, 1960. Pages 594–595.

For details of the first editions of Genet's work, see the Bibliography on page 227.

La Table Ronde, Troisième Cahier, pages 157–167.

Pompes Funèbres—Les Temps Modernes, no. 3, 1945, pages 405–419.

Journal du Voleur—Les Temps Modernes, no. 10, pages 33–56. See

Poésie 46, no. 35, page 145 and SG 164, Tr. 172. Unfortunately, Sartre does not say which surrealist writers protested and where their objections were published.

Page 14. Publication of MR—these details are given on a small slip of paper inside the copy of the 1946 edition which can be consulted in the *Enfer* of the *Bibliothèque Nationale*. This slip of paper also has the following passages from Sartre, which does not appear in SG: '"Since you are not a homosexual, how can you like my books?" asks Genet with his feigned naivety. It is because I am not a homosexual that I like them: pederasts are afraid of this violent, ceremonious work, in which Genet, using long, magnificent, highly decorated sentences, follows his vice right through to the end, making it into an instrument with which to explore the world, and, at the end of this haughty confession, into a passion. Proust presented homosexuality as a fate imposed upon men, Genet demands it as a choice. Everything is choice, in *Miracle of the Rose*, the events and the surprising order of the narration: the author has chosen theft and prison, he has chosen love and chosen to maintain awareness in the midst of Evil (*"la conscience dans le Mal"*). He touches lightly on his subject, he flaunts his own nature, and yet never abandons himself completely: his art lies in holding his readers at a distance. Thanks to this, what we find in the depths of this far-off world, in the hell of warders, cracksmen and punishment cells, is a man.'

Regret at loss of German soldiers—MR 356, Tr. 237.

'Adame Miroir. Genet's own scenario for this ballet was published by Paul Morihien in the same volume as *L'Enfant criminel* in 1949. Its title is a deformation, in Paris slang, of *Madame Miroir*, and it tells of a sailor who dances his own death. As he does so, other dancers imitate his movements, and thus show him to be a prisoner in a hall of mirrors. The original inspiration for this ballet comes from an incident described in JV 282 Tr. 237–238.

Robert Kemp—*Le Monde*, April 24, 1947. He remarked that Courteline would have split his sides with laughter.

Thierry Maulnier—*Le Spectateur* April 27, 1947. Thierry Maulnier was also editor of *La Table Ronde* when it published *La Galère*. He is referred to in *La Revue de Paris*, June 1966, pages 131–134 as having been one of the first, with Roland Laudenbach, to discover Genet. Laudenbach is a well-known theatrical director, who has often worked with Jean Anouilh. Unlike many of Genet's admirers, Thierry Maulnier tends to be conservative in his political views.

Last of the Court poets—*Transition*, no. 4, January 1949, page 152. The same number of *Transition* published Bernard Frechtman's translation of extracts from *The Thief's Journal*. It also contained a full-page advertisement for the privately printed translation of *Our Lady of the Flowers* which Paul Morihien was about to publish. The advertisement carried the following opinions of Jean-Paul Sartre and Jean Cocteau. Sartre: 'French literature is known abroad chiefly in its universalistic, rationalist and humanistic aspect. But it should not be forgotten that it has been marked since its origins with works that are secret and black—in the sense of black magic—and these are perhaps its most beautiful. From the poems of Villon to the works of Sade, Rimbaud and Lautréamont they bear witness of our guilty conscience. It is not sure whether Jean Genet, the latest of these "magicians", is not also the greatest'. Cocteau: 'Jean Genet is a great poet. He is the psychologist of people who do not think and whose darkness lives outside the very pure night which inhabits them. He thinks for them and even thinks them and never thinks them through his own person. Furthermore, he is a moralist in the fullest sense of the term. (A moralist is not to be confused with a man who moralises.) Genet is of a morality severe and inflexible from which he never departs'. The advertisement declared that the 'appearance of this edition will mark an event equal in importance to the Paris production of James Joyce's *Ulysses* in the twenties and Henry Miller's *Tropic of Cancer* in the thirties'. The book cost 15 dollars or three guineas.

Page 15. Simone de Beauvoir, *La Force des Choses*, Gallimard, 1963, page 90. '*Et par-dessus le marché*', Genet said, '*vos employés se permettent de me traiter d'enculé*'.

Genet's own admiration for the *Milice*—PF 51.

Sartre's denial that he actually joined—SG 116, Tr. 119, footnote: 'This quite platonic admiration was not, of course, followed by any actual enlistment.' Simone de Beauvoir, *Force des Choses* page 2, also declares that Genet had no real sympathy for the Germans.

Hoodlums of the worst sort—NDF 56, Tr. 134.

Haute Surveillance—published in *La Nef*, March 1947, pages 97–112. April 1947, pages 92–112.

Originally called *Préséances*—G. Joly in *l'Aurore*, March 4, 1949, who refers to a note in the programme on sale in the theatre.

Page 16. Jean-Jacques Gautier on HS—*Le Figaro*, March 4, 1949.
Marchat's reply—*Le Figaro*, March 7, 1949.

Page 17. To read Genet... spirit of Evil—SG 477, Tr. 517.

Page 18. Difference between first editions and the standard Gallimard text—most of the passages subsequently omitted are, for reasons of good taste if not of censorship, unprintable. It is not difficult for readers to obtain access to the first editions in the *Bibliothèque Nationale*. The 1966 edition of *Notre-Dame-des-Fleurs* reproduces the first edition in its entirety. In particular (p. 37), it gives the same details about Notre-Dame's mother—'*une frutière de la rue Lepic*'—and about the general interest which Genet maintains that he himself felt about incest.

André Rousseaux—*Le Figaro littéraire* September 15, 1951.

Page 19. Other critical writing on Genet—thus Claude Bonnefoy begins his study by assuming rather than analysing the literary value of Genet's work: '*Ouvrez ses livres au hasard, entrez dans un théâtre où l'une de ses pièces est représentée, c'est l'évidence; une scène du Balcon rejette dans l'ombre l'oeuvre entière de Marcel Achard, une page de* Notre-Dame-des-Fleurs *décolore le soufre de François Mauriac. L'écrivain Genet est là, irréfutable, maître de sa langue comme on l'était au grand siècle.*' The subtitle of Jean-Marie Magnan's book, *Pour un blason de Jean Genet*, indicates his intention of using Genet's work in order to build up a picture of his personality.

Re-invented literature—SG 407, Tr. 439.

Philip Toynbee—the *Observer*, February 9, 1964.

Page 20. For production details of Genet's plays see page 223.
Genet's plays may have appeared first because of censorship problems. See *Bath Weekly Chronicle*, February 23, 1963.
Birmingham Public Library—see *The Times*, February 4, 1957 and *The Bookseller*, February 23, 1957.

Page 21. Genet's protest over *The Balcony*—see *Picture Post*, May 11, 1957 for the most complete account of this controversy, together with some photographs of the production. For Peter Zadek's reply to Genet, see the *New Statesman*, May 4, 1957, pages 568–569.
Title of *Les Nègres*—see *Les Nègres* page 93, '*Comme dit quelquefois en termes galants notre garde-champêtre: il y fait noir comme dans le trou du cul d'un nègre. —Oh! pardon, d'un Noir. Il faut être polie.*' Tr., page 49, 'As our constable would say, in that roguish way of his, it's as dark here as up a nigger's hole. Oh! I beg your pardon—I mean a negro's. One should be polite.'

Page 22. Publication of English translation—see *London Life*, January 22, 1966, for the statement about Anthony Blond sending 'a list of potential defendants of Genet to the Director of Public Prosecutions before publication.' Mr. Blond has since confirmed this in private conversation.
Mademoiselle, according to Kenneth Tynan's review in the *Observer* on May 15, 1966, was made from 'an old Genet script' and was 'understandably booed' at the Cannes film festival. It was made

both in French and English, and among those working on the English version was David Rudkin, author of *Afore Night Come*. It was directed by Tony Richardson, and shot in a village called Le Rat, in the Corrèze. It was publicly shown in London in Autumn 1966.

The film opens with a shot of a religious procession which resembles the cortèges which 'on Corpus Christi or Rogation Day, went through the blazing noonday countryside' near the village where Divine/Culafroy spent her/his childhood (NDF 69, Tr. 154). However, the procession is interrupted because the village schoolteacher, played by Jeanne Moreau, has opened the dam and flooded the village. She spends her time committing similar acts of apparently wanton destruction, and the implication seems to be that she does so because of an incident in which a man was burned to death in a fire which she had started by accident (for starting fires in which people die, see MR 196, Tr. 14). Because she leads such an apparently blameless life, suspicion falls on an itinerant Italian woodcutter, whose young brother goes to the local school. After favouring this brother to begin with, the schoolmistress turns against him and makes fun of the short trousers which, like Culfaroy (NDF 64/147), he has to wear to come to school. She even tries to attach blame for her destructive acts on to this boy, who is naturally very upset. She poisons the drinking water and makes all the cattle die in agony (for dreams of revenge or suicide by poison see NDF 60 and 64, Tr. 141 and 147), and shows no moral improvement when she eventually frees herself of some of her sexual frustrations during the night in the woods with the Italian woodcutter. He makes her realise what she really wants by showing her some snakes he has caught (for other sexual connotations of the snake motif, see NDF 78, Tr. 169), and during the thunderstorm which accompanies their violent lovemaking, she licks his boots and howls like a dog (for women howling like dogs, see *Les Paravents*, pages 55, 156 and 190). However, when she returns to the village, everyone sympathises with her because they think she has been raped, and a group of men from the village beat the Italian woodcutter to death. When she finally leaves the village, the inhabitants bid her a fond farewell while the little boy looks pitifully at her for one last glance and is totally ignored.

In addition to reproducing the atmosphere of Culafroy's village in NDF, and to containing a large number of Genet's own semi-private obsessions (woodcutters also occur in NDF 20, Tr. 79), *Mademoiselle* is also heavy with the type of obvious symbolism which clearly places it in the same period of Genet's development as *Deathwatch*. The schoolteacher emphasises her sterile and life-denying activity by crushing eggs, stubbing out her cigarette in apple blossom and putting crosses of sticking plaster across her breasts. The film was nevertheless saved from total disaster by Jeanne Moreau's performance and David Watkin's camera work. As Miss Moreau showed in *Moderato Cantabile*, she can make any film worth seeing, and the camera work bore something of the same relation to the plot of *Mademoiselle* as Genet's prose style does to the plot of his novels: it made it credible by its sheer beauty and technical perfection. In an enthusiastic review in the *Observer* on January 15, 1967, Penelope Gilliatt pointed out how the film echoes Genet's own 'rêveries of revenge', and also made another comparison with his novels. 'The tone of *Mademoiselle* is a very alert transposal of the peculiar lordly trance of Genet's style in his novels, which he has the sense to mix with flashes of brusque sense and rudeness. There are funny equivalents of that in the picture: a grumpy married exchange between villagers under umbrellas, and a priest ripe with the gossip of the confessional bawling for order in church like someone running a fête.' In Genet's films, as in his novels and plays, common-sense will keep breaking in.

Page 23. Genet as a critic of *Les Bouches Inutiles—La Force des Choses*, Gallimard, 1963, page 63.

Selling non-existent manuscripts—see *Carrefour*, September 14, 1955.

Cocteau—see Paul Léautaud, *Journal littéraire*, Vol. XVIII, Mercure de France, page 280.

Interview in the *Evening Standard*, June 6, 1957. He also told the *Daily Express* the same thing on June 7, 1957, and added that he had spent four years writing a film script for which the Duke of Edinburgh would be perfect in the leading part. He is obviously fond of choosing heroes for his films, for he is reported in *Carrefour* on February 9, 1955 as having written a play about prison and found a good actor in the person of Pierre Joly, who had a marked resemblance to Marlon Brando.

Candide—April 25, 1966.

CHAPTER II

Page 25. Rimbaud—*Saison en Enfer*, Garnier edition, Paris, 1960, page 216.

Young ensign—JV 53, Tr. 44 gives the name of this officer as Marc Aubert and describes him as 'a star forever extinguished.' A photograph of Aubert was published in *L'Oeuvre* on March 6, 1939, stating that he had been shot at dawn that very day. He was reported in the same newspaper as saying that he loved what he had betrayed, and this remark may well have made an impression on Genet, who in Sartre's view remained deeply attached to the idea of goodness at the very moment that he was defying it. According to *Détective* (March 2, 1939), Aubert had been systematically handing over military secrets to a foreign power.

Death on the scaffold—MR 189, Tr. 6.

Great social movements their origin in evil—MR 210–11, Tr. 35.

Page 26. Similarities with Claudel—see SG pages 114 and 161, Tr. 117 and 168. *La Quinzaine littéraire*, May 15, 1966. *La Ville*, Seconde Version, Mercure de France, 1946, page 203. Claudélise—see *Cahiers des Saisons*, Summer 1966, page 99.

Ontological failure of evil—SG 175, Tr. 183.

Page 27. Making love after burglary—MR 307, Tr. 168. Sex and crime —JV 13, Tr. 10.

Self-condemnation of criminal—QB 212, Tr. 73.

Page 28. Rejection of the glamorous vision of prison—MR 208, Tr. 31. Disillusion in quest for evil—PF 109.

Page 29. Description of Harcamone—MR 217, 259, 309, Tr. 44, 102, 171.

Harcamone a red rose—MR 391, Tr. 285.

Disreputable areas without mystery—JV 249, Tr. 209.

Page 30. Torn apart by—SG 68, Tr. 64.

Page 31. Sartre on the stupidity of Genet's characters—SG 376, Tr. 406 and 455, Tr. 492.

Neo-Freudianism in SG. Although Sartre is for the most part hostile to Freudianism there is a very close similarity between the ideas which he expresses in *Saint Genet* and those put forward by the Freudian Paul Reiwald in his *Society and its criminals*, International Universities Press, Inc., New York, 1950. Thus Mr. Reiwald, who is Reader in Criminology at the University of Geneva, writes on page 236 that 'The criminal is necessary to man, as we have seen. He needs him for emotional reasons. Consequently, he organises the fight against him so that at the same time it serves the purpose of maintaining crime', and on page 217 that 'the devil and the criminal represent the repressed life instincts; they depict that part of the personality that is suppressed in civilised man.' This corresponds very closely to Sartre's argument on SG 30, Tr. 25 that the 'right-thinking man' will 'give the name *temptation* to the live, vague swarming which is still himself, but a "himself" which is wild, free, outside the limits he has marked out for himself', and that what this man calls evil is 'the unity of all his impulses to criticise, to judge, to reject insofar as he refuses to *recognise* them.' When Sartre asks 'Whom does one lynch in the American South for raping a white woman? A Negro?' and replies: 'No. Again oneself. Evil is a projection' (SG 34, Tr. 29) he is again close to Reiwald's view on page 98 that 'the attitude to the criminal is conditioned by the satisfaction of very clear psychic needs of the law-abiding citizen' and that 'mankind has the criminal which it desires and has him for the satisfaction of psychic needs'. Yet although both Reiwald and Sartre agree in seeing the criminal first and foremost as a scapegoat for men's repressed instincts, Sartre does not go so far as to say that 'if it were really only a question of protection and defence of man, the criminal would long since have ceased to exist'. Indeed, he finally praises Genet for re-asserting the 'irreducibility of evil' and the 'poetic truth of crime.' (SG 455/6, Tr. 492/3).

A monster for social convenience—SG 29, Tr. 23.
Genet predestined to be a criminal—SG 36, Tr. 31.

Page 32. Thought by the spirit of evil—SG 477, Tr. 517.
A deliberate damning of the reader—SG 479, Tr. 519.
Average Frenchman—SG 457, Tr. 494.
Description of Divine—NDF 44, Tr. 116.

Page 33. Mignon—NDF 14, Tr. 43 and 29, Tr. 92.
Bulkaen—MR 199, Tr. 18. See Ronsard *Sur la mort de Marie*, Blackwell, 1946, page 108. Frechtman's translation.
Shadowy with grime—MR 201, Tr. 22.

Page 34. Orwell—*Selected Essays*, Penguin, 1957, pages 141–2.

Page 35. Darnan's Milice—PF 51.
Mau Mau—Preface to *Les Bonnes*, Jean-Jacques Pauvert, 1954, page 15.
Hoodlums of the worst sort—NDF 56, Tr. 134.
Orwell—op. cit., page 139.
Sartre's holistic approach to Genet—SG 523, Tr. 569.
Genius a way out one invents—SG 536, Tr. 584.

Page 36. McMahon—op. cit. page 262.
Sartre's disagreement—SG 537, Tr. 585. It might perhaps be noted that these incidents never actually occur in any of Genet's printed works.
Corrosive cynicism—SG 309, Tr. 331.
Everything reduced to images—SG 521, Tr. 567; do evil without resorting to being—SG 479, Tr. 519; see what it's all about—SG 463, Tr. 501; dead leaves—SG 479, Tr. 519.

Page 38. Malraux on Faulkner—see the preface to the 1933 French translation of *Sanctuary* (NRF 1933), in which Malraux argued that the success of the police in arresting criminals depended less upon the intellectual brilliance of the detective than on '*la délation*'. Sartre also recognises this on SG 167, Tr. 175. Vidocq was a criminal who became head of the Paris police.

Epic of masturbation—SG 416, Tr. 448.

Flaubert—SG 419, Tr. 451.

Page 39. Genet's refusal to meet Gide—SG 230, Tr. 244.

See also Cocteau, *La Difficulté d'Etre*, page 267, which does not mention Gide by name.

Willed himself to be—PF 109.

Page 40. Infidelity of homosexuals—NDF 47, Tr. 120.

Genet sold by Villeroy—MR 368, Tr. 254.

Monstrosity of masculine loves—QB 220, Tr. 86.

The Observer, Magazine section, September 30, 1966. *The Spies who came into Camp*.

Page 41. Poetic description of Pilorge—see *Le Condamné à Mort*, *Oeuvres Complètes*, Vol. II, page 179.

Stilitano's cowardice—JV 68, Tr. 57. Divers syphilitic—MR 256, Tr. 98.

Page 42. Male who—NDF 133, Tr. 253. Female without knowing it—SG 127, Tr. 131.

Homosexual through the power of words—SG 463, Tr. 501.

Just man becomes Jean Genet—SG 477, Tr. 517.

Ideal Just does not read—SG 525, Tr. 571.

Page 43. The *Histoire d'O* is widely considered to be a classic of flagellation. It is generally published with an enthusiastic preface by Jean Paulhan, and a sumptuous edition published in the *Cercle du livre précieux* series in 1963 was illustrated by Léonor Fini. Miss Fini also provided the illustrations for the edition of *La Galère* which Genet had published at his own expense in 1947, and designed the sets for the 1961 revival of *Les Bonnes* at the Odéon-Théâtre de France. The *Justification du tirage* for the edition of *La Galère* reads: '*L'Edition originale de* "La Galère", *poème de Monsieur Jean Genet, a été établie par Jacques LOYAU, libraire à Paris, passage des panoramas, et imprimée sur les presses de l'Hôtel de Sagonne, en juillet M. CMXLVII, aux frais de l'auteur.*

Il a été tiré quatre-vingts exemplaires numérotés à la presse, les neuf premiers sur Vergé de Montval, et huit exemplaires de présent.'

Page 44. Sartre on Genet's description of Bulkaen—SG 463, Tr. 500. Worst enemies among homosexuals—SG 463, Tr. 501.

Laclos's consistent viewpoint—thus it does seem, from his essay *De l'Education des Femmes*, that he was a convinced Rousseauist who believed in the importance of marital fidelity. He was, himself, a devoted husband. The case for him as a moral writer is well argued by Roger Vailland in *Laclos par lui-même*. Editions du Seuil, 1959.

Page 45. Cocteau on Genet—*Combat*, July 16, 1948.
Philip Toynbee—The *Observer*, February, 9, 1964.
Genet seeing himself as a poet—JV 215, Tr. 181.
Subordination of ethical to aesthetic—JV 23, Tr. 18.
My victory is verbal—JV 62, Tr. 52.

Page 46. It is not to be wondered at—MR 384, Tr. 275/6.
Simon Raven—*The Observer*, May 9, 1965.

Page 47. Genet's definition of poetry—NDF 133, Tr. 253 and 159, Tr. 293.
A people invisible—MR 206, Tr. 29. A street—NDF 70, Tr. 156.
Divine—NDF 71, Tr. 159. Each object—NDF 30, Tr. 94 (Bernard Frechtman translates this as: 'Each object brings into the room the fascination of a petty theft that is as brief as an appeal to the eyes').
Silk scarf—Par. 107, Tr. 75.
Papier spongieux—NDF 17, Tr. 73; genoux païens—NDF 23, Tr. 82.

Page 48. Martin Esslin, *The Theatre of the Absurd*, Eyre and Spottiswoode, London, 1962, pages 151–176; page 151.
Robert Brustein, *The Theatre of Revolt*, Little, Brown and Co., Boston and Toronto, 1962, pages 363–411.

Page 49. Lie in order to tell the truth—NDF 115, Tr. 225.

Page 50. *Sainteté* the most beautiful word in the human language—JV 227, Tr. 191; Solange—*Les Bonnes*, L'Arbalète, 1963, page 49, Tr. Faber and Faber, 1947, page 22; Divine a saint—NDF 23, Tr. 83; Genet a saint—JV 222, Tr. 186.
Genet using the word 'saint' to disturb the reader—SG 224/5, Tr. 238/9.
Graham Greene—*The Heart of the Matter*, Heinemann edition, 1948.

Page 51. Sainthood leads to Heaven—MR 215, Tr. 42.

Page 52. Divine causing the death of a little girl—NDF 168, Tr. 308.
Meditation on the Virgin—NDF 160, Tr. 294.

Page 53. The crowd ashamed—NDF 150, Tr. 280; the murderer's body—NDF 156, Tr. 288; the public coming to murder trials—NDF 150, Tr. 279.
Ascension to humiliation and humiliating identity card—JV 97, Tr. 81/2.

Page 54. Mettray a paradise—MR 220, Tr. 49.
Disenchanted visionary—MR 191, Tr. 7.

CHAPTER III

Page 55. Marchetti in the dream—NDF 62, Tr. 144.
Deliberate confusion of genders—NDF 22, Tr. 81. 'Je vous parlerai de Divine, au gré de mon humeur mêlant le masculin au féminin et s'il m'arrive, au cours du récit, d'avoir à citer une femme, je m'arrangerai, je trouverai bien un biais, un bon tour, afin qu'il n'y ait pas de confusion.'

Page 56. Mignon called Paul Garcia—NDF 31, Tr. 96.
Notre-Dame called Adrien Baillon—NDF 154, Tr. 286.

Page 57. Satirising popular novelists—SG 481, Tr. 521.
Genet confirms this when he states on NDF 148, Tr. 277 that his stories are 'born of cheap novels'.
Homosexual prostitution—JV 48, Tr. 39/40.

Page 58. Taking a taxi—NDF 120, 'd'une rentrée en lieu commun.' Tr. 234.
Divine's opportunity—NDF 101, Tr. 204.
Events in Barcelona—JV 71, Tr. 60.

Page 59. Sartre on Divine—SG 315, Tr. 339.
Divine calling herself a whore—NDF 63, Tr. 145.

Page 60. Genet calling himself a whore—NDF 51, Tr. 126.
Genet's reaction to Mettray—JV 185/6, Tr. 156/7.
Epic of masturbation—SG 416, Tr. 448.

Page 61. Decision to write pornographic books—JV 150, Tr. 128.
Culafroy and Solange—NDF 121, Tr. 235.

Page 62. Conversation sous le manteau—NDF 14, Tr. 69 'backstage conversation.'

Page 63. Childhood memories—NDF 39. Tr. 107/8.
Rimbaud, Les Poètes de sept ans, Garnier, 1960, page 95.
Divine what Genet almost was—NDF 21, Tr. 80.

Page 63. Sweet confusion with the world—SG 13, Tr. 5.
Woman always as mother—SG 15, Tr. 8.

Page 64. Ernestine—NDF 67, Tr. 152. Like all provincials—NDF 169, Tr. 308.
Not shocked—NDF 169, Tr. 308.
Baillon strangling Ragon—NDF 155, Tr. 288.
Ernestine's gestures—NDF 17, Tr. 74. Shattered the glass—NDF 18, Tr. 76.
Waiting for the churches to open—NDF 36, Tr. 103; jours de la cloche—same page.

Page 65. Discovery of the hollowness of God—NDF 85/88, Tr. 179/184.

Page 66. Being judged—NDF 59, Tr. 139.
Culafroy stealing—NDF 112, Tr. 222.
Divine imitating boxers—NDF 61, Tr. 143.
Causing the death of a child—NDF 169, Tr. 308.

Page 67. On page 90, Tr. 188, Genet says that Village was killed during a prison revolt at Cayenne, but I have not been able to find any reference to this in the French press. There is a contradiction in the dates which Genet gives for his meeting with Village, which may perhaps be explained by the fact that he is confusing him with another criminal, Ange-Jean-Chrysostome Soleil. Thus on NDF p. 84 (Tr. 178) he states that Village had just spent five years at Clairvaux, but on p. 88 (Tr. 185) he says that he had killed his mistress in May 1939. If NDF was completed by 1942, these two dates cannot both be correct. Ange Soleil, whom Genet also mentions on page 9 (Tr. 61), did commit a similar crime to that of Village. He killed his mistress, Séverisse Joram, from Martinique, and walled up her body, on February 23rd, 1935. He was sentenced to 20 years' hard labour on October 16th, 1936. (See *Détective*, January 28, 1939, *Un siècle de malles-cercueils*).
Swell that made the room pitch—NDF 91, Tr. 189.

Page 68. Bundle of sensations—NDF 93, Tr. 192.
Mignon and Notre-Dame father and son—NDF 26 and 56, Tr. 87 and 135. For more details on Genet's preoccupation with incest, see the 1966 Arbalète edition, page 37.

Page 69. Notre-Dame inspired by Pilorge—NDF 55, Tr. 133.
Pascal quotation—NDF 145, Tr. 272, 'a silence as fearful as the eternal silence of unknown space.'

Page 70. Confession—NDF 147, Tr. 275.

246 JEAN GENET: A STUDY OF HIS NOVELS AND PLAYS

Page 70. L'inutile révélation—NDF 148, Tr. 276.
Histoire ahurissante—NDF 157, Tr. 290.

Page 71. La Santé not a prison for long-term sentences—see Armand Massé, *Les Prisons*, Paris, de Boccard, 1926, page 101. Any prisoner sentenced to more than 1½ years was sent to a *Maison centrale*.
Genet awaiting trial—ten-year sentence—NDF 59, Tr. 139.
Psychiatrist's report—NDF 161, Tr. 296.
Notre-Dame's smile—NDF 157, Tr. 290.
Society protecting rentiers—NDF 162, Tr. 297.

Page 72. The Court cursing a mediocre lawyer—NDF 163, Tr. 300.
Notre-Dame described poetically—NDF 162, Tr. 297, and 164, Tr. 302. For the criminal as expiatory victim, see Reiwald, op. cit. pp. 213–317.
The crowd twisting its face, the judge twisting his hands—NDF 156, Tr. 288.
Good-looking butcher boys—NDF 116, Tr. 228.

Page 73. Names at the trial—NDF 158, Tr. 291.
Misère bariolée—NDF 158, Tr. 292.
Peter Wildeblood, *A Way of Life*, Weidenfeld and Nicolson, 1956.
The Racine of Existentialism—Guy Leclerc, *L'Humanité*, April 25, 1966.

Page 74. Mignon ondoyé—NDF 27, Tr. 90.
Lack of profession—NDF 136, Tr. 257.

Page 75. Close more doors than they open—NDF 137, Tr. 260.
Typical prison smell—NDF 39. Tr. 107; anonymous eye watching—NDF 138, Tr. 261; life longer than broad—NDF 139, Tr. 263.
Inauguration of prison—NDF 43, Tr. 114.
Novels no social reality—SG 479, Tr. 519.

Page 76. Genet's dialogue—NDF 48/9. Tr. 121/2.
Anouilh's Duchess—See *Léocadia, Pièces roses*, Calmann-Lévy, 1947, page 197.

Page 77. Wind kneeling—NDF 139, Tr. 262.
Divine's certainty of being old—NDF 62, Tr. 144.

Page 78. Popular songs—NDF 108/9. Tr. 215.

Page 79. Raphael—NDF 120, Tr. 233.
Poor demiurge—NDF 23, Tr. 82.
Prisoners' New Year greetings—NDF 66, Tr. 150.
Moon rising—NDF 80, Tr. 172.

CHAPTER IV

Page 80. For details of the publication of *L'Enfant Criminel*, see Genet's own preface to the 1949 Morihien edition.
Edwin Morgan, *Sidewalk*, No. 1, Vol. I, pages 63–66. Page 66.
Corresponded to their deepest wish—*L'Enfant Criminel*, page 17.

Page 81. Never to blush—*L'Enfant Criminel*, page 24.

Page 82. Morale des manuels scolaires—*L'Enfant Criminel*, page 33.
Your literature, etc.,—*L'Enfant Criminel*, page 29.
Edgar Wallace—Reiwald, op. cit., page 105.

Page 83. Divers betraying Harcamone—MR 261, Tr. 104.
Harcamone's action deliberate . . . a former colonist—MR 224, Tr. 54/5.
Poet and enemy—*L'Enfant Criminel*, page 25.

Page 84. Mignon serving the police—NDF 60, Tr. 140.
Genet doing the same—*Les Temps Modernes*, No. 10, July 1946, page 39.
Rebel and revolutionary—see *Baudelaire*, Gallimard 1947, page 47.
Sartre and Cocteau—*Combat*, July 16, 1948.
Delights of treason—JV 34, Tr. 27.
Selling a friend to the police—PF 53.

Page 85. Frank Norman, *Bang to Rights*, Pan Books, 1961, page 70.
Christopher Hibbert, *The Roots of Evil*, Penguin, 1966, page 286.
Mettray and Fontevrault—MR 251, Tr. 91.
Mettray is about five miles from Tours. In July 1967, the buildings which had housed the *colons* were still standing, though some appeared to be in the process of being demolished. The grounds were defended by a very large number of *Propriété Privée* notices, and local inhabitants replied to questions in reticent and rather contradictory manner. The phrase *bagne d'enfants* tended to recur, but the buildings were also said to be still used as a *centre d'apprentissage*. According to the dates which Genet gives in MR 356, Tr. 237, Mettray had been closed down as a reformatory as early as 1938. I should be most grateful for any information that readers may care to send me on this point.
The Abbey of Fontevrault is open to visitors as a historical monument, but the visit does not include those parts of the building used for prisoners. It is some thirty miles from Tours.

Page 86. Different punishments—MR 213, Tr. 38.
Affirmed his dignity—SG 60, Tr. 55 'Genet's *dignity* is the demand for evil.'

Page 86. Mettray a hell—MR 213, Tr. 39. A paradise—MR 220, Tr. 49.

Page 87. Prison days poor days—MR 314, Tr. 178/9.
Scurrilous caricatures—MR 206, Tr. 31.
Death on the scaffold and sainthood—MR 189, Tr. 6.
Genet seeing Harcamone—MR 196, Tr. 17.

Page 88. Mystery . . . rose in full bloom—MR 309, Tr. 171.
Harcamone's apotheosis—MR 388/91. Tr. 281/6.
Poetry—NDF 133, Tr. 253.

Page 89. Hated flowers—SG 365, Tr. 393.
Flowers and convicts—JV 9, Tr. 7.
Man who had bullied him the least—MR 224, Tr. 54.
Killing a girl—MR 303, Tr. 162.

Page 90. Treatment of *colons*—1946 edition of MR pages 326 and 457.
Reward for escaping *colons*—1946 edition of MR page 412.
Vile measures—MR 1951 edition 251, Tr. 91; few formalities accorded to humans—MR 317, Tr. 182; children never played—MR 315, Tr. 180; never saw a newspaper—MR 1946 edition, page 331.

Page 91. Mettray as mother—MR 326, Tr. 195.
Elder brothers—253, Tr. 94.
I was sixteen, etc.,—MR 314, Tr. 178.
Visit to Mettray—MR 356, Tr. 236/7.
Clear simplicity of manliness—MR 206, Tr. 27/8.

Page 92. Wild nature always visible—MR 276, Tr. 126.
Imitating thieves—MR 344/5, Tr. 220/1.
Agonising thought—MR 207, Tr. 30.
J. B. Mays, *Crime and the Social Structure*, Faber and Faber, 1963, page 208.

Page 93. Called a thief at age of seventeen—SG 26, Tr. 21.
Simple-minded, theological morality—SG 56, Tr. 51.
Prayers eight times a day—MR 266, Tr. 111.

Page 94. Description of Bishop's visit—MR 299/303, Tr. 158/62.
Brendan Behan, *Borstal Boy*, Hutchinson, 1958, pages 258/9.

Page 95. Tannebaum—quoted by Hibbert, op. cit., page 288.

Page 96. Prestige of the *mac*—MR 287, Tr. 141.
Traditional view—see *Détective*, December 15, 1938. Introduction to the life-story of a *mac*.

Page 96. Hardened cracksman—MR 206/7, Tr. 27/8.
Feeble dreamer... poetry of great birds of prey—MR 311, Tr. 174.

Page 97. Kind of disenchantment—MR 267, Tr. 114.
A book as treacherous—MR 291, Tr. 147.

Page 98. Writing MR without pleasure—MR 298, Tr. 156.

Page 99. Calendars covering twenty years—MR 223, Tr. 53; lying mouths—MR 217, Tr. 44.
Fattened up as for sacrifice—MR 384, Tr. 276.
Man in prison . . . cotton wool—MR 268, Tr. 115.
Divers' voice—MR 280, Tr. 132.
Botchako's voice—MR 200, Tr. 20.

Page 100. Beauty grasped only fleetingly—MR 193, Tr. 10.
Talking slang a male sexual attribute—NDF 34, Tr. 100.
Living youth at thirty—MR 267, Tr. 113.

Page 101. Robert—JV 148, Tr. 126.
Fear into rage . . . poor quality of nervous system—MR 274, Tr. 123.

Page 102. Incident with Botchako—MR 319/20, Tr. 185/7.

CHAPTER V

Page 105. Paulo's Jean's half-brother—PF 20 and 33.
Since there is, at the moment, no published English translation of *Pompes Funèbres*, I am responsible for the English of the quotations from this novel.
Five million young men—NDF 32, Tr. 97.
Mignon's virility—NDF 44, Tr. 116.
MR written on white paper bags—MR 214, Tr. 40.

Page 106. Making camouflage nets—MR 244, Tr. 81.
Innocent people sent to prison—MR 205, Tr. 27.
Cyril Connolly—*Sunday Times*, May 9, 1965.
Date of Decarnin's death . . . Genet's first meeting with him—PF 13.
Lover for three months—PF 161.
Comment on fondness for funerals—PF 9.

Page 107. We act in order to obtain—PF 76, 'Nous agissons aux fins d'un bel enterrement de funérailles solennelles.'
Hatred corresponding to love . . . fearsome brood we call destiny—PF 36.

Page 108. Extracts from PF published in *Les Temps Modernes* No. 3, December 1945, pages 405–419. The extracts describe Genet's visit to the place where Jean was shot, Riton's attempt to kill the cat, Erik's killing of the young child, and Juliette's journey to the cemetery.
Some of the comfortable habits—PF 53.
Hitler . . . an old queen—PF 88–89.
Worthy professor of economics—SG 488, Tr. 529.

Page 109. Would have joined the *Milice* . . . France terrorised by children—PF 51.
Extravagant banditry—PF 75.
Hitler knowing how to use evil—PF 1947 edition, page 221.
The *Milice* . . . three theological virtues—JV 157/8, Tr. 133.
Born to betray—PF 124.

Page 110. Communist poem—JV 184, Tr. 154.
The *Milice* finding its recruits—PF 129. In the 1947 edition, Genet writes that Paulo had not managed to get into the *Milice* because he did not have sufficiently influential friends. 'Pour y entrer,' he writes, 'il fallait être présenté par un de ces macs (Corses or Marseillais) tenant à Montmartre le haut du pavé.'

Page 111. Genet's mistake in thinking that he would be alone in evil—PF 107/9. 1947 edition, page 208.
General Koenig—PF 108. 'Les Allemands avaient déjà rendu légale la délation, et quand il les eut chassés, le Général Koenig la conseilla par voie d'affiche sur tous les murs de Paris.'
Moral solitude—PF 109.

Page 112. Passion for evil—PF 136.
Beauty that men show—PF 108.
France cursed and desired—PF 157.
Weeps when his country suffers—PF 113.

Page 113. The only way Genet has of disposing the mind of his reader—SG 389, Tr. 420.
Tourniquets—Whirligigs—SG 306, Tr. 329.

Page 114. Erik telling himself he is not queer—PF 47.
Praise for homosexuality—PF 13. 'Incomparable avec l'amour pour une femme ou une jeune fille est l'amour d'un homme pour un adolescent.' Also PF 154. 'Jamais je n'aurais la force de supporter mon amour pour Jean si je m'appuyais sur cette fillette malheureuse, par contre je pouvais tout me permettre soutenu par Erik.'
Mourning her son 'à la manière des reines'—PF 12.

Page 115. Jean's mother eating—PF 111, on servants, PF 112.
Real father—PF 35.
Saluting the flag—PF 1947 edition, page 51.

Page 116. Her grief—PF 105.
Meditation on the importance of friendship—MR 215, Tr. 43.

Page 117. Characters in MR real—see 1946 edition, page 299.
Riton killing the cat—PF 55/6.
Erik shooting all the reflections of himself—PF 141.
Reinvented literature—SG 407, Tr. 439.
Neither pleasure, instruction nor information—SG 361, Tr. 389.
'Pourquoi nous comblerait-il? Il ne nous aime pas.'

Page 118. Idea of a literary work of art—JV 115, Tr. 97.

<h3 style="text-align:center">CHAPTER VI</h3>

Page 119. Near to shame—QB 349, Tr. 318.
Gil Turko—QB 273, Tr. 177.
Querelle after his first murder—QB 215, Tr. 78.
Passage used by Sartre—SG 9/10. Tr. 2.

Page 121. The imaginary Assizes—QB 211/2, Tr. 72/3.
Comforting certainty—QB 217, Tr. 81.
Genuinely in love—QB 326, Tr. 267.

Page 122. *Dioscurisme fondamental*—SG 500, Tr. 542.
Inexcusable stupidity of criminals—see Reiwald, op. cit., pages 151 and 159 for the view that criminals make mistakes in order to be caught.
Homosexuals forced to invent women . . . not like genuine love—QB 253/4, Tr. 141.

Page 123. Deep, tender and generous friendship—QB 341, Tr. 304.
Very precious object—QB 343, Tr. 307.
A sort of spirit—QB 348, Tr. 316.

Page 124. So noble an edifice—QB 1947 edition, page 17. See the English translation, page 16. This translation is not based exclusively on the 1953 Gallimard text.
Seblon severe and slightly puritanical—QB 186/7, Tr. 32.
Working-class world—SG 436, Tr. 471.

Page 125. Nobody can go on playing—QB 314, Tr. 246.

Page 126. Théo a skilled workman—QB 198, Tr. 51.
A violent temper—QB 199, Tr. 53.

Page 126. Soldiers and sailors never work—QB 175, Tr. 11.
French navy . . . decorate rather than defend—QB 319, Tr. 255.
World of the stonemasons—QB 200, Tr. 54.
Gil cleaning his bicycle—QB 238, Tr. 116.

Page 127. Placed with a working-class family—SG 17, Tr. 10.
Madame Lysiane . . . Roger—QB 312, Tr. 241.
Living in each other's body—QB 292, Tr. 208.

Page 128. Overcome with confusion—QB 292/3, Tr. 209.
Querelle denying he is queer—QB 303, Tr. 225; Mignon—NDF
56, Tr. 134.
Mystery of the double—MR 320, Tr. 187.

Page 129. Whiteness and warmth—QB 291, Tr. 207.
Prickly with painful angles MR 313, Tr. 177; Bulkaen—MR 335,
Tr. 207; Plaustener—JV 49, Tr. 41.

Page 130. Madame Lysiane not smoking—QB 313, Tr. 206; no
perversions—QB 289, Tr. 204; Robert misunderstanding her—QB
290, Tr. 206.
Anger expressed in a tragic manner—QB 292, Tr. 209.
Cold feet—QB 294, Tr. 211.
Pale light of day—QB 296, Tr. 214.
Lingering lovingly—QB 287, Tr. 200.

Page 131. Problem for translators—QB 288. Gregory Streatham
translates (page 203) as 'fallen women, kneelers, sluts, prostitutes,
strumpets, punks, misses, demireps, jades, skits, mopsies, drabs, rigs,
frails or loose women.'
Allongée, etc.,—QB 288, Tr. 202.
Homosexuality . . . Satan—QB 312, Tr. 242.
Charming invalids . . . delights of love—QB 254/5, Tr. 143.
Milice at the ideal point—PF 130.

Page 132. Querelle and the Navy—QB 192, Tr. 41.

Page 133. Mario . . . prestige of the police—QB 204, Tr. 61; cannot
prevent himself from acting as policeman—QB 338, Tr. 300.
Sexually excited by Bernardini's badge—JV 201, Tr. 170.
Police always too powerful—PF 129.
Roger's naivety—QB 276, Tr. 181.
Stereotyped concept of homosexuality in the police—QB 223, Tr.
90; in the dockers—QB 267, Tr. 167.

Page 134. Mario's childish pleasure—QB 330, Tr. 287.
Police a strong resemblance to those they hunt down—QB 223,
Tr. 91. For further considerations on this point, see Reiwald, op.
cit. pp. 121/3.

Page 134. Vincent de Paul—JV 227, Tr. 191; taking upon himself—JV 220, Tr. 185.
Querelle flesh of our flesh—QB 182, Tr. 25.

Page 135. Cocteau, *Difficulté d'être*, page 267.
Querelle sprung unarmed—QB 248, Tr. 132.
Querelle 'addressed to inverts'—QB 171, Tr .8.

Page 136. Final carelessness about plot—Thus the whole episode of Gil holding up Lieutenant Seblon (QB 320, Tr. 255) is not explained, and no reason is given as to why the police should then arrest the Lieutenant (QB 349, Tr. 318.)
Homosexuality a way out—SG 80, Tr. 78. It should perhaps be noted that in *Les Temps Modernes*, July 1946, page 41 and page 50, Genet himself gives the impression that he regards homosexuality as inborn. He argues (page 41) that it preceded his activity as a thief, and states on page 50 that to give up stealing would be to give up his essential personality his homosexuality.

Page 137. Incident with Joachim—QB 1947 edition pp. 209/19. In the English translation, this is pp. 267/81.
Description of murder—QB 1947, 219.

Page 138. Querelle's smile—QB 194, Tr. 44.
Hugging Querelle—QB 220, Tr. 87.
Supposedly rational—JV 178, Tr. 149.
Still, silent males—JV 191/2, Tr. 161.

Page 139. Gil gives himself away—QB 316, Tr. 250.
Comparison with Oscar Wilde—SG 358, Tr. 386.
Full-dress puttees—QB 181, Tr. 22.
Ten years of literature—SG 501, Tr. 544.

CHAPTER VII

Page 141. Three subjects—JV 181, Tr. 152.
Impossible nullity—JV 100, Tr. 84. See also SG 548/9, Tr. 597/8.
Rigour of composition—JV 65, Tr. 55.

Page 142. Quieter to walk on one's heels—MR 308, Tr. 169.
G. K. Chesterton, *The Man who was Thursday*, Penguin edition, page 45.
Long shudder . . . steeped in idea of property—JV 164, Tr. 139.
Analysis of theft—SG 245, Tr. 261.

Page 143. Pépé—JV 40, Tr. 33. The idea that sexual orgasm calms the nerves is quite widespread. In Ian Fleming's *The Man with the Golden Gun*, 'Pistols' Scaramanga is described as 'an insatiable but indiscriminate womanizer who invariably has sexual intercourse before a killing in the belief that it improves his "eye". (N.B. a belief shared by many professional lawn tennis players, golfers, gun and rifle marksmen and others).' Pan Edition, 1966, page 33.

Page 143. Finally freed himself from moral preoccupations—JV 84, Tr. 70.   Sartre on Stilitano—SG 130, Tr. 135.

Page 144.
Stilitano in Barcelona—JV 67/8, Tr. 56/7.
Stilitano's clothes—JV 127/8, Tr. 108; monarch of the slums—JV 192, Tr. 162.

Page 145. Cyril Connolly—*Sunday Times*, May 9, 1965.
Sylvia—JV 151, Tr. 128.
Malice pédérastique . . . fellatio—SG 123, Tr. 128/9.

Pages 146–7. Light from dead stars—MR 395, Tr. 291 and PF 137.
Life on Uranus—JV 47, Tr. 39.
Un pou avec la conscience de l'être—JV 18, Tr. 14.

Page 147. Theresa the Great—JV 107, Tr. 90.
The Barcelona homosexuals—JV 68, Tr. 58.

Page 148. The Carolinas' shrill voices—JV 69, Tr. 28.
French tourists—JV 171/4, Tr. 146/8.

Page 149. Humiliating anthropocentric card—JV 97, Tr. 82.
The war—NDF 70, Tr. 156.
Cette face crucifiée—QB 241, Tr. 120.

Page 150. No longer the high-sounding—JV 116, Tr. 98.
Hitler's Germany—JV 131, Tr. 111; civil war in Spain—JV 183, Tr. 154.
Perfect coherence—JV 192/3, Tr. 162.

Page 151. Oppressively perfect police system—JV 122, Tr. 103.
Beginning to write—JV 181, Tr. 152.

Page 152. Looking at the world through lowered eyebrows—PF 44.
Moral adventure—JV 121, Tr. 102.

Pages 153–4. Ingrained habit—JV 192, Tr. 162.
Prisons have their foundations in him—JV 94, Tr. 79.
Duality in Sartre's essay—poetic truth of crime SG 456, Tr. 493; making a great to-do—SG 212, Tr. 225.
Rigour of composition—JV 65, Tr. 55; *en vrac*—JV 218, Tr. 183; classical unity—SG 459, Tr. 497; loosely constructed—SG 448, Tr. 484. *Nous souffrons*—PF 73; *une bonne ne fait pas de projets*—PF 74. See *Matérialisme et Révolution*, *Les Temps Modernes*, No. 10, pp. 7/8.

Page 154. *Une giclée qui n'a pas réussi*—QB 285; Genet's mother and father—SG 547, Tr. 596; Sartre's own birth—*Les Mots*, Gallimard, 1963, page 14.

CHAPTER VIII

Page 155. The English translation used here is the Faber and Faber paperback published in 1965; first published in *La Nef*, March, April 1947. For production details, see page 000.

Deathwatch adapted for the cinema—see Albert Johnson, *Dynamic gesture: The New American Independents*, *Film Quarterly* (Berkeley, California), Summer, 1966, pp. 6–11. The film was shown at the 1965 San Francisco Film Festival, but has not been given a general release. Mr. Johnson's article gives the impression that Genet's original text was rather freely adapted, since he describes the prisoners walking around in the punishment cell (as they do in MR but not in the play), mentions how they watch an execution inside the prison (which happens nowhere in Genet's work), and speaks of Green-Eyes and Maurice making love, which again does not happen in the play. He writes of Leonard Nimoy's portrayal of Lefranc as 'pure Genet', and continues: 'Here is the "essential man", branded by thievery, but already carrying within every haunted look his own apprehension of epic evil'.

Page 156. *Signe des monstres*—NDF 11, Tr. 65.

Haute surveillance a technical term—See *L'Oeuvre*, June 14, 1939; 'Rompant la "haute surveillance" à laquelle il était soumis, l'assassin Molinari s'est exécuté lui-même'; *Préséances*—see note to page 14.

Page 157. Effect of the 1939–45 war—MR 205, Tr. 27.

Gift from God of the devil—HS 93, Tr. 39. Page references are to the *edition définitive* published by Gallimard in 1965, not to the first, 1949, Gallimard edition.

Page 158. Tried to be a dog, etc.,—HS 48, Tr. 23.

Famous criminals—Eugène Weidmann, who is also mentioned several times in Genet's novels, was the last person to be publicly executed in France. He was guillotined on June 17, 1939 for murdering a number of people he had kidnapped. Soklay, or Soclet, is referred to in MR 324, Tr. 192 as 'the murderer of the little Marescot girl.' Serge de Lenz was described in *Détective* on December 8, 1938 as 'one of the most authentic stars of the Criminal Courts, whose name has been in lights for more than fifteen years.' He had been arrested for burglary, and had been convicted so often before that, like Genet himself before Sartre and Cocteau saved him, he ran the risk of a life sentence. He had been kept by '*l'opulente sexagénaire, la*

Comtesse de Tessancourt, qui l'entretient largement, lui réservant sa fortune et ses caresses' (*Détective*). For Ange Soleil, see the note to page 67.
All the real signs—HS 81, Tr. 35.

Page 159. Sharing bread—MR 311, Tr. 174.
Sartre on HS—SG 115, Tr. 118.
Harcamone—MR 223, Tr. 53; Lefranc on Boule de Neige—HS 10, Tr. 8.
Poetry of the great birds of prey—MR 311, Tr. 174.
Programme note—quoted by Gabriel Marcel in *Les Nouvelles Littéraires*, March 3, 1949.

Page 160. Marc Beigbeder—*Le Parisien libéré*, March 10, 1949.
J.-J. Rinieri—*La Nef*, March 1949, pp. 137/8.
Bataille—*Critique*, April 1949, No. 35, pp. 371/3.

Page 161. *L'Humanité*—March 12, 1949.
Criminals attain their prestige in prison—PF 129.

Page 162. Merely changed cells—interview in *Paris-Presse l'Intransigeant*, February 24, 1949.

CHAPTER IX

Page 164. *In-car-cé-ré*—*Les Bonnes*, Arbalète, 1963, p. 54. Unless otherwise stated, all quotations are from this edition. The translation published by Faber and Faber in 1957 is based upon the version of the play performed in 1954, which does not include the 'in-car-cé-ré'. According to Genet's *Lettre-Préface* to the volume in which both versions were published together (Jean-Jacques Pauvert, 1954), the 1954 text represents the original version which was pruned down in rehearsal before being put on in 1947. In my view, the play is easier to understand if no attention is paid to any of Genet's cuts; I have therefore made use of the longest text available for whatever part of the play is being analysed.
Les Bonnes, Jean-Jacques Pauvert, 1954 version, page 146, Tr. 42/3. Omitted from the 1946 version.
Said to be based on the Papin case—see *L'Aurore*, April 24, 1947 and Louis Le Guillant, *L'Affaire des soeurs Papin*, *Les Temps Modernes*, November, 1963, pp. 868/913. Page 868 and page 908.

Page 165. *Un peu cocotte*—*L'Arbalète*, 1963. *Comment jouer "Les Bonnes"*, page 11.
La crasse—*L'Arbalète*, 33/4, Tr. 16; *s'aimer dans la servitude*—Arbalète, 48, Tr. 21; Madame's insults—*Arbalète*, 82, Tr. 34.
La Condition Humaine, Livre de Poche, 1946, page 191.

Page 166. Genet deeply attached to the society that condemned him—
SG 27, Tr. 22.
Stealing to be kind—MR 231, Tr. 63.
Easy for Madame to be kind—*Les Bonnes*, 33, Tr. 16.

Page 167. Genet exaggerating our dishonesty—SG 549, Tr. 558.

Page 168. Madame Lancelin putting on white gloves—Louis Le
Guillant, *Les Temps Modernes*, loc. cit. page 879.
Prisoners . . . happy new year—NDF 13, Tr. 67.
Unwholesome exhalations—MR 252, Tr. 92.
Like a bad smell—*Les Bonnes*, 48, Tr. 21.
Exigencies of an ethic—SG 59, Tr. 54.
Robert Kemp—*Le Monde*, January 15, 1954.

Page 169. Preface—Jean-Jacques Pauvert Edition of *Les Bonnes*, 1954,
page 13.

Page 170. Jean-Jacques Gautier—*Le Figaro*, April 20, 1947.
Trying to kill me—*Les Bonnes*, 73, Tr. 31.
Buying new dresses—*Les Bonnes*, 65. This is omitted from the 1946
edition published by Jean-Jacques Pauvert, and from the English
translation.
Genet's reply reported by Sartre—SG 16, Tr. 10.

Page 171. Maxime Belliard—*France Libre*, April 28, 1947.
Austin Clarke—*The Irish Times*, May 3, 1958.

Page 174. *Psyché*—May 1947, pp. 765/6. See also Louis Le Guillant's
article which refers to a full-length study by Ryckene called *La
servante criminelle*.

Page 175. I go to the theatre—*Les Bonnes*, *L'Arbalète*, 1963, *Comment
jouer 'Les Bonnes'*, page 10.
Sartre on *Les Bonnes*—SG 256–73. Tr. 611–25.
Sartre refers to Genet's desire to have the parts played by boys, and
states that it was only a concession to Jouvet that he agreed to have
women. Genet's desire to have women play boys' parts—NDF 119,
Tr. 231.

Page 176. Solange and Claire passive pederasts—SG 116, Tr. 118.
Successive illusions—*Le Monde*, May 5, 1961.
Taking communion—JV 182, Tr. 153.

Page 177. Malraux, *La Condition Humaine*, Livre de poche edition,
1946, page 46.

CHAPTER X

Page 180. Perversions in *Querelle of Brest*—QB 254, Tr. 143.

Slang term for a brothel—See *L'Oeuvre*, January 26, 1939, where a certain Louis Verrechia is referred to as the *'tenancier d'une maison d'illusions.'*

Preface—see the 1962 edition of *Le Balcon*, published by *L'Arbalète*. Last page of the instructions *Comment jouer "Le Balcon"*.

Page 181. Reaction of the Chief of Police to Roger's action—*Le Balcon*, 1962 edition, page 200. English translation (Faber and Faber 1966 edition) page 93/4. These two editions are the ones referred to in this chapter. See note to page 194, however, for details of the 1956 edition of *Le Balcon*.

Page 182. Genet's statements on the political implications of *Le Balcon*— Interview in *Arts*, May 3, 1957.

In losing hope—*Le Balcon*, 183, Tr. 86.

De Tocqueville—*L'Ancien Régime et la Révolution*, Gallimard, Collection *Idées*, 1952, page 236.

Page 183. Lucien Goldmann—*Une pièce réaliste: 'Le Balcon' de Genet*. *Les Temps Modernes*, June 1960, pp. 1885/96.

The Nomenclature—Tr. 86.

Page 184. Anthony Sampson, *Anatomy of Britain Today*, Hodder and Stoughton, 1965, page 21.

The workers chaste—*Le Balcon*, 83, Tr. 39.

Page 185. Stage directions—translation page 70.

Killing arranged by bishop—*Le Balcon* 173, Tr. 81.

First Brechtian play—Goldmann, loc. cit, page 1896.

Page 186. The Bishop on reality and illusion—*Le Balcon*, 171/2, Tr. 80.

Page 188. Madame Irma and Carmen—*Le Balcon* 79, Tr. 37: Divine —NDF 41, Tr. 111.

Jean Fayard—*Le Figaro*, May 19, 1960.

Page 189. The General leaping to a lady's defence—*Le Balcon*, 46, Tr. 22.

The Bishop . . . our holiness—*Le Balcon*, 18/9, Tr. 10.

You live in evil—*Le Balcon* 19, Tr. 10.

Pages 189-90. *Les passes simples*—*Le Balcon*, 65; vi-si-tors—*Le Balcon*, 61, Tr. 29; the one you tie up—*Le Balcon*, 91, Tr. 43.

Cérébraux—See Camus, *Noces*, Editions de la Pléiade, 1965, page 69.

Gilbert Ryle—*Dilemmas*, C.U.P. Paperback, 1960. Page 60.

Madame Lysiane—QB 255, Tr. 143.

Page 191. Bank clerk—*Le Balcon* 67, Tr. 32.

Pages 191–2. Conversation—*Le Balcon*, 71/2, Tr. 34.
Virtually banned—*Combat*, November 7, 1957.
Supposedly rational—JV 178, Tr. 149.

Page 193. Gasman—In the 1962 edition, there is no indication of what the different characters do in real life. Page 79 of the 1957 English translation states that the Bishop is really a gasman, and in this respect it follows page 153 of the 1956 *Arbalète* edition. *Picture Post* for May 11, 1957 stated that a bank clerk came to play the General, and a rich man the person who is humiliated in the fourth tableau.
The Bishop—*Le Balcon*, 21, Tr. 11.

Page 194. T. C. Worsley—*The New Statesman*, April 27, 1957.

Kenneth Tynan—see *Curtains*, The Atheneum Press, New York, 1963, page 171.

Early version of play—this was published by *L'Arbalète* in 1956 in a limited edition of 3000 copies. It differs considerably from the 1962 'édition définitive' used in this chapter, and from the English translations published by Faber and Faber in 1957 and 1966. The 1957 translation clearly follows a very much fuller text, which is only a little different from the 1962 version, and which may well be the version which *L'Arbalète* later published in 1960 as the 'second edition' of *Le Balcon*. However, since I have not been able to consult a copy of this 1960 edition, I should be most grateful for further information on this point. The 1956 *Arbalète* edition is much shorter than any of the later versions of the play. If performed in its original printed form, it would probably arouse unintentional laughter in the scene where three handsome young men, representing blood, tears and sperm (page 110), later turn out to be photographers (page 167).

Carmen referring to Roger—*L'Arbalète*, 1956, page 192. A careful reading of the text does show that this is Roger, the defeated revolutionary leader, but this is a point easily missed by a spectator in the theatre in the speed of the final scenes.

Cuts in the Paris production—see *Libération*, May 21, 1960; for an alternative view, arguing that the revolutionary scenes spoil the play, see Jacques Lemarchand, *Le Figaro littéraire*, May 21, 1960.

Bernard Dort—*Les Temps Modernes*, June 1960, *Le jeu de Genet*, pp. 1875/84. Page 1883.

Page 195. David Grossvogel—see *Four Playwrights and a Postscript*, Cornell University Press, Ithaca, New York, 1962. Page 149.

CHAPTER XI

Page 196. Sympathy for director—see Peter Zadek, *Acts of Violence*, *The New Statesman and Nation*, May 4, 1957, pp. 568/9.
Compliment to Blin—see *Les Nègres*, *L'Arbalète*, 1963.

Page 197. Old beggar woman—*Les Nègres*, 34, Tr. 19. The translation used is the Faber and Faber 1967 paperback.

Page 198. Execution of traitor—*Les Nègres*, 160, Tr. 84: organise the fight—*Les Nègres*, 161, Tr. 85.

Page 199. Corrode the idea—*Les Nègres*, 161, Tr. 85; fight in flesh and blood.

    Poirot-Delpech in *Le Monde*—November 4, 1959.

    Wellington's speech—*Les Nègres*, 76, Tr. 42.

Page 200. Sartre on Fanon—See *Situations V*, Gallimard 1964, page 183.

    Employers peeping through key-holes—*Lettres à Roger Blin*, page 47.

Page 201. Gabriel Marcel—*Les Nouvelles littéraires*, December 24, 1959.

Page 202. Norman Mailer—see *The Presidential Papers*, André Deutsch, 1964, pp. 199–212.

    John Bowen—*Punch*, August 10, 1960.

Page 203. Guy Leclerc—*L'Humanité*, November 4, 1959; Albert Ollivier—*Les Lettres Françaises*, November 11, 1959.

Page 204. Félicité—*Les Nègres*, 111, Tr. 60.

    Puns—Thus on page 20, the Governor says that he is going to '*broyer du Noir*'. Bernard Frechtman translates one of the meanings when he writes 'Stamp out the Blacks', but *broyer du noir* also means something like 'to get gloomy ideas', 'to be depressed.' On page 109, when the Negroes are re-enacting the murder, they say that the victim, on putting out the light, 'fait le noir pour te mettre à l'aise'. *Faire le noir* also means to 'play at being a black person', and Tr. 59 'She's darkening the room to put you at your ease' inevitably misses the joke implied by the fact that the actors are playing at being black although they are black all the time.

    Genet is quite fond of puns, and says of a judge who once refused to discuss crime with him 'Je vis ce juge se dérober: se retirer sous sa robe,' (JV 208, Tr. 175, 'retreating into his robe') misses the fact that *se dérober* has the general meaning of to escape, or to steal away. The plot of *Le Balcon* is also well expressed when one of the characters says on page 124 '*Nous ne sortirons jamais de ce bordel*' ('out of this mess').

CHAPTER XII

Page 205. *Les Paravents* said to have been completed by 1960—*Carrefour*, August 31, 1960.

Page 206. Robert Abirached—*La Nouvelle Nouvelle Revue Française* June 1966, page 1079.

Page 207. Showing the French paratroops the way—*Par* 207. Tr. 142. *A la vieille*—*Par* 256. Tr. 173. For this play, I have used my own translation and not that by Bernard Frechtman, which, in order to provide an English that can be spoken on stage, sometimes diverges somewhat from Genet's text.

Page 208. Kadidja's invocation to evil—*Par* 130, Tr. 86.
Félicité—*Les Nègres*, 154, Tr. 80.

Page 209. Sartre's remark—quoted by Maurice Cranston in *Sartre and Violence, Encounter*, July 1967, pp. 18–24, page 20.

Page 210. In *The Blacks*, etc—*Lettres à Roger Blin*, page 42.

Page 211. *Une déflagration poétique*—*Lettres à Roger Blin*, page 11.
Play not an apology for treason—ditto, page 22.
Half-hiding—*Lettres à Roger Blin*, page 66.
'*S'à demi-dissimuler*' is Genet's own linguistic invention.

Page 212. *Histoire de cinglés*—ditto, page 14.
Certain truths—*Par* 254, Tr. 171.
Un spectacle, etc.—*Lettres à Roger Blin*, page 63.

Page 214. Mustapha's comment—*Par* 24, Tr. 18.
History of Algeria one continuous moment—*Lettres à Roger Blin*, page 24.

Page 215. Dialogue—*Banker*, etc. *Par* 122, Tr. 83.
The Vamp—*Par* 148, Tr. 99. Bernard Frechtman translates: 'That's how a young man in your sphere ought to talk when he's hot in the pants for me'.

Page 216. Asking the soldier if he is French—*Par* 153–4, Tr. 103.
Army too gentle—*Par* 97, Tr. 68.
Genet on the Lieutenant—*Lettres à Roger Blin*, page 15.

Page 217. *Partouze du tonnerre*—*Par* 103, Tr. 72.
Scent of candles, etc.,—*Par* 199, Tr. 134.
Genet's obsession with farting—see QB 260, Tr. 152; PF 126 and 91. For Genet's justification of it see *Lettres à Roger Blin*, page 58. Scene in *The Thief's Journal* when, to express his love for an old beggar woman who he thinks might be his mother, he speaks of vomiting over her hands. This scene (JV 21–2, Tr. 17) is analysed in detail by Sartre in SG 468–9, Tr. 506–7, who presents it as an example of Genet's 'diabolical cleverness'.

Page 218. Georges Portal—*Écrits de Paris*, August 1966, page 126.
De Gaulle's motives for allowing *Les Paravents*—Jean Fabiani in *Combat*, May 5, 1966.